THE GEORGE GUND FOUNDATION
IMPRINT IN AFRICAN AMERICAN STUDIES

The George Gund Foundation has endowed
this imprint to advance understanding of
the history, culture, and current issues
of African Americans.

MUSIC OF THE AFRICAN DIASPORA

Edited by Samuel A. Floyd, Jr.

HARLEM IN MONTMARTRE

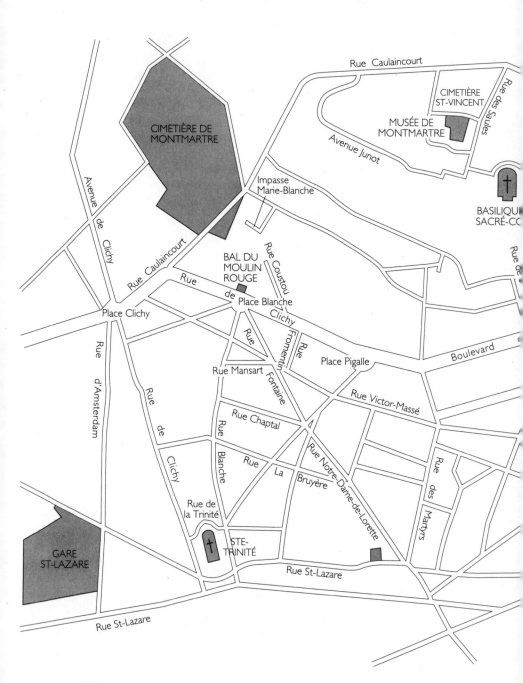

Montmartre, 1919.

# HARLEM IN MONTMARTRE

*A Paris Jazz Story between the Great Wars*

## William A. Shack

University of California Press    Berkeley Los Angeles London

The publisher gratefully acknowledges the
generous contribution to this book provided
by the George Gund Foundation.

University of California Press
Berkeley and Los Angeles, California

University of California Press, Ltd.
London, England

Library of Congress Cataloging-in-Publication Data

Shack, William A.
  Harlem in Montmartre : a Paris jazz story between the great wars / by William A. Shack.
     p.   cm. — (Music of the African diaspora ; 4)
  Includes bibliographical references (p.   ) and index.
  ISBN 0-520-22537-6 (cloth : alk. paper)
     1. Jazz—France—Paris—History and criticism.   2. Afro-American musicians—
France—Paris.   I. Title.   II. Series.

ML3509.F7 S53   2001
781.65'089'96073044361—dc21

                                                                              00-047946

Printed in the United States of America

10 09 08 07 06 05 04 03 02 01

10 9 8 7 6 5 4 3 2 1

*For my father, William Shack, 1890–1997*

# CONTENTS

# ILLUSTRATIONS

# ACKNOWLEDGMENTS

The author wishes to thank the following individuals for their valuable assistance with the preparation of this book: Samuel Adams, Phyliss Bischof, George Bond, Jacques Bureaux, Elizabeth Colson, Maurice and Vonette Cullaz, Alan Dundes, Michel Fabre, John Hope Franklin, Herb Gentry, Jeffry Green, Lynn Hunt, Kendell Jackson, Walton Johnson, Jean La Fontaine, Larry Levine, David Levering Lewis, Herb Lottman, John Middleton, Colette Myles, Dovie Patrick, Robert Paxton, Jeanne Pimentel, Brigitte Porée, Isaac Schapera, Tyler Stovall, Lynn Terry, Elaine Williams, Sally Williams-Allen, Victoria M. Zaldna, and Mike Zwerin.

EDITORIAL NOTE

I wish to thank Lynne Withey of the University of California Press for the special attention she gave to my husband's manuscript as it moved through the editorial maze. I also thank the many staff members at the University of California Press who have played vital roles in bringing the book to its completion. Finally, thanks to Edith Gladstone for her fine editing.

Although the names of many who assisted my husband do not appear here, I sincerely thank everyone who helped him with the preparation of this book. He continued to work toward its completion even in the final weeks of his life. This project was so dear to his heart.

*Dorothy N. Shack*

# INTRODUCTION

I come from that generation of African Americans whose first images of France sprang from stories told by fathers who had served in that country with the American Expeditionary Force, during the Great War. Images were often colored by broken verses of that popular tune American soldiers sang with great delight: "Mademoiselle from Armentières, parlez-vous." Not infrequently, this verse served as a preamble to my father's descriptions of the hospitality French citizens displayed toward black American soldiers. He made sharp comparisons with the racial hostility they experienced in the company of white American soldiers. A constant refrain were his words, often bitterly expressed, that a "colored man" in America had to travel and study in France or England to be recognized as "equal" to a "white man." And he could cite examples of such "colored" men to make the case.

Years later, my opportunity came to experience my father's "theories" on comparative racial relations in the United States, England, and France. It was 1957; I was traveling to Ethiopia to conduct doctoral research in anthropology (which I later completed at the University of London). This was the year when the Little Rock, Arkansas, school incident dominated newspaper headlines across the nation. And in Chicago, in Bridgeport, the neighborhood of the city's mayor, a black man had been stoned to death. After attending church services on a Sunday morning, the victim had entered a white tavern and ordered a drink. It was an innocent act; his mere presence aroused violent hostility from white customers.

But there were *No Green Pastures* in London, to borrow the title of Roi Ottley's study of race relations in postwar Europe. In 1957 I found the city socially cold, and the climate uncomfortable. Londoners appeared to express indifference to strangers, especially black strangers, though perhaps I assumed wrongly. I did not, I believe, misconstrue reasons for the difficulty I had in obtaining accommodations, even in cheap bed-and-breakfast hotels in Bloomsbury. A tour of the famous historical sites of London only sharpened my appetite for Paris.

On my first day in the City of Light, I met Ollie Stewart. A former war correspondent for the *Baltimore Afro-American,* Stewart had remained in Paris after its liberation from four years of German occupation. He gained the reputation as the person an African American visitor to Paris should seek out, if Stewart had not first found the visitor on one of his daily visits for that purpose to the American Express, in rue Scribe. I met him there on that first day. As hospitable as his reputation, Stewart booked me, a stranger, into a small hotel in rue d'Amsterdam in Montmartre. In this quarter on the right bank of the Seine, just after World War I, African American musicians and entertainers had shaped the Harlem-style culture that I would write about forty years later. With Stewart's guidance, I came to appreciate the charm of the city and understand why France had made such an indelible impression on my father.

When I came back to Paris from Ethiopia in 1959, I was fortunate to see Josephine Baker—still the toast of the town—at the Olympia Theater in *Paris, mes amours,* the review that marked her return to the musical world from retirement. The review raised funds to support the several children she had adopted into her multiethnic "Rainbow Tribe."

Years later, a radio broadcast by Lynn Terry, then Paris correspondent for National Public Radio, in Washington, D.C., set me on the literary path that led to this book. An avid fan of black American jazz and its influence on the French jazz scene, Terry frequently broadcast interviews featuring French or American jazz personalities. On this occasion she interviewed Jim Gurley, a white jazz saxophonist from Chicago. Before immigrating to Paris in the early 1960s, Gurley said, he had played in several black nightclubs on Chicago's south side. And Gurley played at the

Mars Club, a club I visited on several occasions in 1959. It was one of the many post–World War II nightclubs that featured African American musicians, who were instrumental in resurrecting Paris jazz after its glory days between two world wars. Those glory days in Montmartre, in the shadow of the Sacré-Cœur, where African American musicians and entertainers created the Harlem-style jazz culture, are the subject of this book.

In the pages that follow, I focus on some of the principal actors who played critical roles in shaping the jazz scene in Montmartre after the Great War. To capture the spirit of the times and particular events, the narrative frequently resorts to what anthropologists refer to as "thick description" of social situations. In the process, it moves back and forth in time and space, telescoping and juxtaposing the periods of ragtime, jazz, and swing that transformed black American popular music. But it does not attempt a musicological study of this era.

Of the African American jazz musicians who figured prominently in the Paris jazz scene that flourished for two decades, few were alive when I undertook this study. The last of the French contingent of leading jazz musicians, the violinist Stéphane Grappelli, died in 1998.

Writing a story of *Jazz Away From Home*, as Chris Goddard characterized the scene of the Harlem-style musical culture in Paris, is rather like sketching colorful must-see images for a tourist brochure. Words invoke the experience of strolling down the capital's most famous boulevards. But descriptive words do not easily convey the characteristics of a jazz nightclub and its swinging sounds that once attracted Parisians out for an evening in Montmartre. The jazz scene that this study encapsulates became a casualty of the German occupation from 1940 to 1944.

Today, historical memories of Paris jazz performed by African American and French musicians in the early days are kept alive by Maurice and Vonette Cullaz and Jacques Bureaux. The Cullaz's reservoir of invaluable knowledge, as demonstrated to me when we met in Paris in June 1998, derives from their personal association with the Montmartre jazz scene. Maurice was jazz critic for Radio Paris. Bureaux's link to the Paris jazz scene is even older; he was one of the five young founding members of the Hot Club of France. In 1928, while attending the Lycée Carnot in Paris, they "discovered jazz," as he put it to me. None of the five young men knew the then-popular musicians or their music by name; they simply "liked jazz" and went on to encourage its acceptance in France. The

Hot Club of France became an integrating force among musicians of different races, an instrument for bringing together black American and French musicians. Assisting in this promotion of racial and musical harmony was Lucien Lévy, who modernized the transmission of his Radio LL, which became Radio Cité during Paris's golden age of radio.

This study turns on the rise and decline of the African American community in Paris during the first half of the twentieth century. Introduced to France by African American soldiers during World War I, the emerging popular musical genre called jazz captivated the French public. That fascination continues to this day.

"Black Manhattan," as the writer James Weldon Johnson calls New York's Harlem, became the crucible for black American literary, artistic, and musical talent from all corners of the United States, attracted by the call of Charles Johnson and Alain Locke, to gather under the banner of what came to be recognized as the Harlem Renaissance. Musicians came and filled New York's speakeasies and dives with the fast, rippling sounds of ragtime music, the precursor of jazz. Harlem's black-owned nightclubs were the training ground for musicians who later became prominent entertainers on the Parisian nightclub scene. After the armistice they transformed the Montmartre quarter in Paris, which Parisians called la Butte, into the jazz capital. Cultural transformation also took other forms in la Butte. Street life, soul food, strolling, clothing, and hairstyles—all familiar elements of Harlem's ambience—gave the quarter the name Black Broadway in Black Paris, or Harlem in Montmartre. Commonly referred to in the Negro press as the "Race Colony," the musicians and other entertainers formed a community that thrived for two decades.

Harlem's patriotic response to America's entry into World War I was to volunteer its men to serve in New York's 15th Heavy Foot Infantry Regiment. In Harlem they were best known by the French designation, the Harlem Hellfighters. As a fighting unit, the 15th's record of valor earned it the distinction of being the most highly decorated American combat unit in the Great War. Having experienced France's version of liberty, equality, and fraternity, many of the 15th's soldiers decided to remain in France after mustering out of the service. Other former soldiers, especially those who had been members of James Reese Europe's military band, returned to France. Better employment opportunities and the chance to live in a discrimination-free environment prompted expatriation. In

Paris, demand was high for black musicians to fill the bandstands of the small nightclubs that began to proliferate along the narrow streets of Montmartre.

Musicians answering the call settled in Montmartre's cheap hotels, close to the nightclubs in which they worked. An African American community soon formed on the Right Bank, consisting mainly of itinerant musicians—young unmarried males. There were few women and, in 1929, perhaps fewer than a dozen children. It featured none of the cultural institutions associated with the black metropolises from which its inhabitants came; and the spirituals and choirs of Negro church, the pillar of black communities elsewhere, were not evident on the Montmartre musical scene.

Harlem-style nightclub culture rapidly paved the streets of Montmartre. Like missionaries of jazz, black American musicians spread the gospel of hot sounds in tiny cafés and a few sumptuous settings that attracted rich and famous British and American tourists and French socialites. In the Parisian music idiom, this era of the Roaring Twenties was often called the era of *le jazz-hot*. During the twenties the black American Josephine Baker rose to stardom in the musical *Revue Nègre*. She later became the toast of the City of Light. Ada Smith, better known as "Bricktop," brought to Paris her experience of nightclub life gained in the cabaret worlds of Chicago and Harlem. Eugene Jacques Bullard, the first black combat pilot, who had flown for France during World War I, held forth at his nightclub, Le Grand Duc, where he served up jazz and soul food in equal proportions. These developments in the Montmartre jazz scene coincided with the making of the Harlem Renaissance to shape the professional and personal lives of black American musicians, composers, writers, and artists. In Paris, their interactions among themselves and with the wider Parisian society molded the day-to-day character of Harlem in Montmartre.

*Le tumulte noir,* the nightclub culture's "black noise," provided less than complete musical respite from the discomforts of racism and job insecurity that black Americans sought to escape in Paris. During the twenties, Jim Crow took flight across the Atlantic: Ku Klux Klan members arrived in Paris intent on shoring up the racial barriers that French tolerance ignored, against intimacy between black men and white women.

The next decade witnessed a fad for black American jazzmen as well as a decline in Montmartre's jazz-based economy. Because of their sheer numbers on the Montmartre scene, black American musicians were most affected by a law to regulate their numbers in resident bands. Intensifying the impact of the Great Depression, the law cut the nightclub bookings of many jazz musicians. They had to find new venues for work in a market that stretched from northern and eastern Europe to North Africa and the Middle East.

The Hot Club of France, a creation of French jazz lovers, restored much of the glitter to the tarnished golden age of jazz in Paris. During the thirties its chapters spread throughout France and western Europe, promoting jazz through sales of the latest gramophone records by black American musicians. Jazz concerts, organized by Hot Clubs, invited the best Harlem talent to Paris. The formation of the Quintet of the Hot Club of France, featuring the guitarist Django Reinhardt and the violinist Stéphane Grappelli, further enhanced the French role in spreading the gospel of jazz, through the collaboration of French and black American jazzmen. In 1939, as war with Germany seemed inevitable, the vast majority of the black community returned to America. German troops occupied Paris on 14 June 1940. Harlem in Montmartre ceased to exist.

The occupation profoundly affected the jazz culture of Paris. A series of Nazi-imposed laws and regulations intended to create a new moral order and rid France of the perceived decadence accumulated in the years after World War I. High on the list of those in need of moral cleansing were French youth, who, like their German counterparts, had acquired a passion for jazz-swing music. The Nazis looked on jazz as the principal source of cultural pollution. Calling it "degenerate negro-jewish" music, they banned American jazz from the airways and nightclubs. French youths, who came to be known as *Zazous,* organized resistance to the Nazi ban on jazz by adopting bizarre clothing and chanting songs that defiantly mocked the repression. At the risk of persecution, they also openly expressed sympathy for Jews.

As black American musicians in James Reese Europe's band had brought the citizens of Aix-les-Bains to their feet, screaming to hear more after their first sounds of jazz in 1918, black American soldiers in the liberation army nearly thirty years later again raised the curtain on jazz. The Nazi ban on black American jazz had ceased. "Black jazz returns to Paris," is how the French and Negro press acclaimed the joy of old favorite tunes being savored in Left Bank bars and cafés. Black American GI clubs, with black American GI bands, welcomed Parisians to experience the waves of black American musical sounds that continue to this day.

The Paris jazz story begins in Harlem.

# 1 | MAKING NOISE AND STOMPING FEET

In Harlem, a narrow stretch of land less than two miles north of New York City's Central Park that James Weldon Johnson calls "Black Manhattan," lived more than "two hundred thousand Negroes" in 1910. In this stretch of upper Manhattan there were more people "to the square acre than in any other place on earth." During the years before World War I, still more black folks moved "uptown." Urban black migrants from the Atlantic seaboard cities, as well as from the rural South, the British West Indies, and the Antilles poured into Harlem month by month, displacing white populations. What lured a great many was the hope of working in factories. Aggressive leasing and purchasing of white-owned houses and large apartment blocks by black realtors provided "Negroes with better, cleaner, more modern, more airy, more sunny houses than they ever lived in before." Attracting migrants of varied talents, Harlem became "the intellectual and artistic capital of the Negro world."[1]

Before the northward extension of Harlem, West 53d Street had been the meeting place of entertainers and musicians who would gather at Jim Marshall's famous hotel at 127–29 West 53d Street. Across the street the Clef Club, formed in 1912 by James Reese Europe and located in rented space at 134 West 53d Street, was beginning to dominate contemporary black music. The Clef Club became a headquarters of sorts, especially in booking jobs for musicians as "colored entertainment" at white society leaders' parties.

"Harlem became a city within a city," writes James Weldon Johnson.[2] And it was a mecca for musical talent. Ragtime pianist Willie "The Lion" Smith recalled that Harlem was "the home and favored stomping ground of the greatest acts in colored show business. During the twenties, people from the world of entertainment, people from all over the country, would go 'uptown' to see the latest techniques in music, dancing and comedy."[3] Visitors from France included the composers Darius Milhaud and Erik Satie as well as popular music-hall entertainers Maurice Chevalier and Yvonne George, who often stopped in Harlem for quick musical tutorials during voyages to New York.

Even before 1914, Harlem's small nightclubs and honky-tonks had begun to nourish talented young black musicians and entertainers. Unlike black Bohemia's notorious clubs in the old Tenderloin along West 35th Street that catered to the common vices of gambling and prostitution, several of these clubs offered a professional and congenial social atmosphere in which artistic ideas were born and exhibited. Leroy Wilkins's club at 135th Street and Fifth Avenue, the oldest cabaret in Harlem, opened around 1910 in the basement of an old brownstone building. Wilkins was the first Harlem cabaret owner to insist on the proper clothes for his floor manager, waiters, and musicians. On weekends *everybody*—including the customers—had to wear formal dress (tuxedos for the men), a fashion in nightlife later seen in black-owned nightclubs in Paris.

This was still the era of ragtime, the precursor of jazz. And New York was a piano man's town. Edward Johnson, a former boxer who ran the Douglas Club on 28th Street, brought in the crowds nightly to dance to the music of his piano man named Jumbo. One-leg Willie Joseph held sway at Mule Johnson's at 108 West 32d Street. Black musicians were not alone in playing ragtime piano; its popularity was growing steadily among white pianists. Jimmy Durante started playing ragtime at Diamond Tony's on Coney Island. Irving Berlin was at one time a singing waiter at Nigger Mike's in Chinatown. Vincent Lopez started as a pianist on the honky-tonk circuit, from which he launched his big band jazz career.

Theatrical talent rarely ventured into these clubs but stayed primarily on the minstrel stage. Small black troupes and duets refined their musical acts to the acclaim of black and white patrons of the Douglas Club, the

Anderson Club, the Waldorf, Johnny Johnson's, Ike Hine's, and other better known clubs before beginning a tour of Europe and performing in the renowned Parisian music halls of Montmartre.[4]

By the second decade of the century, of the cities that would soon become famous for jazz New Orleans alone had established a jazz culture.[5] And until Harlem emerged as a center of jazz, the new sound was nourished in New York at one of the first so-called jazz joints, a café on 37th Street near Seventh Avenue run by William Banks. In 1917 he moved his famous café uptown to 23 West 133d Street between Lenox and Fifth Avenues. At about the same time, James Reese Europe was recruiting Harlem musicians for the 15th New York Infantry Regiment's military band, which he was to lead during the Great War in France.

Despite the relative freedom of movement between blacks and whites in some areas of New York life during this second decade of the twentieth century, racial segregation still barred would-be black patrons from white-owned nightclubs in downtown Manhattan. Even so, black musical talent was all the rage. Risqué songs and dances gained popularity in general society through black entertainers who played ragtime music. Attracted to the experiences of viewing black talent in situ, Vernon Castle, of the famous dance team of Irene and Vernon Castle, was among the many white entertainers who went to Black Manhattan's nightclubs to learn the latest in black dance steps.[6] By the fall of 1913, the Castles led the social revolution of dancing that swept America and reached Paris after the armistice. (In America, the defenders of religious and spiritual values had objected to dancing as an indecent act; in Paris, restaurateurs were the ones who objected because it interrupted a well-prepared meal.)

The wildly popular fox-trot danced by the Castles was based on James Reese Europe's musical scores and dance steps he learned from the "father of the blues," W. C. Handy.[7] Europe called the "One Step," which he created, "the national dance of the Negro." The Castles soon included it in their repertoire. The Castle Lame Duck Waltz and the Castle House Rag, featured in the Castles' performances, brought Europe, the composer, only one cent in royalties for each copy of sheet music or each phonograph record. "A white man," Europe complained bitterly, "would receive from six to twelve times the royalties I receive." On 9 April 1914 the Castles unabashedly displayed their dancing wizardry in an exhibition at the Manhattan Casino, 155th Street and Eighth Avenue, appearing before black

Harlemites from whom they had learned their most popular steps.[8] The performance put on by the Tempo Club, "one of the leading Negro organizations of the city," was for a European benefit tour by James Reese Europe. Before the end of the decade, Europe had created his own revolution in France.

Before the first artillery shell was lobbed in the Great War, the sounds of black music had already crossed the Atlantic. In the summer of 1914 drummer Louis Mitchell, considered "the first man to bring jazz to Britain," and his Southern Symphonists Quintet opened at the Piccadilly Restaurant in London.[9] Featured in the floor show were the dancers Louise Alexander and Jack Jarrett. British journalists and French music critics described Mitchell as "the supreme artist of noise" and as "la plus grande batterie du monde." His drumming style personified the jazz of the age. Born in New York City on 17 December 1885, Mitchell in his youth had sung religious songs, worked in minstrel shows and vaudeville, and become famous as a ragtime drummer. When Harlem entertainers began to move downtown with engagements in swank white-owned clubs, Mitchell's Quintet made its debut at the Taverne Louis, in the Flatiron building in New York, on 15 April 1912.[10] While performing there he met Irving Berlin, who advised him to go to Europe.[11] Mitchell did go, but at the outbreak of war he and his quintet shortened the trip and returned to America. An invitation awaited him to tour immediately with the Clef Club orchestra of sixty musicians directed by James Reese Europe.[12]

In August 1915 Mitchell was again in London, playing drums in the slam-bang style that made him famous, embellishing his act with clowning at Ciro's Club off Leicester Square. Billed as the whirlwind ragtime drummer, he played at the London Coliseum in September 1916, followed by an engagement at the Alhambra in Glasgow. By then Mitchell had formed the Syncopating Sextette, which played in Glasgow in February 1917 (this was at least eighteen months before the Original Dixieland Jazz Band of white musicians crossed the Atlantic). Renamed the Seven Spades, the sextet played at the Liverpool Music Hall and later at the London Palladium. Mitchell's success brought a commission from the Casino de Paris, to organize an all-American Negro orchestra of forty-five men, followed shortly by its cancellation (owing to U.S. State Department restrictions on postwar travel to France). Mitchell, then in New York to recruit for the orchestra, instead formed a seven-man group he called Mitchell's Jazz Kings and headed off to France in 1918 to give free concerts for weary Allied troops. One of Mitchell's sidemen was Crickett Smith, a cornet player who became a legendary figure with the first American jazz bands that toured Europe. A young musician named Sidney Bechet had planned to join Mitchell's group but instead accepted an invitation to join another group on its way to the Continent, Will Marion Cook's Southern Syncopated Orchestra, known as the Syncopates.[13]

Will Marion Cook's bitter experiences in the concert world had cut short his promising career as a classical violinist. Born in Washington, D.C., in 1865, the son of a professor of law at Howard University, Will Marion went to Oberlin's Conservatory of Music at thirteen years of age. His outstanding studies won for him a scholarship to study in Berlin under the famous German violinist Josef Joachim. After five years of study abroad, Cook returned to the United States in 1895 and studied composition at the National Conservatory of Music in New York, then headed by Antonin Dvořák. Cook was the first violinist with the Boston Symphony when the orchestra's soloist died; Cook assumed he would automatically take over the role. But though he could sit in the first chair, the orchestra committee told Cook, as a black man he would not play the solos. Angered by the racist decision, he stamped on his violin and walked out. Turning his talent to the world of musical comedy, Cook became "composer in chief" for a steady stream of black musicals.[14] Bert Williams and George Walker, a famous vaudeville team, were the stars of Cook's black American musical-comedy sketch, the first in America, *Clorindy, the Origin of the Cakewalk*. The musical created a sensation at its opening on Broadway in the summer of 1898.

In 1919 the Syncopates crossed the Atlantic in two parties, sailing on the SS *Northland* and the SS *Carmenia,* the latter carrying Bechet and Cook. Cook was largely instrumental in creating what was to become the vogue for black musicians in England and all over Europe. As the Syncopates docked at Liverpool on 14 June, the city was experiencing terrible race riots; Cardiff, in Wales, with its large black community, was their next stop. In the south of England, London was poised to shed the sufferings and hardships its inhabitants had endured during World War I. The public craved gaiety. "The feeling affected all strata of society; after four years of carnage and tension the time had come for everyone to re-lax," observed one writer. Problems of unemployment and material short-ages loomed, but even those who realized these facts were determined to enjoy themselves. For Britain, the jazz age was about to begin.[15]

Across the Channel, Mitchell's Jazz Kings were engaged by the Casino de Paris, a music hall in rue de Clichy but south of Montmartre, where they stayed five years. The Jazz Kings often accompanied Mistinguett and Maurice Chevalier, feature attractions there (and elsewhere). By the close of Mitchell's engagement at the Casino de Paris, new black American mu-sical talent had entered the developing jazz scene, no longer hauling the baggage of ragtime and "cooning" (performance in blackface makeup). And by the mid-1920s jazz had established a firm foothold.

The landscape of Montmartre had shifted gradually over a half-century between 1870 and 1920 from rural district to artists' and musicians' quar-ter before the jazz era began. Dominating the landscape was the hill on which the famous Sacré-Cœur was built (completed in 1911). The limits of the Montmartre village, known locally as la Butte, were defined south by rue des Abbesses, north by rue Caulaincourt, east by rue de Clignan-court, and west by avenue Junot.[16] Within these boundaries a popular insurrection had taken place in 1871. Peasants suspicious of official regu-lations had set up barricades to protest tariffs imposed by Parisian bu-reaucrats on the movements of persons and goods in and out of la Butte.

In 1900 the little world of la Butte included a notable proportion of landowners, farmers, market gardeners, and the like. The city of Paris off to the south seemed remote. The poverty rate was high: indigents num-bered 7.5 percent of the population. "Misery, oh! yes great misery with no hope of help in sickness or unemployment," writes Crespelle, capturing the despair of this population.[17] Settling into the mélange of proletarians and bourgeois was a colony of young artists who would shape the art world in Paris of the early 1920s. Leading among these artists were Pablo Picasso, Georges Braque, Raoul Dufy, Juan Gris, Max Jacob, Maurice de Vlaminck, and Maurice Utrillo.

Loud brawls and obscene songs issuing from cabarets often punctuated the activities of Montmartre's colony of artists, poets, and amateur actors. Scenes of switchblade fights, gunplay, and pimps punishing their *filles* resembled contemporary Western films but were all too real. On Saturdays and Sundays the place Pigalle and boulevards de Rochechouart and Clichy were hosts to village feasts. Along these streets lined with bars, brasseries, cabarets, theaters, and *cirques,* electric signs began to appear, illuminating the names of Tabarin, Monaco, Le Rat Mort, Royal-Souper, Mirliton, Le Chat Noir, and of course the Bal du Moulin Rouge, the setting earlier for many of Henri de Toulouse-Lautrec's famous graphics. And, between the high and low of Montmartre, were "hot" streets like rue Coustou and rue de Steinkerque, celebrated for their cheap hotels and brothels, where the going rate was 3 francs the visit.[18]

Very soon Le Chat Noir became a sort of literary forum, attracting artists whose talents lay with pencil and paper, not paint and canvas. Neither writers nor painters were wealthy, living just a shade above poverty in cold, drafty, and uncomfortable studios and small rooms. They were served by diverse cafés and restaurants in two categories: very modest and superior. In the long tradition of numerous restaurants and cafés on the place du Tertre, the celebrated Mère Catherine, founded in 1792, is the oldest. The number of cafés in Montmartre relative to its population was incredibly large. For the very poor, also numerous, café-hotels offered wretched accommodations at a price of 1 franc per night. L'Hôtel du Poirier, or Bateau-Lavoir, was temporary home to several people of artistic talent who had fallen on hard times. Many budding artists, including Modigliani, stayed there.[19]

Important to bohemian life in Montmartre was the zone known as the Maquis. Extending on the north flank of la Butte, between the Moulin de la Galette and rue Caulaincourt, the zone was transformed in the nineteenth century to a shantytown. Amidst the flimsily constructed sheds in open fields, the inhabitants—artists, marginals, truants—reproduced country life in town. Rabbits and goats bred and grazed in the marshy jungle of syringa and hawthorn, lilies and roses. To children, this vast no-man's-land, the Maquis, was a paradise of sorts. One child it attracted was Jean Renoir, who went there often to pick mushrooms.

Between 1906 and 1909, Montmartre was regarded as the best place to go to smoke opium and hashish.[20] Modigliani was already taking drugs when he got to Paris and frequented shady cafés on place de Clichy and rue Pigalle, in company with the *bohémiens.* The popular image of Montmartre and drugs remained long after the draining of the swamp, which began in 1902 and took twenty years to complete.

During the summer of 1912 Picasso left the studio in the Bateau-Lavoir where he had painted his *Demoiselles d'Avignon*. After a brief holiday at Céret he moved his belongings to a studio at 242 boulevard Raspail, next to the Montparnasse cemetery in the southern part of Paris. His departure for the Left Bank symbolized the demise of the artists' colony in Montmartre. Only a few stalwarts remained, including Gris, Braque, and Utrillo.[21]

The exodus of artists and writers left intact the grand music-hall tradition for which the area was known. Music-hall revues staged against the backdrop of spectacular colorful settings perpetuated a culture of fantasy, depicting other worlds and other peoples. At the Folies-Bergère, Moorish decorations complete with a Turkish bath and luxuriant green plants created an illusion of a scene from the Arabian Nights.[22] Black Antilleans gave life to static stage props; black Americans gave to musical revues a melange of high-jinks, comic burlesque, and song and dance not hitherto witnessed. The Moulin Rouge and Folies-Bergère in Montmartre, Maxim's near the Champs-Élysées, the Casino de Paris south of Montmartre—all were popular music halls that had engaged black American musical and vaudeville talent decades before Carolyn Dudley's *Revue Nègre* starring Josephine Baker arrived in Paris at the Théâtre des Champs-Élysées in 1925.

The music-hall tradition had its beginnings in the nineteenth century. Nearly four decades before the Fisk Jubilee Singers, the most popular of the early groups to tour Europe, arrived in 1872, the bandleader Frank Johnson of Philadelphia took his musical group to London to perform in 1837. His was the first American group, black or white, to perform anywhere in Europe. Noting the popularity of black musical groups among European theatergoers, white entertainers in blackface—claiming to be "Ethiopians"—appeared as early as the 1840s. It is doubtful, however, that the Jubilee Singers performed in Montmartre music halls during their eight-month European concert tour. A setting with chorus girls in scanty costumes dancing the cancan and delivering boisterous lyrics did not suit the spirituals and sacred religious songs for which the Jubilee Singers had gained a worldwide reputation.

Whether influenced by music-hall culture or seizing on the opportunity for professional bookings, in 1895 a splinter group of the singers, known as the Four Black Troubadours, changed their repertoire of Negro spirituals to comic burlesque and played in concert halls and variety houses.[23] The Troubadours popularized the cakewalk in Europe, and in Paris even the classic waltz was abandoned for the new exotic dance steps.[24] By the turn of the century, the song-and-dance team called Nègres Joyeux was the rage at the Nouveau Cirque in Paris.[25] Clowning, buffoonery, and blackface still characterized the entertainment style of groups like the Four Black Diamonds, originally from San Francisco, who started their European career in 1905 and possibly never returned to America.[26]

From 1900 up to World War I, black entertainers rushed to tour concert halls and music halls in Europe, where race relations were more relaxed than in the United States. Yambo and Dixie Davis were one of several black-and-white song-and-dance acts performing in Europe, where they did not experience overt racial discrimination. The social climate doubtless encouraged many of the early black entertainers traveling in Europe to remain there permanently. Arabella Fields, a contralto born in Philadelphia in 1879, perhaps the first black American to record commercially in Europe, in 1907, made Germany her home.[27] The trickle of black American entertainers who remained in Europe as expatriates increased to a steady flow in later years, especially after jazz became a popular musical form in Paris.

In the early era Will Garland, a musician and comedian with Maharas' Minstrels, toured Europe, eventually settling in England. And after their world tour spreading ragtime, in 1906 Holman's American Serenaders performed in Paris, where some members of the group made their home.[28] Black communities back in the United States would have despised the promotional names that many of them adopted for European audiences: the Four Black Spades, the Four Black Diamonds, Bonnie Goodwin's Picaninies, who all played at the Folies-Bèrgere in 1904, were names with great popular appeal. Advertisements and reviews carried illustrations of grotesque and eccentric black entertainers, presenting songs and dances, shaking tambourines, plucking banjos, and snapping castanets, the descriptive texts liberally sprinkled with "nigger," "coon," and "pickaninnies."[29]

Louis Douglas's arrival in Europe to perform with Belle Davis's Georgia Picaninnies in 1903 symbolically rang down the curtain on the style of black entertainment that Jelly Roll Morton and others called "cooning." "Of course," he once said, "I had burnt cork on my face, and my lips were painted like they were big and white, but since everybody was doing it I didn't let it get to me." With Will Garland's Negro Opera Troupe, Douglas produced *A Trip to Coontown,* which played a European tour.[30] After moving to Paris, Douglas choreographed musical revues and in some of them performed his own dazzling dance steps. (The most famous of his productions—*Revue Nègre*—was staged after the armistice of 1918.)[31]

The Paris Exposition of 1900 had centered attention on the achievements of black Americans other than as musical entertainers. In the Palace of Social Economy, at the edge of the Seine, "the exhibit of American Negroes, planned and executed by Negroes," W. E. B. Du Bois observed, "showed the history of the Negro past and present," illustrated by charts and photographs.[32] A unique and most striking feature of the exhibit, Du Bois insisted, was that of American Negro literature, which traced the development of Negro thought through books, periodicals, and newspapers. A quarter of a century later, the works by writers of the Harlem Renaissance living in Paris—Langston Hughes, Countee Cullen, Gwendolyn Bennett, Jessie Fauset, and Claude McKay—marked the progression of Negro thought.[33] Over time, works by artists and students of classical music joined the outpouring of talent and integrated it with the achievements of black American musical entertainers in the quarter called Harlem in Montmartre.

On 7 May 1915, German submarines torpedoed the British luxury liner SS *Lusitania* off the coast of Munster, Ireland, in the icy waters of the Irish Sea. Plying the maritime lanes of the Atlantic, German submarines were ordered to sink all ships approaching the ports of England and France. The loss of the *Lusitania,* in which 1,198 people were drowned, including 128 Americans, helped weaken American isolationism, creating an emotional fervor to strengthen a common heritage linking two continents. President Wilson's address to Congress in April 1917 asking for a declaration of war against Kaiser Wilhelm's Germany was approved unanimously.

Harlem perceived the sinking of the *Lusitania* and Congress's declaration of war much as W. E. B. Du Bois did: "The last hour of a horrible war has come." [1] Patriotism was high in 1917. It transformed the souls of most Americans during the war, not least the souls of black folks. Harlem joined the clamor to defend democracy abroad, as black voices were raised elsewhere in the Bronzevilles of America. A special 1918 issue of *The Crisis* was dedicated to "the nearly 100,000 men of Negro descent who are today called to arms for the United States." The philosophy of war entailed a double meaning for black soldiers: freedom abroad; freedom at home. Linking the two themes, Du Bois implored: "Patience, then, without compromise; silence without surrender; grim determination never to cease striving until we can vote, travel, learn, work and enjoy peace—all this, and yet with it and above it all the tramp of our armies over the blood-stained lilies of France to show the world again what the loyalty and bravery of black men means."[2] This philosophy was to repeat itself, instilling patriotism in black soldiers responding to the call to arms a generation later.[3]

William Hayward, a white colonel in the Nebraska National Guard, had been appointed to shape black patriotism into action by organizing the 15th Heavy Foot Infantry Regiment (Colored) of the New York National Guard in June 1916. Its eventual fame as the Harlem Hellfighters, the most decorated American fighting unit in the American Expeditionary Force (AEF), belies its meager, indeed shameful, beginnings. Racial opposition arose from the highest military authorities over arming black men to fight Germans or giving black units even the barest essentials for military training. The 15th began "its existence with one white officer and little else; no rifles, ammunition, uniforms, armory to drill in, headquarters for recruitment, or troops. There was also little willingness in either the regular army or the National Guard Quartermaster Departments to assist Hayward in getting what he needed to get started."[4] Eventually, Hayward approached the sympathetic New York mayor, John Purry Mitchell, who used his power of office and old-time political muscle to get City Hall to lease a dance hall in the Lafayette Theatre for use as an "armory," and a former cigar store at the corner of the same building for a recruitment office. A famous landmark on 132d Street and Seventh Avenue, the Lafayette Theatre had been the venue for all the major vaudeville and musical revues that played in Harlem. Recruitment and training of the 15th Infantry Regiment began there on 29 June.[5]

On 18 September 1916 James Reese Europe answered the call to arms. Enlisting as a private, he was assigned to a machine-gun company in the first battalion of the 15th, under the command of Major Arthur Little. Europe's enlistment had less to do with patriotism than with his perception that a national guard unit in Harlem would benefit the entire community. In the common parlance of the times, Europe was considered a "Race Man," a person filled with pride in his race and a strong commitment to racial progress. His perception of blacks' role in creating racial progress stemmed from his own experiences as a founding member and director of Harlem's famous Clef Club orchestra, which dominated the music entertainment world for the pleasure and enjoyment of New York's high society.

The Clef Club (and later the Tempo Club, which Europe founded after resigning from the Clef in 1914) served as booking agent for black musicians in New York's hotels and cabarets. Europe's popularity led to a series of recordings of dance music that his orchestra made for Victor Records; "it was one of the first contracts ever given by a major record company to a black musician and the first ever to a black orchestra."[6] And when Europe's orchestra performed the Clef Club Carnegie Hall concerts, first on 2 May 1912, then in 1913 and again in 1914, his personal reputation as a conductor, composer, and organizer not only elevated him but benefited Harlem as well. A reviewer of the 1912 concert captured the spirit of a delighted audience:

> It was an astonishing sight, that negro audience (a sort of American "Balalaika") that filled the entire stage with banjos, mandolins, guitars, a few violins, violas, celli, double basses, here and there a wind instrument, some drums, eloquent in syncopation, and the sonorous background of ten upright pianos corresponding in efficiency to the *cymbalon* of the Hungarian band. Europe uplifted his baton and the orchestra began (with an accuracy of "attack" that many a greater band might envy) a stirring march composed by the leader. It was the "Pied Piper" again, for as one looked through the audience, one saw heads swaying and feet tapping in time to the incisive rhythm, and when the march neared the end, and the whole band burst out singing as well as playing, the novelty of this climax—a novelty to the whites, at least, brought a very storm of tumultuous applause. After that, the audience settled back with a broad smile of enjoyment.[7]

The Harlemites who clamored for tickets and the best seating at Europe's Carnegie Hall concerts shared Europe's pride in the acclaim from New York society and patrons of the arts. With equal commitment to racial pride, vaudeville star Bert Williams and Lester A. Walton, music critic for the Harlem weekly, *The New York Age,* encouraged Europe to enlist in the 15th. As he bent to their persuasion, Europe could not have anticipated how a reputation in New York's high society would help him, as a line soldier, transform the face of popular music in France. Also attracted to the idea of assisting the war effort in uniform was Noble Sissle, who had once played in Europe's Tempo Club orchestra. Sissle was sworn in as a private in Company K on 26 September 1916; that same day, Europe was promoted to first sergeant.

Despite Du Bois's appeal to patriotism, enlistments were slow among Harlemites in 1917; the call to arms attracted fewer potential recruits than the call to better-paying jobs in defense work. Showmanship, Colonel Hayward thought, might encourage enlistments where parades in Central Park failed. He called on Egbert E. Thompson, brass section director of the Clef Club orchestra, to provide music for several parades and organize concerts, but Thompson's efforts made little progress. Since few musicians had enlisted in the 15th, Hayward convinced Thompson to recruit musicians for the specific purpose of organizing a permanent regimental band. But Thompson did not reach even this seemingly modest goal: "few of the better musicians, the ones who could most easily make the transition from playing in dance orchestras to performing in a military band concert and marching band, could afford to give up their evenings and the high salaries they earned for regular army pay." [8]

Hayward then turned to James Reese Europe, known as the most famous orchestra leader in the city. Europe had passed the officers' examination and was scheduled to be commissioned as a first lieutenant and given command of one of the regiment's machine-gun companies. When Colonel Hayward summoned him, it was not Europe's advice he sought: he commanded Europe "to organize for me the best damn band in the United States Army." [9]

To help Europe in this assignment, Hayward bent army regulations. Aside from fulfilling its role as a recruitment device, Hayward wanted his band to exceed the reputation of the black American 8th Illinois National Guard Regiment's concert band. He secured private donations to augment allocations from headquarters for the purchase of band instruments, and he manipulated assignments of musically talented enlistees to increase the size of Europe's band from the regulation size of twenty-eight pieces to sixty; its final size was sixty-five. Among the private donors were John D. Rockefeller, Jr., and Daniel G. Reid, "the Tin Plate King," who donated $10,000. [10]

As reorganization of the band continued, Noble Sissle, with Hayward's help, was transferred from Company K to Headquarters Company, detailed to special duty with the band, and eventually became drum major.[11] Sissle's new position gave him greater visibility to begin an advertising campaign in national black newspapers, appealing to pride, patriotism, and payment. One such advertisement read:

ATTENTION

NEGRO MUSICIANS OF AMERICA

LAST CALL      GOLDEN OPPORTUNITY

IF YOU WANT TO DO YOUR DUTY IN THE PRESENT CRISIS

. . .

THEN WIRE OR CALL

LT. JAMES REESE EUROPE, CARE OF 15TH REGIMENT, N.Y. INFANTRY, HARLEM RIVER PARK CASINO, 127TH STREET AND 2ND AVENUE, NEW YORK CITY.

P.S. THERE ARE ONLY A FEW MORE VACANCIES LEFT, AND THE REGIMENT GOES TO CAMP, SUNDAY, MAY 13TH.

SO HURRY! HURRY! HURRY[12]

The appeal caught the attention of several veteran army musicians from the 9th and 10th Cavalries, who had fought in the Indian wars, and from the 24th and 25th Infantries. Europe himself went on a special mission to San Juan, Puerto Rico, to recruit reed instrumentalists and after three days came back to New York with thirteen talented young players, none of whom commanded more than a smattering of English. A few days after Europe's return with his newly recruited musicians, the 15th Infantry Regiment embarked at dawn on 13 May 1917 for training camp near Peekskill, New York.

After eighteen days of rigorous field training, the formerly ragged outfit of volunteers was transformed into a regiment that resembled experienced soldiers. The 15th demonstrated its polish at drill on 30 May 1917 as the regiment marched in New York's Memorial Day parade. Eighteen months and eighteen days later, the real spit and polish of a regimental band would shine through when the 15th Infantry marched in the victory parade down New York's Fifth Avenue.

But racism pockmarked the road leading to that second parade. It began when the 15th Infantry was ordered to join the regiments of the 27th Division of the New York National Guard and continued through its training at Camp Wadsworth in Spartanburg, South Carolina. Its members had already experienced disappointment at being denied the honor of joining other regiments of the New York National Guard in making a farewell parade down Fifth Avenue, on their way to final preparation for war service in France. Much later, when the 69th Regiment marched off to join the Rainbow Division of Japanese American and African American soldiers in France, Colonel Hayward was told that "black was not one of the colors in the rainbow." [13]

When Spartanburg's mayor, J. T. Floyd, learned toward the end of August 1917 that the War Department had ordered black soldiers to be among those stationed for training at Camp Wadsworth, he announced his opposition to the presence of the 15th among white troops at the camp. He based his opposition "on the grounds that trouble might result if the 15th refused to accept the limited liberties accorded to the city's colored population." Perhaps he anticipated an outbreak of racial violence like the full-scale riot by black troops stationed in Houston, Texas, that same month. Insults from local white citizens had precipitated a gun battle that left seventeen whites dead; thirteen black soldiers from the 24th Infantry were court-martialed and hanged. Mayor Floyd contended that "with their northern ideas about race equality, [these black soldiers] will probably expect to be treated like white men. I can say right here that they will not be treated like white men. I can say right here that they will not be treated as anything except negroes. We shall treat them exactly as we treat our resident negroes." Backing up the mayor's pronouncement, an official of the Chamber of Commerce proclaimed, "I can tell you for certain that if any of these colored soldiers go in any of the soda stores and the like and ask to be served they'll be knocked down. Somebody will throw a bottle. We don't allow negroes to use the same glass that a white may later have to drink out of. We have our customs down here, and we aren't going to alter them." [14]

Noble Sissle, drum major of Europe's band, soon learned that Southern customs restricting commensalism across racial lines extended even to a black man who entered the lobby of a hotel to buy a newspaper. For the unconscionable act of not removing his hat when entering the lobby of a small Spartanburg hotel, Sissle was attacked by the proprietor and thrown from the premises. The proprietor's actions would have triggered a small riot when white soldiers came immediately to Sissle's defense, if James Reese Europe had not intervened, using the authority of his officer's rank to quell the disturbance. What contained this and other racial incidents while the 15th was in training was the behavior of white soldiers. They closed ranks, courageously defending the rights of black infantrymen against the bigotry of Spartanburg citizens who welcomed an opportunity to repeat the Houston, Texas, riots. And no riots occurred during the unit's stay in Spartanburg. The 15th Infantry Regiment received orders to break camp on the morning of 24 October 1917. After marching in review, the regiment was greeted with the tune of "Over There" as it passed through other camps on the way to the railroad siding.

Now prepared and ready to take up arms on the fighting front, the rank and file of the 15th Infantry Regiment had Europe's regimental band to keep their spirits up. Among the band's sixty-five musician recruits were the famous Chicago cornetist Jaçon Frank De Braithe (De Broit), rhythmic drummer Buddy Gilmore (the first jazz drummer in the modern sense of the word), trumpeter Arthur Briggs, the Harlem dancer Bill "Bojangles" Robinson, and Noble Sissle, "who played the cornet like anything and knows all the tricks of drum majoring, and sings like a lark, and writes verses by the yard." [15] Later, after being mustered out of the army, Sissle teamed with Eubie Blake to form a celebrated piano duo that cowrote to worldwide acclaim the vaudeville spectaculars *Shuffle Along* (with Flournoy Miller and Aubrey Lyles) and *The Chocolate Dandies*. There were also Raphael Hernandez, baritone saxophonist, Ward "Trombone" Andrews, Elize Rijos, clarinetist, and Frank De Bronte, who after Europe himself was called the king of jazz.

"The rest of the band—marimbaphones, the double B-flat helicons, the bunch of French horns and all the rest clear down to the cymbals, were manned by other eminent operators, making what is called a toot ensemble at once hope-reviving and awe-inspiring."[16] The band's personnel included musicians who could sing, dance, and perform comedy or almost any other kind of entertaining. And the band itself ranged from the first-class marching unit led by a strutting Bojangles, to several dance orchestras or a theater orchestra accompanying the versatile talents of its entertainers.

These musicians, now trained as fighting soldiers, prepared to pursue their mission. Adopting the 15th Infantry's nickname, the Harlem Hellfighters, Europe's band embarked with the regiment for France from Hoboken, New Jersey, aboard the SS *Pocahontas* on 11 November 1917. After two days at sea, the *Pocahontas* limped back to Hoboken for repairs but resumed its voyage to France in convoy on 14 December. To avoid German submarines plying the Atlantic, the convoy divided into halves, one making for St-Nazaire, the other for Brest. At daybreak on 27 December the French coast came into view. At about eleven o'clock in the morning, the *Pocahontas* sailed into the beautiful harbor of Brest. The Hellfighters set foot on French soil on New Year's Day 1918.

Europe's band immediately stirred France when it came ashore at Brest. It wanted the French to be aware of its presence, so it blew some plain ordinary jazz over the town, letting the countryside know that hope for defeat of the kaiser's army was not entirely dead. From Brest the band went to St-Nazaire, sowing jazz selections over the fields and cantons en route.[17]

Europe's reputation—as a bandmaster of syncopated style jazz, leader of a popular orchestra for New York society, and accompanist for America's popular dancing sweethearts, Irene and Vernon Castle—had preceded the landing in France. General John Pershing, commander of the American Expeditionary Force, immediately ordered the band transferred to his headquarters, so it could entertain the officers from the British and French armies who were called to conferences with the general. Thus "the Hellfighters were Pershing's personal band for over a year."[18]

Even while Europe's band entertained his headquarters with syncopated sounds, Pershing confronted a political problem that reverberated back home: keeping Jim Crow alive on the western front. As black troops left for France in 1918, some Southern communities were already refurbishing Ku Klux Klan terrorism for postbellum use. In France, Pershing's staff of white officers dutifully carried out his standing order against fraternization—or even a handshake—between black soldiers and French civilians. General Hay assembled his brigade of the all-black 92d Division, and in words echoing those enunciated by Mayor Floyd in Spartanburg, told the soldiers to treat French women as they had been made to treat white women in America. Orders were issued prohibiting black soldiers from entering the homes of the French or talking with women on any subject whatsoever. And though black soldiers were essential to the war effort, they were barred from engaging in combat against the white enemy. Pershing's solution to meeting this restriction was to amalgamate the 15th Infantry Regiment and other black units in combat under French command.[19]

When demands mounted from the rest of the army for Europe's music to raise morale, and French civilians too clamored for the entertainment, Pershing was no longer able to justify keeping Europe's band near headquarters. He ordered the band on a six-week tour, a goodwill mission in provincial France. Between 12 February 1918 and 29 March 1918, the Hellfighters traveled 2,000 miles and played in twenty-five French cities, including Angers, Sancaize, Moulins, la Ferté, Varenne, Créchy, St-Étienne, Lyon, Culoz, and St-German-des-Fossés.[20] Under the regimental command of Arthur Little, then a captain, the band proceeded by train from the base camp to Nantes. Its first concert at the opera house there was in honor of Lincoln's birthday but for the financial benefit of a French charitable institution.[21] The band arrived at Aix-les-Bains on 15 February 1918. It stayed at this resort one full month, two weeks longer than originally ordered.

On the evening of 16 March 1918, the man in charge of entertainment at the casino theater in Aix-les-Bains announced to its patrons that they had heard the last concert by the band of the 15th New York Infantry. It was to rejoin its regiment at Connantre, department of Marne. Captain Little described the near pandemonium that erupted from the audience on hearing the announcement. "The speech was never finished," he added. And a solid phalanx of civilians from curb to curb lined the band's march to the station. As it played its farewell song, "the crowd cheered without ceasing; women and children wept."[22] Twenty-six years later in Paris similar scenes would recur as grateful French citizens celebrated the liberation of their city.

There were few dry eyes in the band as it moved north to rejoin the regiment. In keeping with General Pershing's orders not to permit black soldiers under U.S. command to engage in combat against German soldiers, at Connantre the 15th Heavy Foot Infantry was temporarily detached from the United States Army and assigned to the 16th Division of the French Army. Under French command, it was known as the 369e régiment d'Infanterie U.S.[23]

Europe's band had sounded its last note in concert until it marched in the great victory parade in New York in February 1919. Now with drums silenced, brass horns muffled, the men entered the trenches with other fighters of the 369th. The band said to have "jazzed its way through France" now forced its lines "to the very banks of the Rhine, where the world woke up and found [the hundred master jazzers] on the day armistice was signed."[24]

The regiment won distinction on a number of terrains. Under the command of Général Lebouch, it was the first unit of the Allied armies to reach the Rhine, on 18 November, with the Second French Army.[25] It had been under fire 191 days. Captain Little wrote in his diary,

> They had achieved the impossible! Recruited as fighting men, in
> ridicule; trained and mustered into Federal service, in more ridi-
> cule; sent to France as a safe political solution of a volcanic politi-
> cal problem; loaned to the French Army as another easy way
> out—these men had carried on. France had wept over them—
> wept the tears of gratitude and love. France had sung and danced
> and cried to their music. France had given its first war medal for
> an American private to one of their number. France had given to
> them the collective citation which gave to their beloved regiment
> the honor of flying the *Croix de Guerre* streamers at the peak of
> its colors. France had kissed these colored soldiers—kissed them
> with reverence and in honor, first on the right cheek and then
> on the left.[26]

Finally, New York had a chance to show its long-delayed gratitude. And it did on 17 February 1919, as the band led by regimental drum major Bojangles Robinson marched down Fifth Avenue. Lester Walton's report in the *New York Times* of the tumultuous welcome that greeted the 15th Infantry suggested that the heavens magically responded to the warm cheers of New Yorkers who lined the curb. "Under a canopy of blue with not a cloud in the sky," Walton wrote, "the heroes marched while the February sun, usually cold and unfriendly, beamed down on both soldiers and spectators with springtime cordiality that vied in warmth and fervency with the salutation accorded by the populace." After the lead car of dignitaries passed, the second car in the parade carrying the wounded heroes was greeted by shouts of "Oh, you Henry Johnson," and "Oh, you Black Devil." Their fellow citizens were acknowledging privates Johnson and Needham Roberts, both wounded, who fought twenty-two Germans to a standstill and left several of them in the field; Johnson cut up his attackers with a bolo, after his gun had jammed. For their exploits, France awarded them—the first American privates of the army of France so honored—the croix de guerre. They made a big hit among the dignitaries at the mayor's reviewing stand, who included William Randolph Hearst. And in Harlem the greeting bordered on a riot.

> The 15th New York Infantry . . . marched the full length of Lenox
> Avenue Boulevard [*sic*] through Harlem, to turn a quarter of a
> million men, women, and children of the colored race wild with
> a frenzy of pride and joy and love.[27]

The Hellfighters marched between two howling walls of humanity from 135th to 145th Street, to the martial music of Europe's band of brass and reed and a field music section of thirty trumpets and drums playing a popular tune, with its double-entendre lyrics, "Here Comes My Daddy Now."[28]

Everybody's daddy did not come back then. And some of the unit's survivors never did come back. A racial incident—the single worst racial incident America had witnessed at the time—had occurred in east St. Louis on 2 July 1917, as volunteers for the 15th Infantry were being recruited in Harlem and New York state. During the riot a mob of white men, women, and children drove 6,000 blacks out of their homes and, by "shooting, burning and hanging," killed "between one and two hundred human beings who were black."[29] This incident, and the protest by the city of Spartanburg against the 15th Infantry's black soldiers, were certainly fresh in the minds of the Hellfighters returning home.[30] The seeds of Jim Crow racism that crossed the Atlantic had found a favorable climate in General Pershing's headquarters. The seeds flourished in the acts of commanding officers serving under him: in General Hay's address to the 92d Division prohibiting any contact with French women, or Colonel Hayward's transfer of the 369th regiment's black officers (except the bandmaster and chaplain) out of the unit after it fought in the second battle of the Marne, east of Verdun, near Ville-sur-Turke in July 1918.[31]

Contrasting with the experience of being brigaded with French troops of the 16th Division, who from the very first had treated black soldiers in terms of equality and brotherhood, the specter of returning to the land of Jim Crow dampened the soldiers' enthusiasm for the voyage home. Billeting in small French towns was the greatest single factor in giving black American soldiers social experiences that compensated for the grimness of their mission abroad. These positive experiences were vivid in the minds of black soldiers jammed to the rails aboard a giant Cunarder as it swung up New York harbor, returning from France. "As the ship hove past that unproved symbol, the Statue of Liberty, one of the soldiers reverently snapped a salute to Bartholdi's emblematic creation. An officer standing near, curious to know the reason for such an action, made the query why. 'Because France gave it' came back the firm reply." [32]

So bitter was First Lieutenant Rayford Logan over the treatment of black soldiers in the United States Army and black folks in America that "he managed to be demobilized in France, intending to remain abroad indefinitely." [33] After a long stay in Paris, during which time he served as secretary to the third Pan-African Conference in 1923, Logan returned to America, completed an advanced degree at Harvard University, and began university teaching. Leon Brooks, however, was one of many black former servicemen who stayed permanently in France after the armistice. Discharged from the 303d Stevedore Unit, Brooks went to Paris and eventually to St-Nazaire, where he worked as a salesman for Avenard Wine Company. Still living in France when it was occupied by Nazi Germany, Brooks was interned at Compiègne in December 1941.[34]

Eugene Jacques Bullard, America's first black combat aviator, had a distinctly different training ground for his adventures. Born in Columbus, Georgia, in 1894, at a time when Jim Crow laws and the Ku Klux Klan held sway, Bullard grew restive as a young boy in the racial climate of the South. Eugene's father told him about the country called France, which abolished slavery many, many years before America. Again and again he told his son that in France blacks were treated as well as whites and promised that some day he would take him there. Unable to muster patience for that "some day," at ten years old Eugene made his way to the harbor at Newport News, Virginia. For days he prowled the docks looking for a ship that would take him to France. Eugene stowed away on the German ship *Matherus* en route to Hamburg and abandoned it during a layover at Aberdeen, Scotland. Not yet eleven, Eugene managed to make his way by train to Glasgow, but two weeks after his arrival he was penniless. To survive he sang and danced for organ-grinders with their hurdy-gurdies. The Scots, Eugene said, had never seen a "darky" or a "Jack Johnson," as they called him, referring to the famous black boxer who defeated Jim Jeffries to win the title of heavyweight champion of the world.[35]

After five months in Glasgow, Eugene found work in Liverpool as a target for penny-a-ball tossers at an amusement park in Birkenhead. Induced to take up boxing, Eugene trained at Chris Baldwin's gymnasium in Liverpool. His boxing skills improved, and Baldwin signed him for a ten-round match with Bill Welsh, an Irishman from Wales, whom he defeated on points. With such successes in the ring, Eugene came to the attention of Dixie Kid, a promoter who took him to London and arranged for him to stay at Mrs. Carter's, a boarding house that catered to boxing clientele. There Eugene met Jack Johnson and other renowned black boxers such as Bob Armstrong and Bob Scanlon, who became a lifelong friend. Boxing under the name "Madden," Eugene started as a bantamweight in Liverpool at age sixteen, moving up to lightweight within the year. His career involved more than forty professional fights.

Bullard made his first visit to Paris for a boxing match on 28 November 1913. He won the bout and was determined to return to Paris. Back in London, at Mrs. Carter's boarding house, he joined a troupe known as Freedman's Picaninnies. The troupe's repertoire consisted of singing, dancing, and slapstick comedy. In time he toured Europe and Russia, playing at the Winter Garden in Berlin and the Bal Tabarin in Paris. Eugene returned to boxing in Paris in spring 1914.

Twenty years old when World War I broke out, Eugene Bullard enlisted in the Foreign Legion on 9 October 1914, served in the infantry from 1915 to 1916, and was wounded at Verdun.[36] Finally fulfilling his urge to become a combat pilot, an impossibility in the United States for black Americans until the Second World War, Bullard enlisted in French aviation schools at Cazeaux, Tours, and Avord before serving at the front with the Escadrille Squads 93 and 85, from September 1917 to November 1917. He was sent to the 170th French Infantry Regiment in January 1918, from which he was discharged, having earned the croix de guerre, the *fourrager* of the Foreign Legion, and many more decorations.[37]

None of these wartime experiences prepared Eugene Bullard for his postwar life as a major impresario of black American musical entertainment in Montmartre. By 1919 France was beginning the long recovery from the devastation of war. And the great black musical migration to Paris from Harlem and other jazz capitals in America was starting to gather momentum. A slow trickle of black musicians had begun, adding to the few vaudeville and minstrel personalities already playing Parisian music halls.

One of these was Louis Mitchell from Harlem. After returning home, Mitchell tried to assemble an orchestra to play at the Casino de Paris, but the State Department's postwar restrictions on issuing passports to persons of nonvital importance for travel to France forced him to cancel the project. With dogged persistence, Mitchell got together a seven-man group and left for France. He settled with his wife and son in the heart of Montmartre, at 69 rue de Clichy, a street that would soon be dotted with small nightclubs featuring black jazz. The Mitchells opened their home to the growing expatriate community of black American civilians and former soldiers who remained in France after discharge and extended the welcome mat to musicians fresh from home anxious for advice on "how to do it" in Paris; they became an early symbol of "jazz as family" in Montmartre.

News traveled fast in this small, rapidly expanding community of black expatriates, especially bad news. And the news on the evening of 19 May 1919 stunned everyone: America's first "jazz king" had been pronounced dead of a knife wound in the neck. James Reese Europe had been performing in a concert at the Mechanics Hall on Huntington Avenue in Boston. Europe's assailant was his diminutive twenty-four-year-old drummer, Herbert Wright, one of the Percussion Twins (in a concert billed, ironically, as "Three Jubilee Days of Sunshine in Music").

Hence Europe never witnessed the transformation of the musical scene in postwar France by some of the musicians who had surprised and delighted their French audience in Brest with the first sounds of jazz. After discharge from the army, Arthur Briggs and Buddy Gilmore and other bandsmen decided to come back to France after reading *The New York Age* of 8 February 1919. The headline heralded the new musical era in France: "French Now Want Colored Musicians From the United States." And when those musicians came, they headed straight for Montmartre.

France's victory in the Great War against Kaiser Wilhelm's Germany was tempered by a massive loss of lives, including its flowering youth, who felt the monstrous anger of the guns at Verdun. More than 8 million Frenchmen were mobilized during the 52 months of the Great War that ended on 11 November 1918. Among the casualties, 1.5 million died in combat, and 425,000 died in hospital beds. Four million were wounded, 740,000 of them permanently disabled. France suffered physically more than any other country, for most of the time war raged on French territory. An explosion of patriotic art and architecture set monuments to memorialize the dead throughout the provinces and the City of Light.[1] The monuments' long shadows marked the movements of the widows, the orphans, the invalids, the mutilated, and others haunted by memories of a painful victory. The huge numbers of French women in black widows' weeds were to be a constant feature of urban France for years to come.

But in 1919 the capital was poised for gaiety, and Parisians discovered America. French citizens of all ages looked to the horizons of the Atlantic for symbols of popular culture that fantasized a world divorced from the past. American cinema was paramount in this creation of popular culture, and daily and weekly newspapers had their part as well. In the next two decades, millions of French children of all social classes enjoyed syndicated comic strips featuring Mickey Mouse, Dick Tracy, Tarzan, Little Orphan Annie, Brick Bradford, Flash Gordon, Jungle Jim, and numerous other characters. With their meager weekly allowances the young fans bought frames of colorful images that danced before their eyes, conveying lessons of morality and virtue.[2] Immediately after the war, theaters were packed. Describing the postarmistice euphoria, one young French chorus girl said: "People wanted to forget the war, they spent without counting, went out night after night, living from one day to the next with the sole notion of catching up for the wasted four years that had gone by."[3] But for many thousands of adults, it was the jazz scene developing in Montmartre that set their pulse racing.

And in 1919, Harlem also discovered Montmartre. Like musical missionaries, black American musicians and entertainers from Harlem and other jazz capitals in the Bronzevilles of America descended on la Butte, armed with drums, horns, music scores, and gadgets to make noise. They found accommodations in not too fancy hotels and cheap rooming houses along the narrow streets of la Butte made famous by the bohemian artists and writers of the prewar era. Many of those bohemians had already drifted across the Seine to the Latin Quarter, creating a literary café culture that had been graced by figures from Apollinaire to Rimbaud and Maurice Sachs.[4]

In the small section of Montmartre south of rue Caulaincourt, the sounds of Harlem began to echo in rue de la Trinité, rue Fontaine, rue Blanche, rue Pigalle, and rue des Martyrs, in a triangle of winding streets and alleys. Gare St-Lazare was the principal entry point for those coming directly from America, like Josephine Baker and the *Revue Nègre* troupe in 1925. For many musically talented black Americans mustered out of the army, it was war-battered trains that took them to Gare du Nord, also a short taxi ride from la Butte. By 1924, when Eugene Bullard opened his nightclub, Le Grand Duc, jazz had a firm foothold in Montmartre and several black-owned *boîtes de nuits* were opening up. The gypsy music long identified with la vie bohème barely survived in the tattered cafés near place du Tertre and Sacré-Cœur. It had been replaced south of rue Caulaincourt by the hypnotic syncopated sounds of black jazz.

The streets of Montmartre that were absorbing elements of Harlem's musical culture had not been unfamiliar to Will Marion Cook and other musicians who toured with *In Dahomey* in 1903.[5] Cook wrote the music and the vaudeville comedians Bert Williams and George Walker produced *In Dahomey,* the first all-black musical to play in a major Broadway theater. It opened at the New York Theatre on 18 February 1903 and ran for fifty-three performances before going on tour. On 16 May 1903 the show opened in London at the Shaftsbury Theatre, where it ran for seven months; there was a performance for Edward VIII at Buckingham Palace. In the latter part of the year the musical opened at the Olympia in Paris.[6] *In Dahomey* made the cakewalk a social fad in England and France.

In 1905 Cook was again in New York at Hammerstein's Victoria Theatre, touring with the Memphis Students. It was, James Weldon Johnson exclaims, "the first modern jazz band ever heard on a New York stage, and probably on any other stage."[7] "The Students seemed to have consisted of about twenty instrumentalists predominantly playing mandolins, harp guitars, and banjos (with perhaps three celli added for good measure) . . . , such an instrumentation would be effective both in conveying the kind of syncopated music that Will Marion Cook was then composing as well as sound authentic in the southern African-American musical tradition from folk music through minstrelsy."[8] After an unpleasant legal struggle to gain control of the Memphis Students from Ernest Hogan, who created the national fad for coon songs following release of his famous (or infamous) "All Coons Look Alike to Me," sixteen of the singing players, now renamed the Tennessee Students, sailed with Cook for Europe, where in the course of the next six months, they appeared at the Palace Theatre in London, the Olympia in Paris, and the Schumann Circus in Berlin.

Cook's great talents as a classically trained composer enabled him to identify exceptional musicians for his European tour in 1919. The group he organized, called the Southern Syncopated Orchestra, consisted of thirty-six instrumentalists and twenty singers.[9] One of his clarinetists was Sidney Bechet. When the orchestra split up, Benny Peyton, the drummer, formed his own group from members of the band who stayed on in London.[10] It was called the Jazz Kings and included Bechet, who played with Peyton's group for about two months in 1920 at the Apollo Theater in Montmartre.[11]

During his tour with the Syncopates, Bechet and a young trumpet player named Arthur Briggs became close friends. Born in 1901 in St. Georges,

Canada, and raised in Charleston, South Carolina, Briggs eventually became Europe's most celebrated trumpeter and a founder of *Jazz-Hot* in Paris. Perhaps Noble Sissle brought Briggs to Cook's attention, since he and Briggs had been members of the 15th infantry band led by James Reese Europe.[12] During the Syncopates' London tour in the summer of 1919 they played in major concert halls and performed before King George V.[13] When Cook's Syncopates broke up in 1921, Briggs remained in London and formed his own group, the Five Musical Dragons, which played at Murray's Club. After a brief return to America that same year, when he played with Leslie Howard's band, Briggs once more sailed to Europe, linking up with his friend Bechet. In London he played with George Clapham, Jacob Patrick, and Andy Clarke. But the fascination with Paris that Briggs acquired during military service with the 15th Infantry was too strong to resist. He crossed the Channel, settled in Montmartre, and formed the Savoys Syncopated Band in 1922. His international array of musicians consisted of members from Canada, Haiti, Italy, Belgium, Trinidad, and Guadeloupe.[14]

Until Bullard opened Le Grand Duc at 52 rue Pigalle in the early autumn of 1924, there was no "home" in Montmartre with a "soul flavor" where the growing community of black musicians could congregate after hours or between gigs at other nightclubs in the quarter. In the hustle for bookings at the most popular nightclubs in Paris and elsewhere in France and Europe, small musical groups like Briggs's Savoys were constantly on the move, spreading the gospel of jazz. For a time the Savoys became a musical fixture in Brussels, where they played at Le Perroquet de Paris, a ballroom of the Théâtre de l'Alhambra (boulevard Émile-Jacqmain).[15] A short train ride from Gare St-Lazare, Brussels was rapidly developing a jazz scene of its own, employing black American musicians who had made their home in Montmartre. Briggs's Savoys and a new group he formed later, the Creole Five, toured Belgium, playing a long engagement at Chez Pan, in the boulevard Van Iseghem in Ostend.

Bullard's Grand Duc was the place musicians back in Paris between engagements went to "jive," to receive messages, to swap gossip and tales from home, and to meet other black musicians or folks newly arrived in Paris. It also nurtured the musical talents of the stars of the Paris Harlem Renaissance.

The sequence of events that brought Bullard to Montmartre's nightclub scene—including a stint as a musician—remains unclear. One source claims that he saw so many "colored Americans making good money in Paris, he decided to take drum lessons." After mastering the basic techniques of the drum, perhaps more in the slam-bang style of Louis Mitchell than in the smooth rhythmic form of Buddy Gilmore, he was hired to play in the band at the Chez Florence in the Théâtre Caumartin at 17 rue de Caumartin.[16] Another source places Chez Florence in rue Pigalle—and thus in Montmartre—founded as Mitchell's by Louis Mitchell in 1924 but renamed for the singer and hostess, Florence Embry Jones.[17]

In time Chez Florence was sold to Joe Zelli, an Italian American who had come to France from London. A jazz impresario, Zelli owned and managed several other Parisian clubs, including the Royal Box at 16 rue Fontaine and the Tempo Club above Zelli's in rue de Caumartin.[18] Zelli's reputation as being "the only place in Paris that was open all night and everybody who was anybody went there," passed shortly to Bullard's Grand Duc and Bricktop's soon-to-be-opened club, both without the sleaziness of Zelli's. His was "a big, raffish, cavernous room lined with tables decorated with B-girls whose business was to 'mount the check.'" It resembled a dime-a-dance hall on San Francisco's old Barbary Coast, including a mediocre jazz band and gigolos to guide women "of a certain age" up and down the dance floor.[19]

When Bullard was hired to manage Le Grand Duc, he had high social class in mind (the club's first owner in the early 1920s was Georges Jamerson, said to be a small-time gangster from an important French family).[20] Only one club rivaled Le Grand Duc's popularity: Mitchell's, one block away in rue Pigalle. Bullard reaped the harvest of his past generosity to scores of black musicians and entertainers when they dropped into the club to entertain guests at no charge. Among the frequent guests were Dooley Wilson, Buddy and Mattie Gilmore, composer Spencer Williams, and the black British singer Mabel Mercer. Cole Porter once said of Mercer that no one could sing his song "Love for Sale" better than she did.[21]

As Le Grand Duc's success grew, Bullard hired "the exactly one female Negro entertainer in Paris," Florence Embry Jones, wife of the pianist Palmer Jones.[22] Pretty, perky, and said to be arrogant, Florence was the singer, hostess, and all-around star of Le Grand Duc. Parisians loved her style. A similarly creative, flamboyant fashion in clothing would become a trademark of Bricktop's and Josephine Baker's. Night after night, Florence Jones filled Le Grand Duc with celebrities, making the club an enormous success.[23]

When she departed for Mitchell's, who renamed his club Chez Florence in her honor, Palmer Jones suggested to Bullard that he bring over a singer from Harlem. And so Ada Beatrice Queen Victoria Louise Virginia "Bricktop" Smith came to take the job. Bricktop had been a partner of Florence Mills and Cora Green in a singing-dancing trio called the Panama Trio.[24] Bricktop was "the second Negro female entertainer to arrive in Paris."[25] It was her bright red hair and freckles that earned her the nickname "Bricktop," when she gained fame entertaining in the big and exciting clubs in Chicago's south side and Harlem.

Born in Alderson, West-by-God-Virginia (as she labeled it), at age sixteen Bricktop joined Flournay Miller and Aubry Miles's comedy team, then playing at the Pekin Theater in Chicago. It was the first theater of any consequence devoted to black drama. Young entertainers nourished their talents in Chicago cabarets, which included boxing champion Jack Johnson's Café de Champion, at Armour and Dearborn Streets since October 1911. Hugh Haskins's saloon at 32d and State Streets, another popular place, was where Alberta Hunter got her start before going on to become a star in Montmartre. When Bricktop moved to New York and began singing at Barron's Exclusive Club, at Seventh Avenue and 134th Street, it was a training ground for her years as one of the most popular nightclub hostesses of Paris. Barron Wilkins's customers were "the 'who's who' of New York's roaring twenties, when gangsters rubbed elbows with high society and people in show business came uptown after the Broadway theaters closed." Barron's customers John Barrymore and Charles MacArthur (who married Helen Hayes) were later to meet Bricktop again in Paris in her own nightclub, which carried her name.

But the places where Bricktop had performed—Barron's, the Cotton Club, or Small's Paradise—were no preparation for a stint at Le Grand Duc. She sailed on the SS *America,* landing in Le Havre on 11 May 1924. On seeing Le Grand Duc, Bricktop described it as a hole-in-the-wall, the size of a booth in Connie's Inn in Harlem. It sat in rue Pigalle, at the angle where Pigalle met rue Fontaine. The tiny room contained "about twelve tables and a small bar that would feel crowded with six pairs of elbows leaning on it." [26] Seeing Bricktop in tears at the sight of the small club and on the verge of returning to Harlem, Langston Hughes rushed to her aid and prepared a meal for her. On his first trip to Europe at the time, Hughes had not yet become a leading poet and writer of the Harlem Renaissance. He was virtually penniless after his trip across the big sea when, thanks to Rayford Logan's introduction, he found work at Le Grand Duc as dishwasher, backup cook, and waiter. Hughes assured Bricktop she would love Paris, Bullard, and Le Grand Duc. And she did.

At some point, with the money saved from playing music, Bullard bought Le Grand Duc. The partnership of Bullard and Bricktop shaped Le Grand Duc into one of the favorite nightclubs of international celebrities in the 1920s and early 1930s. Bullard brought tough, genial management and hospitality; Bricktop brought exciting musical entertainment glossed with the flair of a table-hopping hostess who made every patron feel like a celebrity. A list of the club's patrons—a blend of European royalty with rich and famous Americans who had discovered Paris's Harlem in Montmartre—includes Elsa Maxwell, Fatty Arbuckle, Mistinguett, Ed "Strangler" Lewis, the prince of Wales, W. E. Leeds, Horace Dodge, Jimmy Walker, Barry Pilsen, the Dolly sisters, Richard Reynolds, Charlie Chaplin, Pearl White, Gloria Swanson, Sophie Tucker, and Nora Baynes.[27] To F. Scott Fitzgerald, Le Grand Duc was home away from home. He was soon followed by the Montparnasse crowd of writers, Ernest Hemingway among them. Louis Bromfield and Picasso were in the first contingent of the Montparnasse artistic crowd to discover Le Grand Duc; Man Ray and Kiki soon became regulars. Black American jazz had yet to gain a firm foothold on the Left Bank, where the literary cafés of the Latin Quarter and Montparnasse still dominated nightlife. But that ambience would soon change.[28]

Bullard's success in attracting to Le Grand Duc patrons from among the rich and famous gained him an entrée into the Parisian social world. His musical talent for drumming could not compare with the style and polish of Buddy Gilmore, who came to Paris with Irene and Vernon Castle and stayed on to form his own group. Bullard "specialized as an impresario in furnishing dance bands and attractions for private parties, marriages, and so on, and was often called on to furnish bands and attractions for high society people. He hired the most talented of black musicians and entertainers for social functions held by titled French families as well as by important businessmen like Paul Chapotin, owner of the Café de la Paix."[29]

When Bricktop arrived in Paris on 11 May 1924, it took her only two nights "to see just about every Negro American," she stated: "Opal Cooper, Sammy and Harvey White, Charlie 'Dixie' Lewis, Bobby Jones and maybe ten other Negro musicians were the only Negro men in Paris." And all of them were in Montmartre. By 1925, Paris had its own version of the Harlem Renaissance. Drawing on the title of Paul Colin's book of early jazz age Paris, Bricktop called it *le tumulte noir*. The black commotion was the "noise" in Montmartre stirred up by the stream of black musicians and entertainers coming from America's Bronzevilles and finding steady employment in race-blind France. "All the nightclubs in the area of Pigalle," Bricktop recalled, "had at least a few blacks in their orchestra."[30] At the Casino de Paris, 16 rue de Clichy, where jazz was regularly featured from late 1918 when Louis Mitchell appeared with his Jazz Kings, the orchestra was entirely black.

The sounds of black jazz that underlay *le tumulte noir* re-created a street culture reminiscent of Harlem, in which strolling was not merely going out for a walk along rue Pigalle or rue Fontaine; it was more like going on an adventure.[31] It was the feeling of adventure along the streets of Harlem in Montmartre that attracted Sidney Bechet, who found it more to his liking than London. Much of the excitement of Paris was to be found in the street life of Montmartre, he said:

> Any time you walked down the streets you'd run into four or five people you knew—performers, entertainers, all kinds of people who had real talent in them . . . you'd start to go home, and you'd never get there. There was always some singer to hear or someone who was playing. You'd run into some friends and they were off to hear this or to do that and you just went along. It seemed like you just *couldn't* get home before ten or eleven in the morning.[32]

Joel A. Roger, in his column "The Pepper Pot" for the *Pittsburgh Courier*, sketched a picture not dissimilar to Sidney Bechet's.

The Boulevard de Clichy is the 42nd and Broadway of Paris. Most of the night life of Paris centers around it, and most of the colored folks from the States, too. If you hear that some friend from the States is in Paris, just circulate around this boulevard from the Moulin Rouge down Rue Pigalle as far as the Flea Pit [at the corner of Pigalle and La Bruyère]. And it is a hundred to one shot that you'll encounter him or her, at least twice during the night. Most of the colored folk live in this neighborhood. There is a surprising number of them, and it is increasing every year. Just now with the "Blackbirds" at the Moulin Rouge, this section reminds you more of Harlem than ever.[33]

Harlem-style black life on the streets of Montmartre aided Bricktop's adjustment, and she moved out of the small hotel room that Langston Hughes had booked for her to an apartment at 36 rue Pigalle. As Hughes predicted, Bricktop would come to enjoy the absence of racial discrimination; in fact, she experienced "a strong pro-Negro prejudice," as Parisians identified the new musical sounds of jazz with African Americans. "If there had been a lot of average white Americans around," Bricktop said, "*they* might have influenced the Parisians, but they weren't."[34]

As the sounds of *le tumulte noir* were beginning to be heard across the Seine in Montparnasse and the Latin Quarter, two dozen black musicians, singers, and dancers (including Sidney Bechet) arrived in Paris. Sailing from New York on 15 September 1925 on the SS *Berengaria,* the *Revue Nègre* troupe arrived in Paris seven days later. The musical, staged by Rolf de Maré, who had branched out of ballet into chic music-hall promotions, opened at the Théâtre des Champs-Élysées on avenue Montaigne in October 1925. It starred Josephine Baker. The artist Fernand Léger, a devout jazz fan, is said to have suggested the idea of importing a black troupe.

*Revue Nègre* opened at the time when the Parisian music hall had reached its postwar zenith. Jean-Claude Klein depicts the music hall as a receptacle of the images of *modernité,* a break from the past and the terrible memories of the Great War. Artists like Picasso, Braque, Modigliani, and other modernists in the Left Bank colony had already discovered *l'art nègre* at the turn of the century. In 1925 black jazz was in full form in

Montmartre and awakened Parisians' interest in popular culture. Reflecting this shift, and responding to the public's taste for new music and choreography, in April 1925 the Théâtre des Champs-Élysées converted its prestigious stage to a *théâtre music-hall*. And in turn these transformations inspired Caroline Dudley Reagan, heir to an American fortune, to produce *Revue Nègre*—"a show of authentic Negro vaudeville"—at the renovated music hall.[35]

Caroline Dudley brought to her production of *Revue Nègre* an understanding of black musical culture. Dudley was the daughter of a liberal Chicago physician who often invited blacks to dinner. In the early 1900s, his was an unusual display of interracial commensalism. And Dudley liked to boast that she grew up "on Booker T. Washington's knee." She "went with her father to black vaudeville shows on State Street in Chicago and fell in love with the music, the ragtime, the beginnings of jazz, and the raunchy humor. This early exposure to black vaudeville gave her an experience, at the time rare among whites, of seeing authentic black entertainment originated by blacks and performed by blacks."[36] With considerable luck and a wide range of exceptional black talent available, especially in Harlem, Dudley recruited a cast of dancers, singers, acrobats, and musicians for the production.

Many of those recruited had gained their experience on the minstrel and vaudeville circuit. And among the twenty-five musicians and entertainers in the *Revue Nègre* troupe were those who had already performed at European nightclubs, particularly in Berlin and Paris. Sidney Bechet had played in Britain and Belgium, and Louis Douglas, the choreographer, had lived in London since 1915; composer and pianist Spencer Williams, and orchestra leader Claude Hopkins both had European experience before joining the *Revue Nègre* show. Maud de Forest, a singer of blues and spirituals, was the intended star of the tour but was unable to perform on opening night. She was replaced from within the troupe by Josephine Baker, who had danced in Noble Sissle and Eubie Blake's *Shuffle Along*.[37] Dudley had found Baker at Sam Slavin's Plantation Club, above New York's Winter Garden Theater at 50th and Broadway, where she had been a chorus girl in Ethel Waters's show *Dinah*.[38]

With Josephine Baker as its star, *Revue Nègre* opened at the Théâtre des Champs-Élysées on 2 October 1925. The musical played to rave reviews, though not without considerable controversy and caustic criticism from

Mistinguett, the darling of French music halls; its run was extended twice before it moved on 19 November to the smaller Théâtre de l'Étoile on avenue des Champs-Élysées, where it ran through December. After the show's run at the Alhambra in Brussels and the Nelson Theater in Berlin ended, Baker quit the troupe and prepared to open at the Folies-Bergère in rue Richer in Montmartre. Now she was to star in a Paul Derval production, *La Folie du Jour,* which launched her into orbit, in her own galaxy. Appearing semi-nude, she mixed her dances with acrobatics and "the shimmy." Miming sex, wearing outlandish costumes from grass skirts to a skirt of plush bananas set in motion by jiggling like perky, good-natured phalluses, Josephine Baker became the rave of Parisian music halls and beyond.[39]

Baker's fame as an international celebrity benefited from the discovery by the French, long before anyone else, that black is beautiful. Henri Varna, director of the Folies-Bergère, realized the marketing possibilities of including an exotic black act in his show. Baker had that potential. Under his direction she became one of the Folies-Bergère's most sensational successes. Swinging her elegant brown body to blue music was of less consequence than the newsworthy persona she created of her public life. Indeed, everything about Baker was newsworthy. Her gold fingernails led the comtesse Mathieu de Noailles (a socialite and, some said, France's greatest poet) to christen her "the pantheress with golden claws." For her leopard, Chiquita, Baker bought a different collar to match each of her dresses; snakeskin upholstered her chauffeur-driven Delage limousine; fur wraps and striking jewels embellished her high-fashion wardrobe. Women imitated her close-cropped slicked-down hairstyle and bought trademarked products *pour se bakerfixer les cheveux.* At Deauville, a whole vogue of sunbathing was created by women trying to emulate her caramel skin color.

By 1926 a cult of Bakerism centered around her, stimulated by her public persona. "Josephine Baker dolls, costumes, perfumes, pomades" were in vogue, including hair curls and skin anointed with walnut oil in lieu of weeks in the sun.[40] Noble Sissle said he often observed her strolling down the Champs-Élysées, one day with two cheetahs on a leash, another day with two swans: all part of the menagerie including boa constrictors and monkeys that she kept in her apartment.

Despite *la Baker's* phenomenal popularity, she was not one of the missionaries of jazz. Jazz was going strong when the *Revue* troupe arrived in Paris. "The jazzmen who played in 'la Butte Montmartre,' who knew Bessie Smith, Ethel Waters and Adelaide Hall, did not take Josephine seriously. Being musicians, we knew she stank," one said, "she was a chorus babe, a big-shot dame, but a lot of it was luck."[41] Almost at once, her career ceased to have anything to do with jazz. She danced to jazz numbers and swung her "sensational waxed brown body to blue music" but that was incidental. She was not a great singer and her dancing relied more on comedy—crossing her eyes and doing the shimmy—than rhythm. As fellow artist Jimmie Daniel remarked, she had even more important qualities than these: "She had balls! She was born to be a star. . . . As far as jazz was concerned, Josephine was an exception to the rule. She was alone in making a sensational success out of not being a good jazz singer and dancer."[42]

Baker's triumph in *Revue Nègre* shaped the climate of receptivity that other black American musical troupes would later enjoy: Louis Douglas's *Black People* in 1926; Florence Mills in *Blackbirds,* called "the second *Revue Nègre,*" in the same year at the Ambassadeurs; Lew Leslie's revival of *Blackbirds* in 1929 at the Moulin Rouge at place Blanche.[43] Baker was comfortable on the stage of the big spectacle: the orchestra pit, the floodlights, the velvet stage curtains, and her appearance in lavish jeweled costumes adorned with peacock feathers. The typical wooden platform found in Le Grand Duc and other handkerchief-size nightclubs on which small black jazz bands made noise until the early hours in Harlem in Montmartre was not for her. She belonged in the fashionable theaters of Paris.

*Le tumulte noir* was in full noisy form when Baker opened Chez Joséphine in December 1926.[44] Each night after finishing her act at the Folies-Bergère she would go dancing in the early morning hours at l'Abbaye de Thélème, at Milonga, or at l'Impérial. L'Impérial was owned by Harot and Léonard, who had changed the nightclub's name to Joséphine Baker's Impérial when she was booked as the lead performer.[45] Though this small cabaret featured her name in electric lights, it proved to be a short gig en route to realizing the dream of opening her own nightclub in Montmartre. With the assistance of Pepito (later her husband), Baker acquired

the financial backing of an admirer, Gaston Prieur, and opened Chez Joséphine in rue Fontaine on 10 December 1926. She usually finished at the
music hall and arrived at her cabaret at one in the morning.[46]

Chez Joséphine was another Montmartre hole-in-the-wall, the size of
Le Grand Duc. The menu set by Pepito charged outrageous prices, "the
most expensive in Paris": 45 francs for one dozen oysters, a few drops of
caviar, or the day's special.[47] And a chance to see Josephine Baker up close
and at her best. "She danced, clowned, and teased her clients, pulling the
men's moustaches and stroking their bald heads. She acted as though
everyone there was her personal friend," a style that Florence Jones had
introduced to Paris and Bricktop had perfected. Taking its cues from Bullard's Grand Duc, Chez Joséphine also mixed its Cordon Bleu cuisine
with a taste of soul. Chitlins, greens, and black-eyed peas had equal bill-
ing with *canard à l'orange* and shrimp pâté.[48]

Baker was not the first superstar to popularize black style in Paris. When
Battling Siki, a black boxer from Senegal, defeated France's Georges Carpentier in six rounds before sixty thousand cheering fans at Buffalo
Stadium on 25 September 1922, the victory was wildly acclaimed on the
streets of Montmartre. American and French celebrants of color poured
into Montmartre's small bars and nightclubs. Crowds cheered Siki's victory much as later crowds in Harlem and America's Bronzevilles would
celebrate Jack Johnson's defeat of Dempsey and Joe Louis's victories. After the event, one Parisian observed that "almost every Race man seen on
the streets is mistaken for Siki and is surrounded by an admiring crowd
until the poor fellow—he is usually a jazz band player—is forced to take
flight in a taxi in self-defense."[49]

Battling Siki's victory resurrected the "black craze" that gripped many
French cities during the Great War when black American soldiers came
over in the AEF. In the era launched by Siki's intense popularity, black
was the color of designer high fashion for women: black stockings, black
dresses, black hats, black blouses. Consistent with the latest mode, wom-
en's hair was dyed black, bobbed, and carefully kinked. Dark-skinned men
became even more popular as companions, as French women asserted
that "dark-complexioned men understand women so much better."[50]

After Siki's untimely death, his flamboyant presence on the streets of
Montmartre was quickly filled by Panama Al Brown. Born in Panama,

Alfonso Brown immigrated to Harlem in the early 1920s and established an impressive record of victories as a welterweight boxer. An invitation to fight in Paris brought him his first victory on French soil, on 10 November 1926. Several more boxing victories brought Brown acclaim as the new star of the Paris boxing world. He lived on his predatory moniker— "the Black Widow Spider."

Like Battling Siki, Panama Al dressed elegantly, enjoyed public appearances immensely, and frequented bars and jazz clubs. He drifted away from professional fighting and tried his hand as a circus entertainer, engaged by the Cirque Medrano to tap-dance, sing, lead a jazz band, and skip rope to swing tunes under the big top. He made his cabaret debut as a song-and-dance man at the Caprice Viennoise. According to Janet Flanner, Jean Cocteau wrote "charmingly" of Brown that he was "a miracle who refuses to cease being a miracle . . . a phantom, a shadow, more terrible than lightning and the cobra." Flanner continued, "Unfortunately he ceased being both a miracle and lightning in his singing and dancing, one being slow and the other off beat."[51]

Though Josephine Baker's star quality drew clients both white and black to her own club in Montmartre, neither the setting nor the cuisine at Chez Joséphine could compare with the more auspicious establishment opening across the Seine that was to become Hemingway's legendary hangout: La Coupole. Ernest Fraux and René Lafon signed a twenty-year lease in October 1926 on the large lot at 102 boulevard du Montparnasse where they began building La Coupole in January the next year. Three thousand invitations were sent out for a *coupe de champagne* to inaugurate La Coupole late in 1927 and, along with Le Dôme and La Closerie des Lilas, it became one of the favorite cafés of the literary crowd and intelligentsia of prewar Montparnasse.

The decade after President Poincaré had, in the company of his wife, inaugurated the boulevard du Montparnasse on 10 July 1913, the quarter experienced its own fling with nightclubs and jazz music. Before the Great War, painters, writers, and actors from Montmartre had drifted across the Seine, joining students from the Sorbonne to re-create in Left Bank cafés the bohemian atmosphere once found in la Butte. In later years the cafés included such famous names as Les Deux Magots, Le Café Flore, La Closerie des Lilas, Le Dôme, La Coupole, and La Rotonde. Pleasure and crime, though never as notorious as writers and observers reputed for Montmartre, soon became established, and during the twenties La Rotonde and Le Jockey were noted as the grand centers of drug trafficking in Montparnasse.[52] To accommodate itself more to the pleasure of the dancing craze than to the crime in drugs (which mainly changed hands in the lavatories), La Rotonde underwent total transformation, creating a bar, grill room, brasserie, and on the entry floor a vast dancing hall. Jazz-swing had arrived at the first nightclub in Montparnasse.

Wambly Bald, an American observer of the Left Bank and Montparnasse during the age of the Lost Generation, described the social transformation of Montparnasse street life as having gone very Harlem. Montmartre invaded it with "Black and Tan cabarets," he wrote, "and the noise of jazz bands is steadily driving the old guard out of town." The Hemingway crowd of writers and artists who sought idyllic inspiration in studios in the south of France found little refuge in their escape to Menton, the last retreat on the French Riviera. Noisy jazz bands traveled there too, if only seasonally. The literary crowd sought escape from the street scene in Montparnasse, where the gigolo was everywhere, but it was a black gigolo, "the sheik à la [Battling] Siki, who corners the market. Sometimes he is a boxer who has wearied of being mutilated for a few hundred francs; sometimes he is just a dishwasher . . . who moves about in a svelte African way and knows the inchoate anxiety of neurotic women vacationing from their husbands. These gigolos satisfy, apparently, like a well-known cigarette, and a visit to the Bal Nègre, the Boule Blanche, or the Antilles may prove more amusing than a visit to Harlem. There you will discover the Martinique tom-tom of jazz bands, blue smoke, and ladies swaying luxuriously in the long arms of dark cowboys."[53]

Dark cowboys and Red Indians in sinister silhouettes decorated the walls of Le Jockey. An inspiration of the American painter Hilaire Hiler and his partner, former jockey Miller, their nightclub transformed Montparnasse overnight in November 1923. They took over the Café Camélon on boulevard du Montparnasse, at the corner of rue Campagne-Première, and decided to open a nightclub. They left the dingy interior unchanged but decorated the exterior walls in vivid colors, covering them with posters and paintings of Mexicans, Indians, and cowboys.

Le Jockey's popularity drew on Montparnasse's artists closely associated with Kiki and Man Ray. The dada-inspired New York artist Man Ray arrived in Paris on 22 July 1921 and was quickly accepted into the inner circles of Parisian dadaists. But lack of funds soon led him to turn his talents to photography. Six months after his arrival in Paris, Man Ray met Kiki in a Montparnasse café and she moved in with him as his mistress and model. "Kiki came to dominate and symbolize the Montparnasse era. Born in a poor family in Châtillon-sur-Seine in Burgundy, she came to Paris when she was thirteen and was sent to work a year later. By the age of seventeen, Kiki had gravitated to Montparnasse and had found her place there."[54] Her "Paris was the open society of Montparnasse, which offered individuals the opportunity to be themselves artistically, intellectually, politically and sexually." Kiki's naughty performances of the cancan at Le Jockey—wearing nothing underneath her billowing multilayered skirts, and singing outrageously dirty songs in a way that offended no one—led fashionable Paris, including Americans, to the club. "Innumerable people, English and American and French congregated there nightly. Les Copeland, an ex-cowboy, who had a great assortment of songs, cowboy, jazz—blues and comic, was at the piano. . . . Almost anybody of the writing, painting, musical, gigalong, whoring, pimping or drinking world was apt to turn up at the Jockey."[55] Bald wrote that "the place became a 'night joint,' and despite its eccentric appearance, its exiguity of space, its intolerable atmosphere, its negroes and jazz-band, was and is the most fashionable rendezvous of Montparnasse." It attracted frequenters of all colors and of all races but not because it served up hot jazz. It offered loud unusual jazz and nostalgic accents of Negro spirituals.[56]

The Jockey's success was rapid; so too was its decline. Madness and folly characterized its brief existence, shutting its doors in 1930. New nightclubs, all more or less ephemeral, followed: Le Cri-Cri; La Horde; La Boule Blanche; La Cigogne; College Inn; Normandy; La Ville. La Coupole at 102 boulevard du Montparnasse, and La Jungle at 127 opened in 1927. The last one, also decorated by Hilaire Hiler, was all the rage by the next year. Packed into a gloomy but vaguely exotic setting, people danced to blues cheek to cheek in an area the size of three tables. Le Monocole, on boulevard Edgar-Quinet, had an orchestra of women and its clients were dedicated to an exclusive "cult of Sappho."[57]

It was "a celebration in blues" when the singer Alberta Hunter sailed to Paris from Harlem on the SS *DeGrasse* on 5 August 1927. Florence Jones,

Bricktop, and Josephine Baker (whom Hunter had known when both were young singers in nightclubs on Chicago's south side) had been keeping excitement at home alive with frequent gossip about Harlem in Montmartre. Disembarking at Gare St-Lazare, Alberta was met by musician friends from Chicago, the singer Nettie Compton and her ragtime pianist husband, Glover, and taken to their apartment at 35 rue Victor-Massé. Later she moved to the Hôtel de Paris, at 55 rue Pigalle. The real celebration in blues came when Alberta strolled with the Comptons to the Flea Pit, at the corner of Pigalle and La Bruyère. The Pit was unmistakably a slice of Harlem transported to Montmartre, "a combination poolroom, public bar, cigar stand, and place to drop in and hear news of home, of friends."[58] It also sold small Sterno stoves; many people on a budget—those waiting for their first big paycheck—put the stoves on the square of floor tiles normally found in hotel rooms underneath the sink.

The second child of a Pullman porter, Alberta Hunter was born on 1 April 1895, in Memphis, Tennessee. Alberta moved to Chicago and began her first singing stint at Dago Frank's, at Archer Avenue and State Street in Chicago in 1911. She earned ten dollars per week. Then she sang at Hugh Hoskins', a small club that catered to an exclusive black clientele at 32d and State Street. A move in 1915 to the Panama Café at 35th and State Street, owned by Isadore "Izzy" Levine and Izzy Shorr, pointed Hunter in the direction of Paris. The Panama Café attracted whites from Hyde Park's university community as well as entertainers from downtown who flocked to hear the best black singers and musicians Chicago's south side had to offer. Among the singers in the Panama's downstairs saloon were Florence Mills, Nettie Compton, Bricktop, Cora Green, and Mattie Hale; except for Mills, who died in 1927, all of them would meet again in Montmartre. One of the first to sing composer Maceo Pinkard's "Sweet Georgia Brown," Hunter worked at the Panama from 8:00 P.M. to midnight. Then she headed for the after-hours clubs to perform: the Deluxe Club and the Dreamland Café, whose band included Joseph "King" Oliver, Sidney Bechet, Warren "Baby" Dodds, Lilian "Lil" Hardin and, later, Louis Armstrong. After hours and on off-days she worked at the Pekin, Packy McFarland's, and the Elite no. 2, all popular State Street nightclubs. (Hunter would find this routine of playing multiple gigs in a single night familiar and well established on the Montmartre cabaret circuit.)

Moving back to New York years later, Hunter was to learn that Bricktop had thwarted Hunter's first opportunity to work at Le Grand Duc in 1924. Eugene Bullard was seeking a singer to replace Florence Embry Jones, and her husband, who knew the Harlem entertainment scene very well, suggested that Bullard invite Alberta to join his club. At Bullard's urging, Palmer Jones sent a telegram containing an offer to Hunter in care of Eva Blanche, a former chorus girl who operated a typical Harlem-style "buffet flat," serving meals around the clock to black entertainers in the large dining room of her Harlem apartment. Blanche held messages and mail for musicians who were on the road. Hunter stated that Bricktop picked up the telegram, saying she was going to deliver it but instead read it, then took off immediately for Paris. Telling the story in a matter-of-fact way, Alberta said, "in those days you had to survive." [59]

She opened her first large engagement in France at the Princess Palace in Nice with the Tourmanoff Sisters on 10 December 1927. The New Year found Hunter still on the Riviera, at the Knickerbocker Club. After leaving the Riviera she traveled to London to appear in Noble Sissle's show at the London Pavilion on 27 January 1928, to raise money for victims of the Thames River flood. Crossing to Paris on 5 March 1929, Hunter played at the newly opened Cotton Club at 6 rue Fontaine, managed by Jack Landorff. The club closed several days after opening. She sang for a few weeks at Le Florence, owned by Peppy d'Abrew, and then went back to New York on 22 May 1929 aboard the *Île de France*. Resettled in The Big Apple, Alberta sang at Harlem's famous Small's Paradise in February 1930.

A Harlem-Paris push-pull involved Alberta Hunter in frequent transatlantic crossings. Neither the City of Light nor the Big Apple seemed satisfying for the long stay; it was a replay of her early life in show business. In France after her most recent crossing in late May 1933, she went to work at Fred Payne's Bar, 14 rue Pigalle. Payne, a white American expatriate, offered afternoon bridge, a cabaret all night long, and a solid reputation for the best barbecue cooked by a black American. Fred Payne's Bar became Hunter's base for engagements outside Paris. And there were many such engagements: the Casino Excelsior in Alexandria, Egypt; the Continental Cabaret in Cairo; the Garden-Petit-Champs in Istanbul; the Femina Music Hall in Athens. Hunter was in Italy in February 1937 when Il Duce imposed a ban on performances by black Americans. Two years later, as war clouds threatened the sanctity of Europe, Hunter sailed once more for New York on the *Île de France*, not anticipating a return soon to Paris. There must have been a twinkle in her eye as she recalled the story of Bricktop's return to New York in late October that year. Lady Mendl and the duchess of Windsor, she said, chipped in to pay Bricktop's way home because she was penniless.[60]

One view of the exodus of musical talents across the Atlantic to Montmartre from the jazz capitals in America is that of small-scale voyages in the middle passage—but in reverse. The image of Paris as a place to work and enjoy unfettered life filled black passengers with exhilaration. One such traveler was Henry Crowder. On his first voyage to France in 1928, he proclaimed: "No color bar there. No discriminations! Freedom! A chance to live as every other man lived regardless of his color."[61]

In the 1890s times were hard for the family of a poor, devout Baptist Georgian working man, and Henry Crowder, the youngest son, decided to get away at the first opportunity. Learning his music by singing in church and playing piano for the YMCA, Crowder soon made his way north, to Washington, D.C. After a stint playing in honky-tonks and brothels and managing several orchestras, he found work as the piano player in a new quartet, the Alabamians, with the well-known jazz violinist Eddie South (one of the finest classically trained violinists ever to play jazz, South was born in Louisiana, Missouri, in November 1904 and studied at the Chicago Musical College before becoming the music director of Jimmy Wade's Syncopaters in 1924).[62] Recruited to join the Alabamians for the Paris engagement, Crowder landed in Cherbourg in 1928 with 1,500 francs in his pocket. This sum, which he earned playing with South as a jazz piano and violin duo to entertain rich white shipboard passengers, proved to be a blessing indeed. The white "manager" in New York who signed a "contract" to sponsor South and his Alabamians' trip to France and set up an engagement in Paris was nowhere in sight when the almost penniless group got to Cherbourg. Anxious to leave America for work in Paris, the group had agreed to pay its own boat fare, expecting reimbursement in Cherbourg. After docking and clearing customs and finding no manager to greet them, they got directions to Montmartre from a friendly black American stranger at the quai. They met—as the stranger predicted—many old friends and acquaintances in the musical entertainment world from New York and Chicago. "There were a great many American Negro musicians in town at the time and the night life was gay," observed Crowder.[63] In 1928 the high demand for black American musicians by managers of theaters, cafés, restaurants, and music halls soon brought Crowder and the band a two-week booking at the Empire Music Hall in Paris. From this successful engagement came a number of offers, among them one from Venice for an eight-week stand at the Hotel Luna, next to the Royal Palace and near St. Mark's Cathedral.

During the Hotel Luna engagement Henry Crowder met Nancy Cunard, the rebellious daughter and heir to the Cunard steamship fortune. "And for the next few years [they] foundered around in one of the most intractable and serious human problems; the sexual, social and political attractions and antagonisms of whites and blacks."[64] Henry transformed Nancy's life and found his own turned upside down in the process. Their relationship gained international notoriety.

When the Hotel Luna engagement ended in early October, the band returned to Paris. Crowder stayed on in Venice, as did Cunard. By the time Crowder rejoined the quartet, news of his affair with Cunard had spread around Paris, nourishing the grapevine of gossip and fact that entwined black Montmartre.[65]

Crowder and the band were booked at the Plantation, a nightclub that had just opened up. After playing through the entire night, finishing work at 5 A.M., some musicians would wander to the Costa Bar or to Bricktop's for a drink. One night at Bricktop's an argument arose between Mike McKendrick, the banjo player from Chicago, and Sidney Bechet. At issue were unflattering words about Crowder. McKendrick and Bechet, each armed with loaded revolvers, fired wildly. Bullets sprayed the area outside Bricktop's. Glover Compton, the well-known pianist from Chicago, who played regularly at Freddy Payne's and Harry's New York Bar, was wounded by a stray bullet, as were a French and an English bystander.

Displaying the usual generosity for which he was known in the black community of Paris, Eugene Bullard provided money for lawyers' fees. As Bechet recalled of Bullard, "he'd made himself the kind of man people around Paris had a need for. The cabarets, the clubs, the musicians — when there was some trouble they couldn't straighten out by themselves, they called on Gene." In the Bechet-McKendrick incident Bullard's help was to little avail. Each man was sentenced to eleven months' imprisonment and fined 10,000 francs. After release from prison, both were deported.[66] (Bechet went to Germany and played at Haus Vaterland in Berlin, then back to the Wild West Bar in Montparnasse. There he received a wire from Noble Sissle to return to America and join his band. Another twenty years passed before Bechet returned to Paris.)

The Bechet-McKendrick incident capped Henry Crowder's growing disillusionment with the cabaret scene in black Montmartre. On a small scale it seemed to mirror nightlife in the rest of Montmartre: raucous, drunken street behavior that broke out almost nightly and often ended in fights resulting in serious injury or even death. Before the turn of the century, even before the Paris Commune of 1871, Montmartre had gained the image of a mix *du plaisir et du crime.*[67] Crowder was sick to death of night hours, of the fatigue attendant on adulation, of all the drinks sent to him at his piano, and of those interminable "crap games" he and other musicians would be playing at the Flea Pit at dawn, too weary to go home and sleep. So Henry was susceptible to Nancy's invitation to get away from all that.

He followed her to her country place, Puits-Carré, at Chapelle-Réanville in Normandy, to help in printing and publishing manuscripts at her Hours Press. She had purchased an ancient Belgian Mathieu handpress that used Elzevir type. Henry also wanted to play and compose, and in time Nancy hired a piano for him. Working at Hours Press, Crowder drifted away from the hectic nightlife of Montmartre. He was, as Nancy said, "invaluable." He painted the house, oiled the press, repaired it when necessary, packed and wrapped and posted publications, and drove on errands to Vernon and Paris.[68] And he devoted time to creating musical compositions.

By 1930 Nancy, tiring of the frequent journeys to Paris and the boredom that Réanville's quietness provoked, handed over the management of the press to Wyn Henderson, a woman friend also involved in publishing. Cunard and Crowder went off to southwestern France, settling in the tiny village of Creysse, in the Dordogne. They rented two primitive rooms and hired a piano, which arrived drawn by two oxen. Crowder worked on his compositions in the course of their four-week stay, so that he went back to Paris with the opus almost finished.

Before the year ended, Nancy published her second series of books. One of them was "Henry Crowder: Six Piano Pieces with Poems by Richard Aldington, Walter Lowenfels and Nancy Cunard." And his opus,

*Henry Music,* a collection of songs and poetry, was Hours Press's last publication for 1930. Man Ray created the photomontage in black and white for the cover, showing Crowder's dark head and neck encircled by Nancy's white arms wearing a selection from her fine collection of African ivory bracelets.[69] Walter Lowenfels's song was a rallying cry about Sacco and Vanzetti; Samuel Beckett's poem, "From the Only Poet to a Shining Whore," was subtitled "For Henry Crowder to Sing," and Nancy contributed "my own small effort at a rather sophisticated 'Blues,' which Henry sang with all the nostalgia the words imply":

Back again between the odds and ends,
Back again between the odds and ends,
what once was gay's now sad,
what was unknown's now friends.

Each capital's not more than one café
Wherein you lose, wherein you lose
Yourself in what you have and have had
why worry choose, why worry choose?

The Waiter waits, he will wait all night
And when you're tight he will set you right
Back in tomorrow, or even yesterday.
Time plays the piper, but what do we pay?

Oh Bœuf sur le Toit, you had one song,
But when I look in the mirrors it all goes wrong—
Memory Blues, and only back today
I'm a miserable travelling man.[70]

In time, the press at Réanville would play an instrumental role in Cunard's fight for racial justice of black Americans, in which Crowder was her tutor.

After Crowder and Cunard returned to Paris in 1930, he went back to the nightlife of Montmartre. His first booking was at the Bateau Ivre, a popular club that often remained open after the music ended at about 2 A.M. After-hours affairs kept Crowder and other musicians and entertainers in touch with the Harlem Renaissance writers in Paris in 1930.

And when he decided to return to America for his first visit since leaving home in 1928, it was the Harlem Renaissance black American writer Countee Cullen who offered to help him make travel arrangements.[71] The trip, once postponed, occurred later that year.

Crowder was to make two other transatlantic voyages; the first one in 1932, in the company of Cunard, included a visit to Harlem. Three years later their stormy relationship ended. The two never met again. Crowder remained in Europe, falling back on his musical talents to keep afloat as a competent jazz pianist with occasional bookings in nightclubs and musical revues. He headed a racially mixed orchestra for a revue produced by Buddy Bradley, brother of dancing instructor Arthur Bradley, in which there was a spot for someone identified only as "Mrs. Henry Crowder." It suggests either that Crowder married after he and Cunard separated or that he introduced the woman in the show as his "wife." In fact, Crowder's wife remained in Washington, D.C., during the years in which he mainly lived and worked in Paris. It was not uncommon, however, for many married black musicians to take on a "wife" while abroad. After Crowder's death in 1955, Cunard received a letter from Mrs. Crowder stating that "she, the wife, was Crowder's only true loving wife."[72]

Recognized for his talents as a jazz pianist, Crowder was hired by Frank Withers, who was in charge of the band for Louis Douglas's ill-fated all-black revue that opened in the Mediterranean Theater in Nice for the 1936 spring season. After a short run, the revue moved to Liège, Belgium, where it closed. Crowder formed a small band in Brussels, adding to his floor show the Four Harmony Kings, who had been performing in Douglas's revue. The spread of jazz clubs in Brussels and Ostend gave Crowder ample work and enabled him to keep the distance he desired from the turbulent nightclub scene in Montmartre. He was in Belgium when Germany invaded France.

While in Paris, besides working in Montmartre, Crowder played the piano bar at the popular Bœuf sur le Toit, the center of a different but highly influential jazz scene. *Le bœuf sur le toit* was the title of a ballet devised by Jean Cocteau with music by Darius Milhaud. The nightclub that carried its name prospered as a lively meeting place for everyone in the artistic movements then and outlasted the many restaurants and bars that fashion made and unmade in Paris of the 1920s. Louis Moÿses (Moysès), a bartender from Charlesville, created Le Bœuf in rue Boissy-d'Anglas, off the place de la Concorde. Moÿses had managed and then become proprietor of the Bar Gaya, in rue Duphot, which offered as a nightly feature ragtime and Broadway sounds played by pianist Jean Wiener. The Gaya was noted for attracting such celebrities as the prince of Wales, Arthur Rubenstein, and Prince Murat to listen to Jean Cocteau and Jules Pascin playing drums. Pascin and Cocteau, like the prince of Wales, would not hesitate to take over the drums, mixing with accomplished musicians, many of whom were regularly engaged to play in black Montmartre.

Moÿses's official inauguration of Le Bœuf on 10 January 1922 was met with wild enthusiasm by Jean Cocteau, Constantin Brancusi, and Raymond Radiguet.[73] Cocteau is said to have selected the club's name because the action in Milhaud's ballet takes place in a bar. Milhaud was inspired by the Spanish, Portuguese, and black Latin music he came to appreciate after several years' service with the French diplomatic service in Rio de Janeiro.

James Harding captures the brashness of this era as it shaped the making of Le Bœuf's reputation by its creators, les Six—Arthur Honegger, Louis Durey, Germaine Tailleferre, Darius Milhaud, Georges Auric, Francis Poulenc—the half-dozen young French composers who had collected under Cocteau's intellectual stage management. The artists, writers, and classical composers that les Six represented

combined to produce an intellectual climate which, for a while, was uniquely suited to a favorable reception for jazz. For a start it appeared to sound an appropriately irreverent note to people who had recently passed through hell and survived. It appealed to the rather phony "populism" of men like Jean Cocteau; its "primitive" sound and "savage" quality attracted the surrealists; and the musicians adopted it as a way of thumbing their noses at the ponderous pretentious of the Wagnerian school. It was therefore quite in keeping that Paris should produce the first jazz club and entirely fitting that it should be given the surrealist name Le Bœuf sur le Toit. This became the main meeting place for all the leading intellectuals of the day, particularly the younger ones, for whom jazz had become an almost obligatory intellectual affectation. It was here that Ravel was first introduced to jazz by the piano duo of Jean Weiner and Clement Doucet early in 1922.[74]

For the Regency period's generation of young lions, the Rocher de Cancale captured its outlook; for the symbolists it was the Closerie des Lilas. Le Bœuf was for the generation of *les années folles*.[75] For a brief time during these "crazy years" of 1919–29 Paul Deschanel had his pathetic presidency, going mad in office and resigning. Once in an earlier stage of his madness, the president of the Republic was found wandering through the night in pajamas. Deschanel's last days in office symbolized the era of Le Bœuf, in which surrealism, gaiety, and bodily abandonment swept aside old ideas of dignity and tradition. Young girls frequented public places far from the eyes of mothers or chaperones, smoked cigarettes, and danced in nightclubs like Le Bœuf to hot jazz. Freud's advice to get rid of inhibitions was accepted and became a rationale for women to grant their favors to lovers; the delinquencies by wives and mistresses were even viewed sympathetically by husbands.

New words and expressions flowed into the popular vocabulary, reflecting the rapid changes in mores as well as a distinctly American influence on Parisian daily life.[76] "A nurse was the female you employed to look after your children. In the afternoon you went to a 'tea-room' for your 'five o'clock.' Later in the evening, amidst your 'modern-style' furnishings, you offered 'un cocktail' (not an *apéritif*) which you poured from 'un shaker' and called perhaps 'Bosom caresser' in your eagerness to keep 'up to date.' Then you might go on to 'un dancing,' where 'un jazz-band' discoursed 'one-step' and 'shimmy.' At the Folies-Bergère you could watch . . . Josephine Baker throw herself into a frantic 'Charleston.' Her compatriots were everywhere on the Paris stage in the 1920s."[77]

At the height of its fame, Le Bœuf was where one met all the city's celebrities: besides Maurice Ravel and Jean Cocteau, Pablo Picasso, Max Jacob, Fernand Léger, Jean Wiener, Erik Satie, Jean Lurçat, René Clair, Léon-Paul Fargue, André Derain, Marcel Duchamp, and a score of others might be mingling about or occupying the dozen or so tables. Maurice Sachs, a chronicler of the era and himself a habitué of Le Bœuf, described the nightly social mix at the club:

> It was the only place . . . where one could go in full dress or grey flannels as one chose, and the women in evening gowns or tailored suits. Society mingled with painters and actors, men of affairs with writers. It was not unusual to meet these working men

in sandals come down from Montparnasse.[78] Parisians as well as tourists had only to consult a reputable Paris guidebook to encounter Le Bœuf and its wonders. As one tourist guide described, there one would find "the artistic trend of the moment, the literary trend of the moment, and . . . *the* trend of the moment, whatever it may be. If one hears here the most outstanding declarations that are being made in Paris, one is at the same time certain to eat exceeding well. There are Alsatian specialties, such as *foie gras* in pastry; and there are excellent Rhine wines, not to mention quetsche and mirabel, to transport you far away from Paris. Average price of a meal: 25 francs."[79]

To the youth of the time Le Bœuf blazoned enchantment, for in its crowds they found their real masters. And they also found jazz. "Throughout the twenties, the Bœuf had the loudest jazz, the prettiest women, and the latest art gossip to be found in Paris."[80] But its neighbors' complaints against the nightly sounds blaring from Le Bœuf forced its move to rue de Penthièvre in 1928, and with that its magic vanished. "In the rue Boissy-d'Anglas—it attracted a famous clientele—the champions of the art movements like Dadaism and Surrealism, diplomats, English dukes, music-hall artists like Maurice Chevalier and Mistinguett, Diaghilev, and the flamboyant André Citroën of the car firm. In the rue de Penthièvre the 'Bœuf' drew only tourists curious for the personalities who had by then deserted it."[81] Ragtime and Broadway sounds played by pianist Jean Wiener at the old Bar Gaya continued as a feature in the nightly music repertoire of Le Bœuf in its new location.[82]

Harlem-style jazz was ill-suited for the craze that swept Paris in the mid-1920s: dance music. And yet it was as dance music that jazz finally triumphed against an older generation's dismissal of jazz as the ultimate in decadence and barbarism. Many young Parisians still preferred the accordions and violins of the *bals musettes,* cheap dancing places where customers paid a few sous, each time they asked a woman to dance, to cover the musicians' expenses.[83] And as small nightclubs began to mushroom in la Butte, many featured what the French called *un dancing,* a term that became synonymous with "nightclub" or "public hall." One of the first *dancings,* an observer of Montmartre's changing nightclub scene claimed, was a second edition of the Clover Club in rue de Caumartin opened in 1922 by Maurice Mouret and Leonora Hughes. The nightly routine—with audience participation orchestrated by some American singing—proved a great attraction to Parisians and well-to-do foreign visitors after the war.[84] *Dancings* were advertised all over Paris in this era, not only in Montmartre. A nightclub, public hall, or supper place might be *un dancing*, but patrons seldom really danced: there was no room. As Basil Woon observed at the time, "what one does is to stand still and wiggle wearily. Variations of this are called the 'foxtrots,' 'crawls,' and the like."[85]

Dancing to the jazz beat accelerated the transformation of Montmartre. Even at the end of the nineteenth century Montmartre, with its seamy reputation, attracted few tourists. A few windmills still remained as vivid reminders of la Butte's past. Converted to a nightclub, Moulin Rouge symbolized the transformation. Artists, poets, and singers whose life and spirit were essentially French had been the last to bend to the winds of change and migrate across the Seine to Montparnasse. Critics of the transformation deplored Montmartre's becoming a sort of pleasure fair, its sole purpose to exploit English and American visitors.[86] And visit they did. An end to the 9:30 P.M. wartime limit on dancing and music in Parisian restaurants had attracted large numbers of well-to-do tourists. The visitors flocked to Montmartre, where Harlem-style jazz was featured in jazz clubs owned and managed by black Americans.

Shortly before such clubs became permanent features in Montmartre—beginning in 1924 with Mitchell's Chez Florence and Bullard's Grand Duc—entrepreneurial white expatriates, among them white American former soldiers discharged in France, had already established themselves in the dining-dancing night world of Paris. After the armistice, Jed Kiley of Chicago opened several clandestine members-only night spots that the French police more or less tolerated at first because they were supposed to be strictly limited to American soldiers. Kiley's, at 6 rue Fontaine, offered dancing from midnight to breakfast, drawing capacity crowds every night. So popular was his place that the *New York Herald Tribune–Paris,* widely read by Americans, regularly listed Kiley's as one of the best bars in Paris. Seeing the profit being made at Kiley's, Billy Arnold, who sought to book an American band for its *dancings,* and Billy Kenley, a soldier with the AEF stationed in France, recruited a band from among his fellow army privates. The band called themselves the White Lyres and made the dubious claim to having played the first jazz ever heard in Paris at one of Kiley's clandestine dances.[87]

Dining, dancing, and jazz continued to gain in popularity among Parisians. Patrons of nightlife entertainment relished the excitement of making noise and stomping feet in clandestine clubs operated by somewhat shady characters. In Paris, the formalities for obtaining a license to start a nightclub were not onerous but included payment of a special tax to remain open after midnight. *Dancings* and bars changed their ownership quickly, a fashionable and popular resort one month being deserted or closed the next. Typical was Harry's New York Bar, a tiny cabaret in rue Daunou. It was sold in 1923 by Nell Henry to Harry McElhone, who had lived in France for many years before the war and then became head bartender at Ciro's in London.

When Kiley abandoned jazz, Joe Zelli (who later influenced Eugene Bullard's entrance into the world of Montmartre nightlife) opened a clandestine club in rue de Caumartin. A patron gained entrance by paying 30 francs for a "membership card." Zelli's was crowded every night, raided several times by police, and eventually closed. He then moved to a new legitimate club, featuring black jazz musicians, and brought most of his following.[88] After a refurbishing to produce the first really smart club in rue de Caumartin, Harry Pilcer's Sans Souci opened in Zelli's old site, but it too was short-lived.

Maurice Chevalier and Saint-Grenier, famous comedians of the Casino de Paris, also entered the lucrative market for *dancing* patrons by opening the Acacias, at 49 rue des Acacias. For a time the black American composer Edmund Jenkins held forth with a small jazz band at the club.[89] But the Acacias' location near the Bois de Boulogne—on the far western side of Paris with few other nightclubs in its vicinity—did not attract late night revelers who preferred to go from midnight to dawn visiting several *dancings,* never approaching dawn in the place where the evening began. Much of the attraction of night reveling derived from stumbling down the street with glass in hand, going in one bar for a drink and a spin on the dance floor, then onto the next, a pleasurable ritual that a taxi ride would violate. After a typical night, the score or so of white musicians in Paris made Harry's New York Bar their headquarters.[90]

For black American musicians, Bullard's Grand Duc in Montmartre was home away from home. Langston Hughes, working there as a dishwasher and general kitchen hand, recalled that "when all the other clubs were closed, the best of the musicians and entertainers from various other smart places would often drop into Le Grand Duc, and there'd be a jam session until seven or eight in the morning—only in 1924 they had no such name for it."[91] Between jam sessions in the early morning hours, Bricktop said, Bullard served three things that could be found in most all-night Harlem clubs: corned-beef hash with a poached egg; creamed chicken on toast, or a club sandwich—all courtesy of the house.

After the arrival of the Charleston in 1925, Parisians were no longer content with the waltz, the java, or the fox-trot, and the new dance craze became de rigueur for young and old. Chez Florence in rue Blanche was popularized as the headquarters of the Charleston, doubtless a claim disputed both by Bricktop and Josephine Baker. Bricktop was in such high demand to teach the new dance steps that she booked Charleston lessons weeks in advance for high-society patrons of Le Grand Duc. The rage among Parisians to learn the Charleston generated a friendly rivalry among Josephine Baker, Bricktop, and Frisco Bingham, all self-styled teachers, to garner the most students. Frisco Bingham was hailed in a *Paris Soir* article by Stephen Manier as being the first to show the Charleston in Paris. He taught Parisians the rhythm of the dance, first demonstrating the dance to Nikitina and giving lessons every Friday afternoon at Chez Florence. Students were not wanting for Bingham's crowded dance courses, which charged wealthy Americans 200 francs a lesson.[92] Anxious to perform their latest dance steps but often too timid to take the plunge, visitors to Chez Florence, willing or unwilling, were sometimes made to dance by "a gigantic nigger tapping people on the shoulders to remind them that participation in the dance is one of the rules laid down by Florence."[93]

At times the band of black musicians who held forth at Chez Florence from 1:00 A.M. had already finished an evening's stint, playing for the dancing crowd from 9.00 P.M. until after midnight at La Michodière, at 4 rue de La Michodière. When Florence Jones was still the star at Le Grand Duc, her husband worked at Les Ambassadeurs and arrived at her place of work about three in the morning. Until he came she sang with the orchestra a couple of songs an hour between dances, but her star performance of special numbers that attracted nightly crowds began when Palmer came and accompanied her at the piano.[94] The hustle and bustle of the most popular musicians and entertainers moving from one club to another between midnight and dawn, often bringing in tow a trail of devoted musical fans, added to the flavor of what Bricktop called *le tumulte noir*.

The craze for dancing at mealtimes seriously affected business in some of the fine old eating places in Paris. Dancing was anathema to the true gourmets. Echoing the prejudice of restaurateurs against the noisy disruptive atmosphere generated by this new fad, one *maître de maison* stated that a fine French chef has the pride of an artist. He carefully prepares a dish and sends it fragrant and steaming to the table. But with the dancing innovation, just as the waiter serves the culinary creation, the jazz band strikes up and everyone rushes to the dance floor, the meal forgotten in the frenzy of wiggling.[95]

The Café de Paris, 41 avenue de l'Opéra, was the first grand luxurious restaurant to yield to the dancing craze, beginning with exhibition dances at suppertime. Maxim's, 3 rue Royale, soon followed the trend, as did Les Champs-Élysées at 63 avenue des Champs-Élysées. Dancing at Le Bœuf sur le Toit started several years earlier, when it was in rue Boissy-d'Anglas. From the time it opened, Le Bœuf was popular with sophisticated young literary men and their female admirers who crowded the tiny dance floor wiggling to loud jazz played by black musicians until after dawn. Dancing to the tempo and style of black jazz musicians served as a common denominator, a musical joining together of different social classes with different reasons for a night of enjoyment to the same musical beat. *Dancings* at the Florida, 20 rue de Clichy, an exclusive club where Leon Abbey led a resident band in 1929 and most popular with members of the American colony in Paris and English visitors, and Le Perroquet at 16 rue de Clichy, which occupied premises above the Casino de Paris, appealed "to visitors who liked to take their wives, or other people's wives," a reputation also enjoyed by Zelli's, in rue Fontaine.[96] The popularity of Le Perroquet remained unimpaired, doubtless enhanced by the long engagement of Louis Mitchell's Jazz Kings. When Mitchell left the group in 1923 it was renamed the Real Jazz Kings and came under the leadership of the cornet player Crickett Smith. Smith became a legendary figure with the first black American jazz bands that toured Europe, starting an engagement at the Casino de Paris.

The public preference for jazz caused the gradual disappearance of the high-kicking *quadrille excentrique,* known to tourists as the French can-can. At the turn of the century, the cancan was the chief attraction at pub-lic halls—the Élysée Montmartre, Jardin de Paris, the Moulin Rouge. For a time it resisted the invasion of jazz and the tango and managed to survive at the Bal Tabarin. New *dancings* pervaded the length and breadth of Montmartre in order to suit the taste of foreign patrons. In popular *dancings* at clubs like the Florida, on a typical night they numbered more than two-thirds of the customers.[97]

Though the craze for dancing first took root in night haunts in central Paris, south of la Butte, as new restaurants and dancing places like the restaurant Volterra on the site of the Théâtre de l'Étoile at 7 Champs-Élysées introduced tango and jazz bands, it next gained a foothold north of la Butte and invaded almost every café and restaurant in Montmartre, adding to the boom in nightclub entertainment that proved an economic blessing to black jazz musicians. The cabaret du Lapin Agile, 4 rue des Saules, in the shadow of Sacré-Cœur, a favorite place of writers, poets, musicians, painters, and sculptors before their drift across the Seine to Montparnasse, engaged jazz bands and singers.

The clamor for Harlem-style jazz to be played in Parisian nightclubs and restaurants opened the market for black American musicians often strug-gling for work in the Bronzevilles at home. Word spread that there were no shortages of gigs on both banks of the Seine. First-rate musicians like Elliot Carpenter and his Red Devils were in high demand and could bar-gain for the highest wages. Carpenter would learn to do so on his first trip to Paris in 1920. Opal Cooper and Sammy Richardson had just come back from France and talked to him enthusiastically about Montmartre; they themselves were eager to return. Carpenter was approached by Mr. Wickes, president of New York's Clef Club, looking for musicians for a new club in Paris. Wickes offered the band's members $50 each. In Paris Carpenter met Crickett Smith, who criticized him for accepting an offer of $50 and offered $150 to join his band. Smith himself, working at the Casino de Paris, was earning $250–300 a week. Two weeks later Carpen-ter's Red Devils were signed for an engagement in London for $350 a week. Soon, nightclub work brought earnings of $750 a week on both sides of the Channel.[98]

Paris's infection with black-American-style jazz had not escaped the notice of the Great White Hopes in the white American big-band world of the mid-1920s. When Paul Whiteman, the self-styled "King of Jazz," introduced his big band at the music hall of the Champs-Élysées in August 1926, the program presented jazz renditions that were mostly unfamiliar to a Parisian audience accustomed to the Harlem-style black jazz found in Montmartre. As one writer described Whiteman's orchestra, it had "the elegant precision of a well-oiled machine, a kind of 'Rolls-Royce of dance music' but whose effect remained pedestrian and predictable." [99] The instrumentalists who made up Whiteman's aggregation were more suitable for listeners seated in a large auditorium, not wiggling in the small space of a crowded nightclub, which jazz lovers relished. Paris music critics judged Whiteman's performance as a further attempt by the orchestra leader to establish himself as "chef du jazz." [100] His flashy, novel style of musical presentation never posed a serious threat to black musicians on the Parisian scene.

Whiteman's concert came at a time of lively debate in Parisian intellectual circles among writers, music critics, and classical musicians on the cultural and aesthetic merits of this new musical sound. Some critics characterized jazz as only noise and cacophony, and dancing to it the death of intelligence; others raised the question, is it music? The League against the Jazz Band, under its president Princess Anna de Saxe, vowed never to engage a jazz orchestra for one of its soirees. But Jean Cocteau's search for a "music for everyday" discovered jazz tailor-made for his intellectual scheme of things. "Jazz was unquestionably music of the people, with the added attraction of being exotically Negroid." He argued that the jazz band was like the music's soul; others sought to claim that, in due course, jazz would become French. [101]

As the great jazz debate raged on, other Great White Hopes of jazz showed up on the Paris music-hall scene with somewhat sanitized versions of ragtime jazz, still the popular form in Montmartre nightclubs. Billy Arnold, Jack Hylton, and Enoch Light kept fully engaged performing in Paris music halls, combining jazz presentations with modified stage shows by dancers and choral groups. Fred Warring and his Pennsylvanians arrived for their concert in Salle Pleyel in July 1928. Decked out in blue jackets, red vests, and white flannel trousers, like those of navy officers, Warring and his sprightly jazz orchestra played to the curiosity seekers but attracted few true jazz lovers.

More successful in stamping his signature on the local white jazz scene was Ray Ventura, a French pianist. He and four other students of the Lycée-de-Sailly formed for their amusement a small jazz quintet, titled Le Collegiate Five, in April 1924. In January 1929 he became leader of the group and shortly reshaped it, claiming as his jazz heroes Jimmy Dorsey and Eddie Lang, whose style of music shunned the slam-bang noisy beat notable in Paris's Harlem. Ventura retained his style of jazz music after his quintet days; and as his band enlarged, becoming increasingly popular as a dance orchestra with great versatility, his separation from Montmartre-style jazz became even more apparent. Unlike white American big bands that left no visible mark on the Paris musical scene, Ray Ventura filled the niche of the Great French Hope of the big band scene, introducing jazz to a large audience in France through gramophone records, radio broadcasts, and international touring.

Although black jazz musicians favored the intimacy of clubs—their most accustomed venue in the Bronzevilles—over the concert halls of the big bands, they did aspire to theatrical presentations of their own. Some black artists and entertainers saw Montmartre's Harlem-style nightlife as a setting for great musicals and inevitably focused on the 1903 smash hit *In Dahomey* produced by vaudeville stars Bert Williams and George Walker, which would become an even greater hit in London later. A stream of theatrical successes had followed on the black theater circuit, leading the way with Noble Sissle and Eubie Blake's hit musicals, *Shuffle Along* and *The Chocolate Dandies*. Josephine Baker toured in both these reviews before coming to Paris in 1925.

Excitement captured the black community's imagination, conjuring up other images, when word spread of efforts to found a Negro art theater. For many members of the black community in Paris, this was no longer a dream deferred but an inspiration resurrected by the former director of the Cincinnati Art Theater, Ruth Allen. Her view of a Negro art theater was on the lines of the swift-moving, flitting acts of the Moscow Chauve-Souris modified to accommodate African American and African themes. Launching an aggressive promotional campaign to gain converts to the idea of a Negro art theater, Allen claimed the black theatrical company would divert Parisian audiences from traditional music-hall spectacles, with "American and African decorations, dances, songs, spirituals and real 'blue' music."[102] She solicited endorsements by prominent members of Montmartre's black community, not only to legitimize her purpose of leasing a theater in the district, but also to gain an affirmative nod from the black community—a requisite Seal of Approval. Prince Kojo Tovalou of Dahomey, who shared with Eugene Bullard the reputation of always being ready to promote the cultural activities of black American writers and artists in Paris, was sympathetic to Allen's proposed production. Writer Claude McKay, Florence Jones (then singing at Bullard's Grand Duc), and other "musical colored lights of the Paris colony" came to Allen's support.

The curtain never rose on the Negro Art Theater. In the financially risky, highly competitive arena of Parisian musical productions, unforeseen factors often undercut the most carefully orchestrated and financed schemes. It is possible that Ruth Allen's inspiration for the Negro Art Theater's first production was too far removed from the Harlem-oriented jazz-vaudeville culture that black American entertainers had forged in Montmartre. African decorations, spirituals, and "blue" music were not items of Harlem culture that the missionaries of jazz carried in their baggage on the voyage to France. Negro spirituals were the domain of groups like the Fisk Jubilee Singers, whose European tours became less frequent after the turn of the century. By 1919, tenor Roland Hayes and his piano accompanist Harry Burleigh filled Paris concert halls with renditions of spirituals, "plantation songs" and classical songs.[103] Even raunchy "blue" music did not enter the repertoires of Bricktop and Florence Jones, whose sultry, seductive, jazzy lyrics aimed to delight, not shock, tourists and provincials with seemingly unlimited francs to spend during a night on the town. The Cincinnati Art Theater had ill-prepared Allen for the jazz-based, Harlem-style music-hall scenes Montmartre had come to enjoy.

Two years after the successful *Revue Nègre* closed, Lew Leslie returned to Paris with another of his *Blackbirds* stage productions. His earlier revue of that name played at the Théâtre des Champs-Élysées (which had closed during the Great War and reopened on 25 October 1920). Edmund Sayags's presentation of *Blackbirds of 1926* was still remembered fondly by the Parisian theater public. It starred Florence Mills and, as one reviewer wrote, her "beautiful Zulus." Shrimp Jones and Johnny Dunn were featured dancers and the entire production was accompanied by Johnny Hudgins's jazz orchestra from the Plantation Club in New York. Witnessing the arrival of the train bringing *Blackbirds* to Gare St-Lazare in June 1929, a press reviewer wrote ecstatically that the windows of the convoy were garnished with a quantity of unusual black figures, saluting Paris with large laughs of white teeth and numerous faces of attractive, outlandishly charming women. Leaving the train, the *oiseaux noirs* performed the "Aunt Jemima Stroll" as they moved down the quai toward Montmartre.[104] For Florence Mills, this would be the last stroll at the head of her company.

In her brief twenty-four-year stage career, Florence Mills, born in the nation's capital, had captivated audiences all over America and Europe. Her first big show engagement came at the age of four at the Bijou Theater in Washington, D.C., in an act called Bonita and Herren.[105] Appearing in the *Sons of Ham* as "Baby Florence Mills, an Extra added attraction" she sang "Miss Hannah from Savannah," a song taught to her by pioneer show performer Aida Overton Walker.[106] By the time Florence was six she had captured cakewalking and buck dancing championships on nationwide tours. After the Mills Sisters team, which she formed with two sisters, had toured the country, Florence had joined Bricktop and Cora Green as the Panama Trio at the Panama Café in Chicago.

Bricktop and Mills were to meet later in Paris, both then as popular stars. The successful New York season of Lew Leslie's *Blackbirds of 1926* gained for the troupe an invitation to Paris, where Mills starred in the production, its scheduled four-week engagement extended to sixteen weeks. The show opened in London at the Pavilion on 14 May 1926, playing for an uninterrupted three hundred performances. The prince of Wales, exhibiting his fondness for black American jazz and musical performances, visited the show no less than twenty times. Florence Mills's popularity was so great that "dolls were named after her and shops designated light brown goods as the Florence Mills shade."[107] She died at the peak of her fame on a London operating table in the summer of 1927, after a routine appendectomy. She left behind no recordings, only her most popular number: "Bye Bye Blackbird." It was a song that tragedy seemed to haunt. Isadora Duncan had danced to it before setting off on her fatal car ride in

Nice. And as the funeral procession for Mills passed through Harlem, a low-flying plane released a huge flock of blackbirds.

Adelaide Hall was seen as the natural successor of Florence Mills in the black show-business world. Hall played music halls in Europe about five years before *Blackbirds,* as early as 1924. Born in Brooklyn of British parents on 20 October 1904, she made her debut with Sissle and Blake in *Shuffle Along.* Later she played the principal female role in Miller and Lyles's *Runnin' Wild.* Singing blues on Chicago's south side at some of the most famous nightclubs along the half-mile stretch of State Street, clustering at 35th, had been Adelaide Hall's rehearsal for a debut in Montmartre. She could point to the opulent Dreamland Café, which opened in the early 1920s with its mirror-hung dance floor; or the Elite Café, where Glover Compton and Tony Jackson played as a ragtime duo and Jelly Roll Morton was the resident pianist when he first arrived in Chicago around 1914. State Street's vaudeville theaters also contributed to Hall's education in the blues; she sometimes performed there herself and often attended the Grand Theatre to listen to such prominent vocalists as Bessie Smith and Clara Smith, or the Monogram Theater where Ma Rainey, Ethel Waters, and other jazz musicians appeared, including a band from New Orleans of which Sidney Bechet was a member. From Chicago, Hall signed a five-year contract under Lew Leslie, becoming the leading lady in *Blackbirds of 1928.* The show's return to Paris, opening at the Moulin Rouge in place Blanche, ushered in a new wave of black American theatrical entertainment talent. Leslie's review carried a story line that featured singing and dancing stars, a chorus line, and a choir set against the musical backdrop of a hot jazz orchestra.

The *Paris Tribune's* theater critic predicted that the returning all-black American show "bids fair to become the big hit of the Paris summer season." [108] Brought to Paris without change from the New York production, primarily to appeal to the tourist trade and the resident British and American colony when music-hall patronage was at a low ebb, the show about black American life caught the fancy of the French. Theater critics remembered how Josephine Baker became the toast of Paris through a single act in *Revue Nègre,* which was predominantly in French; *Blackbirds* captured and held audience interest for an entire evening though the songs and dialogues were in English. With more than one hundred artists, *Blackbirds'* company was accompanied by the red hot jazz band of the Plantation Club in New York and the chorus. Universally and enthusiastically acclaimed a musical success, *Blackbirds* engendered none of the caustic criticism that was heaped on *Revue Nègre*. Tim Moore, the leading male star, received critical praise equally with Adelaide Hall and Aida Ward. Later Moore went on to play in the radio show Amos and Andy as the cunning, comic "Kingfish," whose fast, slippery, money-making schemes inevitably failed. The abundance of male talent appearing in solo performances included Mantan Moreland, Earl "Snake Hips" Tucker, Crawford Jackson, Blue McAllister, Eddie Rector, Clayton "Peg-leg" Bates, the Berry Brothers, and the singer Louis Cole. Cole was to return the next year in a starring role in *Revue Noire* at the Embassy. In the grand finale, the entire company of 150 *Blackbirds* filled the stage: the solo performing artists, the Cecile MacBride choir, the show's chorus, and a dance troupe of eighteen "girls" and eighteen "boys."

After the 1929 summer season ended on 1 September, *Blackbirds* closed.[109] And the Moulin Rouge also closed its doors after the last performance, to be transformed into a cinema installed with talkies. On "Black Thursday," 24 October 1929, share quotations on Wall Street tumbled. On 11 December that year, at the Bœuf sur le Toit, "the ox came down from the roof."

# 4 | JIM CROW

*Sans Domicile Fixe*

As the 1920s opened, a galelike force of racial intolerance blasted African American communities throughout the Deep South and the border states, especially in rural areas. Bands of white-robed masked figures roamed at night, instilling the Ku Klux Klan's brand of vigilante justice. Lynchings were commonplace. Black communities were often sacked, their inhabitants put to flight, usually heading north to the relative safety and security of expanding black settlements above the Mason-Dixon line. Harlem and other black metropolises welcomed their share of displaced rural black folks whose experiences, recounted by the Negro press and retold from church pulpits, were later to provide story content for much of the Harlem Renaissance writings. The horror of these experiences served as the backdrop of Claude McKay's indignant poem "If We Must Die."

> If we must die let it not be like hogs
> Hunted and penned in an inglorious spot,
> While round us bark the mad and hungry dogs,
> Making their mock at our accursed lot.

Enjoying wide circulation through black American publications, "If We Must Die" gained the status of a Negro anthem of sorts, even making its way into the pulpits of black churches. "Ministers ended their sermons with it, and the congregations responded, Amen. It was repeated in Negro clubs and Negro schools and at Negro mass meetings."[1]

Racism often set its "mad and hungry dogs" on black men accused of having raped white women. Underlying these accusations were issues of sex and morality. Whites' fears of bending the color line accompanied the flood of American tourists to London and Paris, where they found that black men consorting with white women was as acceptable a pleasure of life as gaiety and strong drink. A spur to tourists' anxiety over a weakening color line in Gay Paree was the fact that there were somewhere between one thousand and two thousand marriages between black American soldiers and French women during the Great War.[2]

In this "dark age of bigotry and discrimination," as Mercer Cook called it, French interest focused on the two most prominent black Americans of the time—Booker T. Washington and W. E. B. Du Bois. The *New York Age* carried Washington's glowing observations of his Paris visit in 1899, infused with accounts of cordial treatment by American ambassador General Horace Porter and at the American University Club where he dined. His French audience's concerns with the plight of colored Americans matched his compatriots' cordiality.[3] Washington's *Up From Slavery* was reviewed in several Paris periodicals before the French translation was published in 1904. And no French authors could write on race relations in the United States without mentioning Booker T.

Two decades after Washington's strolls on the boulevards of Paris, Du Bois convened the first Pan-African Congress in Paris at the Grand Hôtel, boulevard des Capucines, on 19–21 February 1919. Fifty-seven delegates representing fifteen countries attended. For Du Bois, the destiny of humankind centered in Paris. Not a single great, serious movement or idea, he proclaimed, has omitted to send and keep in Paris its "Eyes and Ears and Fingers!" The congress afforded the French minister of foreign affairs an opportunity to emphasize that "the sentiment of France on equality and liberty, irrespective of color, was shown by the fact that she had six colored representatives in the French Chamber."[4] It was a policy, the minister emphasized, that France pursued even before the Revolution. What Americans saw as bending the color line was France's policy of racial tolerance. And many white Americans arriving in France felt it their duty to shore up the barricades of racial separation weakened by French impartiality to peoples of color.

Neither Booker T. Washington's exuberance nor Du Bois's triumph twenty years later prefigured the migration of Jim Crow across the Atlantic. By 1925 transatlantic arrivals of American passenger liners discharged on average five thousand Americans in French ports of call each week, and nearly all went straight to Paris. Hundreds of the denizens of white American society came to France on the *Île de France,* the *Leviathan,* the *Majestic,* the *Mauritania,* the *Berengaria,* and the *Aquitania;* the passenger manifests read like a social calendar reprinted from the pages of the *New York Times.* Basking in the triumph of the Allies' victory over Kaiser Wilhelm's Germany, white Americans with old money and new set out to discover France. Not a few tourists envisioned exotic adventures in Paris, stimulated by having read F. Scott Fitzgerald's *Tender Is the Night.* The City of Light was said to be a banquet for the senses and it was one that Americans could enjoy for very little money. The dollar was strong on the currency market. After 1924 the exchange rate, which had stood at 7 francs to the dollar in 1919, started to soar. It reached an all-time high of 50 francs to the dollar in 1926, stabilized at a little over 20 francs in 1927, and remained at that rate through the stock market crash of 1929 and well into the thirties.[5]

American puritanical inhibitions faded as the Statue of Liberty slipped below the horizon on the transatlantic voyage. Once in Paris it was the Champs-Élysées, avenue Montaigne; dinners at La Pérouse, Voisons, the Trianon, the Café de Paris, Harry's New York Bar; shows at the Lido and the Casino de Paris. For budget-minded tourists, a cheap three-course meal came to about twenty cents. After dancing until dawn in Montmartre, where jazz had already taken a firm hold, it was a must to visit Louis Mitchell's or Le Grand Duc at dawn for soul food; on another night, onion soup in Les Halles bistros was an adventure as tuxedoed carousers stood next to meat and produce porters in the early morning crowd. In Vichy, Aix-les-Bains, and the Côte d'Azur cities popular with white Americans—Juan-les-Pins, Fréjus, Menton, Nice, and Cannes—nightlife was shaped by black American jazz musicians who toured provincial France in the summer tourist season, spreading the gospel of jazz from home bases in Paris.

Black Americans discovered France with similar excitement and hope for adventure. They, however, were not spurred to cross the Atlantic by memories of *Tender Is the Night* but by stories from black soldiers who had served in France during the Great War. Frequent reports in the leading Negro newspapers or in journals emanating from the growing black community in Paris also glorified French color-blindness, enhancing the French courtesy that reputedly transcended race.[6] A long article that read like a primer for African Americans anticipating a visit to France appeared in the *Chicago Defender*. Its author, the black Frenchman M. Cornnick, noted his compatriots' delicate regard and consideration for racial courtesies, as vouched for by black American soldiers who served in France. White American troops, Cornnick argued, considered preposterous the French conception of the black soldier being equal to the white. In the postwar era, Cornnick explained, this attitude toward "the black races is being given to France by [white] Americans [despite] the brilliant exploits of France's black troops." And as a final reassurance of the welcome African Americans would experience on the boulevards of Paris, Cornnick reminded the reader that "France had coped with and solved the race question long before the thirteen American colonies had freed themselves from England."[7]

Society columns in the black press took note of the French courtesy and hospitality extended to black folks, reporting the arrival and itinerary of prominent black American families, many of whose sons and daughters attended summer courses at the Sorbonne before beginning a tour of Europe. If racial incidents marred the visits of black American tourists to France, the Negro press gave these occasional discourtesies little attention. Instead, articles stressed the "symbols of democracy" that Cornnick glorified in his reports of racial tolerance and freedom of movement of black Americans.

Ironically, prominent black visitors to Paris were exceptionally critical of the public behavior of certain members of the Montmartre community who cast a bad light on the Race. Robert Abbott, publisher of the *Chicago Defender,* noted these street spectacles in the Paris portion of his report, "My Trip Abroad." Unlike his Paris experience, his visit to London was marred by racism: several first-class hotels refused shelter and service. Protests launched official investigations by a member of parliament and editorials in the *London Daily Express,* but public concern and embarrassment failed to erase the seemingly indelible color line, which Abbott was not to experience in the City of Light.[8] His glowing report on Paris and French hospitality in general echoed Cornnick's commentary. Abbott's criticism turned on the black community in Paris, which, by the time of his visit in 1929, had been in the making for at least a decade and exhibited both the good and the bad elements of cultural life that its members brought with them from the Bronzevilles. "Most of the Colored people live in the Montmartre," he wrote, "and if the truth be told, some of them are everything but a credit to the Negro group. They indulge in fights and shooting scrapes, and [referring to the Bechet-McKendrick incident], two of them were recently given a long prison term for shooting at one another. . . . It would be an excellent thing if there were some way of keeping out the riff-raff, for, as the Negro is a marked man, this type makes it bad for the respectable Negro." Especially critical of the behavior of black musicians, Abbott proposed forming an organization with the authority to place restrictions on its members, to raise the tone of the profession, and keep the members from hanging about "cabarets and other loafing places."[9]

Montmartre, with its Harlem-style character of nightlife and black community, experienced a disproportionate share of racial incidents. Black Americans and French citizens of color were attracted to the district for much the same reasons as white Americans. In New York, white Americans journeyed uptown to such famous nightclubs as the Cotton Club, Small's Paradise, and Connie's Inn to enjoy jazz played by black musicians; white American tourists journeyed to northern Paris to enjoy jazz music played in Montmartre's Harlem-styled nightclubs. However, the interracial climate in Paris differed radically from the ebb and flow of colorful street life characterized by Harlem's chocolate dandies of the 1920s. If whites attacked blacks in Harlem, the catalyst was not resentment over blacks having crossed the color line; in Paris, it was.

An outbreak of racial attacks on black Americans and Frenchmen of color by white American visitors in France became the subject of comment in leading French and American literary journals. The French public's intolerance of racial prejudice countered white Americans' intolerance of the notion and practice of a color-blind French society. White American tourists' arrogance in forcing black patrons out of public accommodations—but often with the subtle connivance of French proprietors—drew much controversy. The racial incident involving Prince Kojo Tovalou Houénou, maternal grandson of the last king of Dahomey (now Benin), became a cause célèbre in 1924. A waiter in the barroom of a Montmartre café in rue Fontaine approached Prince Kojo and his party (a cousin, Prince Benhanzin, and two white women) with the statement that black men might not dance with white women in that café. A white American customer who had demanded the party's ejection then assaulted the prince. The prince took the matter to the courts, with the result that the café lost its all-night license.[10] When the incident came to the attention of Premier Briand, he issued the statement that "discrimination against people because of their color will not be tolerated in France. Those who cannot observe this fact may leave France at all speed. France does not want the dollars of those who cannot respect her laws and customs."[11] French news commentators asked whether "tourists from Dollar-Land have turned Montmartre into an American colony?"

Incidents of white Americans' attacking blacks increased in frequency, with some French proprietors initially taking sides with white Americans protesting the presence of black customers. Catering to white American bigotry for the obvious benefit in profits, the Bal Tabarin advertised as the single place in Paris that admitted only white customers. The bigotry of certain white customers made no distinction between American or French customers of color, treating them alike. The large presence of black French troops in Paris, particularly Senegalese and Antillean former servicemen, generated more intolerance and identical display of antipathy shown toward black Americans. On more than one occasion a nightclub in Montmartre refused admittance to a black customer in order not to displease its white American clientele. Once reported to officials, punishment was always swift, followed by a letter from the prime minister, reasserting the policy of France in racial matters.[12]

The Prince Kojo incident prompted Claude McKay to examine the part played by the American press in Paris in fostering racial sentiments. The Paris edition of the *New York Herald,* McKay claimed, took "a malicious joy in poking fun and dropping asides about Negroes in general." When the French public learned that their American guests were eager to give them lessons in the American way of handling colored people, protests were launched through their press against any American "School of Prejudice" established in France. The *Herald* was the foremost defender of racial prejudice, McKay wrote, insisting that mingling with "Negroes in the bright cafés" might "spell very, very bad business."[13] That racial equality at home and abroad was "bad business" was frequently expressed in the Paris *Herald*. Though disassociating himself from an editorial attacking Clarence Darrow's liberal views on race that appeared on 7 July 1926, Ogden Reed, owner and editor of the Paris *Herald*, issued a tempered statement critical of the editorial. Darrow, a celebrated lawyer and champion of civil rights for black Americans, had taken an uncompromising stand at the Chicago conference of the National Association for the Advancement of Colored People against "continuance of Negro disenfranchisement in the southern states."[14]

The Paris *Herald* was not the only newspaper to depict African Americans in Paris in unsavory situations. The combined Paris editions of the *Chicago Daily Tribune* and the *New York Daily News* shared its prejudice. To the *Chicago Defender,* their reports held more than "malicious joy"; rather it was unbridled hatred. White Americans in Paris were carrying out an unceasing war against "American Race men."

When Eugene Jacques Bullard, the highly decorated African American combat pilot who had flown for France in the Great War, became a casualty of the Paris *Tribune's* racial rhetoric and misinformation, he challenged the newspaper in court. In a front-page story, the *Tribune* had alleged that Bullard struck a white American, Harry McClellan, on the nose with brass knuckles and that McClellan's companion, Ronald Reuter, also suffered contusions. The incident occurred outside Ciro's restaurant in rue Daunou. A French woman sitting at McClellan's table in Ciro's had spoken in French to Bullard, who was also dining there. McClellan objected to a "damn nigger talking to women in his company." Reporting the incident, the *Tribune* exhibited its racist propaganda against African Americans in Paris. Writing that "dozens of Negroes are now said to be infesting Montmartre," the paper claimed that American authorities here, cooperating with the police, could see to it that many of the men, "nearly all of whom have prison records, were deported."[15] Ignoring Bullard's heroic war record, the article claimed that he had avoided combat both in the trenches and as an aviator and since the armistice frequented Montmartre, playing in jazz bands. In Bullard's legal suit brought against the Paris *Tribune,* the court decided the newspaper had distorted the truth and ordered Bullard's version of the incident printed in the same length and in the same place given the original story.[16] His suit for damages against the *Tribune* for 50,000 francs was settled for 10,000 francs and an apology.

Bullard's legal rebuttal of the *Tribune*'s malicious "dirty way"—though a symbolic victory for black Americans in Paris—did not slow the rise of racism in France. The war against black American men reported in the *Defender* was fueled by stories carried in Paris editions of American journals of raucous nightlife in Montmartre and fraternization between black men and French women. The daily spectacle of black men and white women strolling arm-in-arm down Montmartre streets led to frequent fights between white Americans and members of the Parisian black community. Reacting to these interracial public spectacles, the Ku Klux Klan was prepared to defend French women against violation as it had protected white women in America. The popularity of celebrated men of color provided no defense against racist encounters.

When boxer Battling Siki defeated Georges Carpentier in 1922, his victory was not received with the same enthusiasm by all Americans in France. Some white Americans protested his victory not only because a white man, even though French, had been soundly defeated by a black man, an intolerable event by racist standards. Even worse than the victory itself was the color-blindness of French women who exhibited no restraint in joining the Parisian black community's celebrations in Montmartre.

Siki's popularity as a national hero and unwitting source of a "black is beautiful" craze in feminine fashion and male companionship were ineffective defenses against racial prejudice. His popular habit of wearing stylish, elegant fancy dress and strolling through Montmartre arm in arm with his attractive French wife as his pet lion and tiger walked beside them incited the worst behavior of racially intolerant white Americans. Siki was refused service in an American bar (later closed by French authorities) and was frequently involved in street fights stemming from racial insults. Racial incidents followed him from Parisian bars to the lower West Side cabarets in New York's notorious Hell's Kitchen. He was often seen wearing a long black overcoat with a stovepipe hat and a monocle, strutting down Seventh Avenue with a monkey riding on his shoulder and a lion cub on a chain leash following along behind him. At the slightest unpleasant exchange of words, which most often occurred in a bar, Siki would turn his lion cub on the offender. On one such occasion he set his

cub on the manager of the Capitol Bar, where he had been drinking. Later he wandered over to Tenth Avenue and set his pet after a tough Irishman. These might have been the last few minutes of his life, spent in a
saloon-restaurant brawl with eight men whom he had called "damned
white trash." The next morning Siki was found dead in the gutter. The
"white trash" accused of Siki's murder was eighteen years old; Siki was
said to be twenty-three or twenty-four.[17]

In the early 1920s racial incidents involving white Americans and the
black community were nearly always attributed to the Ku Klux Klan. The
frequency of racial encounters in Montmartre turned rumor into believ-
able fact, underpinned by the rash of known violent Klan activity taking
place in black community members' hometowns across America. When
word spread that the Klan was actively seeking to establish itself officially
in France by opening a branch in Paris, the government moved swiftly to
block this effort and on 5 January 1923 a French official declared that no
secret society having the announced aims of the Ku Klux Klan would be
permitted to operate under the existing French laws. With the *Déclaration des droits de l'homme* clearly in mind, the official said, "the whole idea
of the French republic is equality. Not only of classes, but of sects and colors too. Therefore it is not permissible to organize any campaign against
dark people."[18]

While Jim Crow found no *domicile fixe* in France, across the Channel
John Bull had met his acquaintance briefly during the Great War. The
British military command objected to giving temporary service and train-
ing to the 92d all-black division due to arrive in France. Despite General
Pershing's protest, the U.S. War Department bowed to the wishes to ex-
clude the 92d on racial grounds from training assignment in Britain.[19] (In
France, instructions by American authorities to effect the segregation of
black American soldiers from local citizens tended to be ignored by the
French and often triggered angry protests from some sections of the government.) White American officials' overriding dread of sex relations between black men and white women hovered not only over black American soldiers but over British blacks as well. The race riots in Cardiff in
1919, which involved British blacks, had undercurrents of that white fear.
It was a fear nurtured when the postwar jazz scene took hold in the British Isles.

Anti-German sentiments erupted throughout England as war with the kaiser's Germany came to seem inevitable. African American musicians and entertainers were beckoned to take the places of Germans playing in London's hotels and cafés and at summer resorts. Joe Jordan of New York and Chicago was among the first of several popular entertainers to replace German musicians ousted from the local scene. But as the war lingered on, the once lucrative employment opportunities for African American entertainers in London and the British Isles declined. More and more nightclubs closed for lack of patronage, owing to the wartime economy, before the armistice in 1918 brought relief to the drought in public entertainment. The war's end signaled the return of black American jazz musicians who found bookings not wanting on either side of the English Channel. Weekly dispatches from London by Norris Smith, European theatrical representative for the *Chicago Defender,* portrayed a lively entertainment scene created by the leading "Race musicians" and entertainers touring the British Isles.

Norris Smith's own musical career brought a personal note to his dispatches from London and the continent. Through his long residence in London he developed a close relationship with the expatriate community of black musicians and entertainers in Paris as well. Smith's stage career began as a "boy baritone" in 1896. In 1903 he went to London where he later became a member of the Four Black Diamonds, a singing group formed by Strut Payne in 1905. Smith's exceptional voice came to the attention of Paul Robeson, for whom he was an understudy in *Show Boat* at the Drury Lane in 1927–28. Smith's experience in France began in late 1929, when he teamed up with Marino Barreto, from Cuba, and recorded duets in Paris.[20] A typical Norris Smith dispatch from London was an update of the black world of entertainment in the British Isles, listing such entertainment events of black artists as Will Marion Cook's orchestra, now joined by Abbie Mitchell in Liverpool; the Southern Syncopated Orchestra booked for the Philharmonic Hall, Great Portland Street, London; the Exposition Four now playing in Nottingham, after sellout performances in Dublin and Belfast; Louis Douglas and Sonny Jones with an act of twelve Shurley Girl dancers; the Versatile Four booked for the Palladium in Oxford Circus, London; Buddy Gilmore at Ciro's. Smith's dispatches to *Defender* readers were all the more popular when they were laced with statements that appealed to racial pride: "Colored entertainers

PLATE I   James Reese Europe with his Clef Club
Orchestra, 1914. (Maryland Historical Society,
Baltimore. MS 2800, Box 72.)

PLATE 2  Members of James Reese Europe's Hellfighters Band. (Maryland Historical Society, Baltimore. z24.1575, Eubie Blake Collection.)

PLATE 3  *Below:* James Reese Europe and his band entertaining wounded soldiers at the Red Cross Hospital, Paris, September 1918. (National Archives at College Park, Maryland, Still Pictures Division: 111-SC-20417.)

PLATE 4 Some of the men of the 15th Heavy Foot Infantry Regiment who won the croix de guerre for gallantry in action, 12 February 1919. (National Archives at College Park, Maryland, Still Pictures Division: 165-ww-127-8.)

PLATE 5 *Below:* The famous 15th Heavy Foot Infantry Regiment returns from France on the *Stockholm,* 1919. (National Archives at College Park, Maryland, Still Pictures Division: 165-ww-127-22.)

PLATE 6  Lieutenant James
Reese Europe, 1919.
(National Archives at College
Park, Maryland, Still Pictures
Division: 168-ww-127-41.)

PLATE 7  *Below:* Mitchell's Jazz
Kings, Casino de Paris, 1921.
*Left to right:* Louis Mitchell
(leader), drums; Dan Parish,
piano; Cricket Smith, trum-
pet; Vance Lowry, banjo;
Walter Kildaire, bass; Frank
Withers, trombone; James
Shaw, alto saxophone.
Courtesy of the Frank Driggs
Collection.

PLATE 8  Bricktop at her nightclub, Bricktop's, Paris, circa 1925. Courtesy of Beinecke Rare Book and Manuscript Library, Yale University Library.

PLATE 9  *Below:* Josephine Baker and Sidney Bechet *(right),* La Revue Nègre, Théâtre des Champs-Élysées, Paris, 1925. Courtesy of the Frank Driggs Collection.

PLATE 10  Josephine Baker. Courtesy
James Weldon Johnson Collection,
Beinecke Rare Book and Manuscript
Library, Yale University Library.

PLATE 11   Nancy Cunard and Henry
Crowder at the Hours Press, Paris, spring
1930. Courtesy of Anne Chisholm.

PLATE 12   *Below:* Photomontage cover
for Henry Crowder's *Henry Music* (1930).
Courtesy of photographer, Collection
Moorland-Spingarn Research Center,
Howard University.

PLATE 13   *Foreground, left to right:* Louis Cole, Bricktop,
Jimmy Donahue, Mabel Mercer, and Alberta Hunter
at Bricktop's, Paris, 1933. Courtesy of the Frank
Driggs Collection.

PLATE 14   *Top:* Duke Ellington arrives in Paris, 6 April 1939.
Courtesy of the Frank Driggs Collection.

PLATE 15   Jam session at Hot Club of France, Paris, 1939.
*Left to right:* Rex Stewart, Django Reinhardt,
Duke Ellington, Louis Vola, Max Geldray,
Joseph Reinhardt. Courtesy of the
Frank Driggs Collection.

were a credit to the Race" was a frequent accolade. But it was a credit devalued by the lingering racism exhibited by white American tourists visiting London.

The Four Mills Brothers were among several leading black American entertainers denied accommodations after arriving for their engagements in London. They met with refusals at more than twelve major hotels in the capital before they checked into a small railroad hotel on condition that they leave the following morning. Investigations of the discrimination revealed that white American tourists had registered their objections to the Mills Brothers' being accommodated at the hotels.[21] This was not an isolated incident. Duke Ellington and Cab Calloway, booked with great excitement to play in London, were also denied hotel accommodations on racial grounds, being obliged to settle in second-rate hotels during their tour.

Cyclone Billy Warren, a black American boxer who lived in Dublin several years and throughout the Great War, charged that a climate of racial prejudice existed after armistice all over the United Kingdom. He bitterly described the worsening of conditions since the war's end, which, he said, brought "all the beachcombers, bums and tramps from the far corners of the earth." And when they see "a Race man, it is nothing but 'nigger,'" with threats of how he would be treated in America. Warren stressed that the early good fortunes of France's Battling Siki and his fellow boxer Bob Scanlon (the black American heavyweight champion who, like Bullard, joined the French Foreign Legion and fought and was wounded at Verdun) were unique. Unlike in France, he said, "a Race boxer has a hard time of it" in England, where some places would not use a black pugilist at any price. And if booked for a sporting event, he would likely experience difficulty in finding accommodations, for "only one in a hundred in Great Britain would put up a Race man for lodgings and board."[22]

London attracted the vast majority of white Americans touring the British Isles after the armistice. They stayed in the finest hotels and resented the presence of black Americans as guests but swung nightly to their jazz music in famous clubs like Ciro's and the Piccadilly. But Jim Crow found cold lodging in Britain's provincial cities. They had no Aix-les-Bains or Vichy, where wealthy white Americans could combine the reputed health benefits of bathing in hot springs and drinking naturally purified water as well as stomping their feet each night to jazz music played by black American orchestras. Most curiosity seekers were content to take day trips from London, and fleeting visits by a few white Americans tourists did little to shape locals' negative racial attitudes toward black American entertainers. Doubtless most citizens of a London suburb were appalled when confronted with a racial show bill in spring 1930:[23]

HALLELUJAH. THE TRUE STORY OF A NEGRO'S LIFE.

AWAY DOWN SOUTH

SEE REAL BLACK NIGGERS

LIFE IN THE PLANTATION

THE SWANEE RIVER

THE REAL BLACK JAZZ GIRL DO A REAL BLACK JAZZ DANCE

HEAR THE NIGGERS SING

Arriving in London, white Americans could unleash racial prejudice and find sympathetic hotel and café proprietors willing to act on their complaints over the presence of black patrons. Claude McKay's difficulties in getting lodging in Bloomsbury, when studying at the British Museum in the mid-1920s, echoed Cyclone Billy's complaints and were typical experiences for blacks. McKay quickly discovered that signs shouting Rooms For Rent meant blacks were not desired. "For England is not like America," he said, "where one can take refuge from prejudice in a Black Belt. I had to realize that London is a cold white city where English culture is great and formidable like an iceberg. It is a city created for English needs, and admirable, no doubt, for the English people. It was not built to accommodate Negroes."[24] This formidable English culture suited the preferences of white American tourists; it was not Paris. An American observer of the city in the mid-twenties noted that Paris accorded "black men an equality of treatment unknown in the United States, even in the North. Consequently, the Negroes of Paris have become one of our American obsessions. Every summer the presence of Negroes in Paris gives rise to a crop of unpleasant incidents in which visiting Americans always figure."[25] Unlike their English counterparts, French hotel proprietors were guided in their behavior toward people of color by the *Déclaration des droits de l'homme*, if not by genuine moral considerations for the meaning of human dignity.

French citizens' belief in human rights explained their interest in Booker T. Washington's account of the fate of former slaves in America. The same principle guided Du Bois's choice of Paris as the venue for the first Pan-African Congress. It also led William Monroe Trotter, a graduate of Harvard University, who founded the *Boston Guardian* in 1901, to carry the cause of black Americans to Versailles in 1919.[26] And this belief underpinned the interest of French intellectuals in the Scottsboro boys' trial. The questionable trial and conviction of nine young black men between the ages of fourteen and nineteen charged with raping two white women in a railroad boxcar near Scottsboro, Alabama, gripped the attention of much of the literate world. Appealing to all workers and intellectuals to intensify the fight for the lives and freedom of the Scottsboro boys, thirty-five leading French writers, artists, and university professors issued a statement calling for reversal of the Scottsboro verdicts. The signers of the appeal called the verdict "judicial murder."[27]

A decade later, French novelist Paul Morand created an imaginary scene of the Ku Klux Klan's version of judicial murder on French soil. In his book *Magie noire* (Black magic), white women and black jazzmen set the story line, a theme that triggered the race hostility the Klan imported to France. A black American, a member of a jazz band playing in a small town on the Côte d'Azur, is summarily executed near Antibes. His body is found at dawn riddled with eighty-six bullets, bearing the scribbled words "Respect our white women! K.K.K." The corpse is brought to rue Fontaine in Montmartre.[28] And the band plays on.

In spite of catastrophic world events at the beginning and end of the decade, and the turmoil they caused in the music industry, the thirties were some of the richest years for jazz. On the morning of Tuesday, 29 October 1929, front-page news in *Le Figaro*—a brief report on the financial crisis in Wall Street—did not slow the Parisians' ritual consumption of large gulps of *café au lait* to wash down hunks of bread. A crisis in Paris was not financial but political, ministerial. The Wall Street crash heard by Parisians was more a squib than a great explosion but it sent shock waves throughout the community of expatriate Americans. Customarily, they relied on the Paris edition of the *New York Herald Tribune* for their daily intake of world news and morning coffee. Poring over the most recent transatlantic passenger lists of celebrities or friends from home that appeared each day alongside stock market quotations, they verified the favorable exchange rates of the dollar against the French franc. Now the economic news provided no joy for the American community. Daily reports of the wealthy forced into bankruptcy spelled an end of the strong dollar that had kept the good life Paris offered within the expatriates' reach.

It *had* been a good life since the end of the Great War—unfettered by Christian crusades against a perceived decline in moral values (brought on principally by dancing and hot jazz in Montmartre cabarets). The styles and sounds of these pleasures no longer entertained the somber passengers filing aboard ocean liners to make the return voyage from Paris. In the *années folles,* grand passenger liners had maintained a steady weekly flow of American tourists to Le Havre, Cherbourg, and other French ports of call. Now anxious Americans scrambled desperately to reach home. There, they could monitor the daily attrition of their capital. For some, no longer able to witness the ruin of family and personal fortunes, suicide became an acceptable response.

Harlem in Montmartre was no comfort zone, no shelter from the impact of economic depression on the black entertainment community. Unlike white Americans in Paris, members of the black community had their wealth in musical and entertainment talent, not in marketable commodities or assets bought, sold, and exchanged on international monetary markets. Black jazz in Montmartre nightclubs had spread like wildfire arranged to a musical score in the age of *le tumulte noir.* But the popularity of making noise and stomping feet masked the precariousness of the black jazz scene that the Great Depression now pushed to the edge of the economic abyss. The morning coffee ritual of black entertainers at the popular Chez Boudon and Chez Liseux was usually replete with gossip or scandals stemming from outlandish behavior observed in this or that cabaret the night before. Talk now turned to nightclub owners unable to fulfill booking contracts, leaving musicians and entertainers unemployed and stranded.

As the economic depression of the 1930s began to make itself felt in Paris, the glitter of Harlem in Montmartre revealed signs of tarnish from the effects of France's "10 percent law" on the black jazz scene. The law limited the number of foreign musicians employed by an establishment to 10 percent of the total number of French musicians employed there. In 1919—when Louis Mitchell was commissioned by the Casino de Paris to import a large orchestra of black musicians from the United States— French audiences had already fallen "willing victims" to jazz. "French Now Want Colored Musicians," blared the headline in the *New York Age.*[1] But French musicians did not uncritically share the public's taste for ragtime and jazz. They had long complained of being denied employment because black Americans had so dominated the jazz scene, especially in Montmartre. Restaurant and dancing hall managers quickly scorned

French musicians' offer "to do the jazzing themselves with banjo, motor car horn or any other instrument of moral torture to their own artistic temperament." French musicians called it the "Black Peril." Jazz brought with it, they claimed, a certain kind of music and the public listened to no other. Compositions from America—and especially from black American musicians—had ousted French compositions. To fight back against the Peril, a "salon of French musicians was formed to popularize the works of French composers."[2] When their complaints of being driven out of employment by the "colored jazzmen" reached President Poincaré, he took the matter to the National Assembly. Enacted in spring 1922, the 10 percent law passed by the assembly was, by agreement, to become effective at the end of the summer season.[3]

In fact, ten years passed before the law made its force felt, dissolving all foreign orchestras. During that summer, popular black American ensembles headed by Eugene Bullard, Leon Abbey, Freddy Johnson, and other favorites departed Montmartre for the Côte d'Azur, following the tourists who gathered at Cannes, Juan-les-Pins, Monte Carlo, Nice, and other Mediterranean resorts.

In summer 1933 Montmartre faced a drought of patrons and jazz. According to an American reporter stationed in Paris, owners of hotels, cafés, and cabarets paced nervously about their establishments, "their troubled countenances betraying their innermost grief, suffering, and loss of patronage." They greeted the summer season's end with joy and satisfaction, welcoming the return of musicians and entertainers to a nightclub scene now tightly regulated by law. French jazz bands anticipated being the beneficiaries of the law, but French-owned restaurants and cabarets that normally employed orchestras experienced a decline in patronage as a result of a decline in the quality of jazz music offered by the new plan. Desperate to stem the tide of low patronage, cabaret owners and musicians devised transparent schemes to bypass the law, but often these backfired, with severe penalties imposed on the conspirators. Trumpeter Arthur Briggs became involved in such a scheme and was expelled from France in 1933. While engaged in a cabaret in Paris, he signed himself as part-owner of the establishment to defeat the 10 percent labor law and remain employed there. Business went bad, and two months after returning from Biarritz he secured papers in another cabaret in Paris but was removed from the job because his papers granted him permission to work only in an establishment of which he was part owner. Inspectors discovered him on another job and he received the customary fifteen-day notice to leave France.

To Edgar Wiggins, "the Street Wolf of Paris," correspondent for the *Chicago Defender* who prowled the night scene, it was the black community itself, not French laws, that rubbed thin the glitter of the jazz scene they had created in Montmartre.[4] Loud complaints that their lack of employment was caused by the economic depression, French laws, and other restrictions were only partly correct, Wiggins said. The unfortunate conditions Race musicians were experiencing were the result of their own folly, the Street Wolf wrote:

> When [the black community] had Paris "all sewed up" the heavy
> money they earned plus the unlimited freedom they enjoyed
> went to their heads. They became boisterous and unapproach-
> able, and thought themselves indispensable. They cut many ca-
> pers and their wrongful attitude toward citizens was tolerated for
> some time but finally certain steps were taken to eliminate them.
> So when conditions reached the point where certain musicians
> would arrive at their places of employment in one of the best au-
> tomobiles made, which they had bought or rented, accompanied
> by at least two prostitutes and dared to raise hell with the door-
> man, traffic cop and even the patron if objections were raised to
> their car being parked in front of the establishment, it was con-
> sidered more than enough. Soon afterwards a law was passed re-
> stricting the salaries of musicians and artists to a limited amount.
> This law was designed to halt the wild advances of our entertain-
> ing group, but they made it appear weak, so law after law, to cope
> with every rising situation, was passed until finally the 10 percent
> law was created. The law became effective 1 June 1933. It is evi-
> dent that they are not particular about having many of our enter-
> taining group as permanent residents of Paris.

The 10 percent law aimed to snare those black entertainers whom Carter Woodson observed on the boulevard des Italiens and labeled "chocolate dandies." They might have come straight from the pages of James Weldon Johnson's *Black Manhattan*. Seeing such a dandy strut up and down the grand boulevards dressed in loud colors and above all, Woodson noted, with "his hair straightened and packed about his head as if it had been dipped into tar and then ironed out around his empty poll," made the average Parisian wonder whether the black man belonged to a jazz orchestra or figured as a clown. The Parisian might begin to think how well this black man could dance the Charleston or the Teddy and might even—if circumstances suggested it—call on the man to perform. A dandy "who stayed in Europe long enough to become acquainted and to impress himself on the people [was] too often the shiftless immigrant, the scullion or the 'Jazz spreader,' who managed 'to give race several black eyes.'"[5]

The summer of 1933 was the worst season for black American musicians and entertainers who had left Montmartre for the French Riviera. Many got no pay for their efforts and were obliged to borrow train fare back to Paris. The Côte d'Azur's popular resorts were quiet, attracting few American and English tourists with their now discounted dollars and pounds. On the Atlantic coast, evenings at the large municipal casino in Biarritz—with a ten-piece orchestra dispensing classical music and an occasional popular jazz selection—might draw only six customers. The decline in tourist business, as well as the absence of musicians, also severely affected the jazz scene in Montmartre. Many visitors to Paris had made the clubs their first stop, where they learned the latest dance steps before heading for the dance floors on the coast resorts.

From 1 June 1933, when the French 10 percent law went into effect, until 20 April 1934, when Willie Lewis and his entertainers opened their engagement at Chez Florence, "there was not one Negro jazz orchestra entertaining in Paris." Most of the black American musicians who remained fared badly.[6] But French jazz orchestras, with one or two exceptions, failed to prove a big attraction, as the majority of cabaret patrons showed their preference for the rumbas and beguines of Martinicans and Cubans that became the rage throughout Paris as black jazz withered. Don Castellano, owner of the Cabane Cubaine, popularized the rumba and beguine with an all-Cuban orchestra, claiming for the group's right to work that each member had a financial interest in the business. Madame Régine, new owner of Chez Florence, created a loophole in order to employ Willie Lewis and his orchestra by designating them "entertainers" for a French orchestra. Lewis's success in the eventual rebirth of black jazz in Montmartre led the once popular Cuban and Martinican rumba and beguine specialists into becoming jazz musicians. During the drought of black musicians, several jazz orchestras conducted by black Americans had a full complement of Cuban and Martinican musicians.

Before the 10 percent law was lifted, the economic status of black American musicians in Paris worsened, with many seeking more permanent engagements in other major cities around the globe. In Shanghai's international community, for example, the dominant presence of French expatriates paved the way for black American musicians and entertainers to escape France's 10 percent law and spread the gospel of jazz in Asia. During the age of *le tumulte noir,* a few musicians like pianist William Hegman had become missionaries of jazz in Shanghai. In 1924 Hegman played with the band at the Hotel Cathay and eventually opened the largest music store in Shanghai. As this port city's international community grew, new cabarets, dance halls, and country clubs featured jazz, attracting black American musicians and entertainers to a musical scene no less enthusiastically receptive than that of Montmartre. By 1934 the roster of black jazz musicians playing in Shanghai exceeded that in Paris, where the 10 percent law was in effect. For eight years Jimmie Carson's nine-piece band played at the Lafayette Gardens, Teddy Weatherford and his band were at the Candrome ballroom, and Harry Langmum was at Rector's Country Club. Singers and dancers once familiar on the Montmartre scene found steady bookings in Shanghai. The dancers Bob and Teddy Drinkard headlined the floor show at the Candrome; the singers Nora Holt Ray and Al Baldwin were featured for six years in Shanghai clubs' floor shows. After Florence Mill's death, her husband, dancer Ulysses S. Thompson, entertained for several years at Shanghai's Little Club. Harlem had brought to Shanghai the same slam-bang music that invaded Montmartre after the Great War. Shanghai was enjoying a renaissance of jazz, joining European capitals in their fascination with the syncopated beat of black musicians.

Back on the Montmartre scene, Paris's celebrated black entertainers were experiencing a roller coaster ride. Even Bricktop's popularity as the "toast of Harlem in Montmartre" could not slow her plunge into the economic chaos of Montmartre's black entertainment world. On 14 December 1933, one month after she opened her new cabaret at 42 rue Fontaine, she made her last appearance there before heading for Cannes. Freddy Johnson, the "boy wonder pianist" who for five years had been bandleader of his Harlemites at Bricktop's, became owner and manager of the cabaret with a racially mixed orchestra, hoping to bury the cabaret's reputation of "being jinxed." But Bricktop herself could not shake loose the jinx. Unable to make a success as a cabaret hostess in Cannes, Bricktop returned to Paris and reopened her old nightclub in rue Pigalle on 26 May 1934.

The nightclub scene in Montmartre was in flux. Old cabarets were shutting their doors and new ones toasting grand openings. Only the most talented black American musicians who had made their reputation during the heydays of the jazz craze found steady engagements now. By June 1934 a new club, the Pigalle, opened its doors directly across from Bricktop's reopened rue Pigalle nightclub, featuring the blues singer Myrtle Watkins as the star entertainer. Frisco Bingham, once the only black owner of a nightclub in rue Fromentin, the Grand Écart, reopened the club only to close it a few months later and move to London. Across the street the Russian café Monte Cristo opened, engaging the Browning and Starr songs and rhythm act (which had encountered labor permit complications during its engagement in London). The Monte Cristo's clientele, composed chiefly of the numerous white Russians in the city, was apparently content with the café's reputation for *not* offering hot jazz.

In imitation of the short-lived Jockey across the Seine in Montparnasse, the Wild West opened in Montmartre. It was said to be designed for "the peculiar type of Americans that come abroad feeling they have the right to break up something wherever they go." And place Pigalle, never suffering a drought of jazz clubs, became the location of yet another cabaret, the Cotton Club. Imitating its Harlem namesake with exciting floor revues, the Cotton Club attempted to co-opt the nightclub scene in Montmartre by opening with Leon Abbey's band, which had just returned from a second six-month engagement at the Taj Mahal Hotel in Bombay, India. Abbey opened the Cotton Club revue with a reduced orchestra of seven pieces, the maximum that Henri Dajou, the owner, was permitted under the labor law to engage, along with a fourteen-piece French orchestra.

The 10 percent law was no deterrent to Eugene Newton, who married millionairess Dolores Ford and opened his Gaiety Cabaret at 25 rue Fontaine in May 1930. Many in the black community anticipated that Newton's entry into the cabaret scene would revive Montmartre's pre-

Depression nightlife. He brought in Eugene Bullard, with his genial reputation in Montmartre cabaret life, to manage his Gaiety Cabaret and S. H. Dudley, Jr., to produce the elaborate floor show. The chorus consisted of dancers who remained in Paris after Lew Leslie's *Blackbirds* and Dudley's own *Revue Noire, Hot Stuff,* ended their runs at the Embassy theater.[7]

The crowded field of jazz musicians tightened the control of a few black band leaders over bookings in the best of Montmartre nightclubs. In this role Willie Lewis acquired bookings to maintain steady employment for his band. He was assisted nonetheless by the 10 percent law itself, and by aggressive cabaret proprietors like Madame Régine, who had acquired Chez Florence. Named after Florence Embry, the club kept its popularity in Montmartre by booking the best black American bands and featuring the most talented entertainers in its floor shows. When Willie Lewis and his band were hired as "entertainers" to skirt the 10 percent law, Chez Florence did its best business since the start of the depression. Rather than turn away latecomers to its packed shows, the cabaret provided them with chairs on the sidewalk where they could listen to Lewis's band while waiting for a vacancy inside.

Louis Mitchell's club in rue Pigalle, with the first quick-lunch café in Paris and still a favorite early-morning, wind-up haunt in Montmartre, came under white ownership. In the wake of the Wall Street crash, black faces other than those of Americans began to appear increasingly in positions off the bandstands, owning and managing cabarets in Montmartre. The Melody Bar, once a popular cabaret with a black American proprietor, came under management of Martinicans. Antilleans and Cubans gradually became the dominant black faces in Montmartre cabaret life. They were already prominent in Montparnasse, competing with whites in acquiring ownership of black American establishments, even reaching into the world of small cafés typically found in black Montmartre.

Though Le Bœuf sur le Toit still attracted great musical talent from among the race colony's musicians before the thirties ended, the number of small black-owned nightclubs that opened in Montmartre lessened Le Bœuf's domination over the jazz scene. Leon Abbey and Benny Carter were among the highly popular visiting musicians there between 1930 and 1938. Beginning in 1937, Le Bœuf was the Parisian home of the jazz pianist Garland Wilson.

For Garland Wilson, born in 1909 in Martinsburg, West Virginia, the road from the American South to a Parisian piano bar was long and rough. At age sixteen he went to Atlantic City to play with a five-piece band in a beer garden. On the road again he headed north to New York to play for Jenny Dancer, who once sang with Earl Hines, and then found engagements on Loews and the B. F. Keith circuits. As with many other young black musicians, Wilson developed his signature style of rhythm and blues in Harlem, beginning at Covan's Dew Drop Inn. Prohibition came in and money was to be made in speakeasies and honky-tonks where risqué singers like Detroit Red and the blues singer Monette Moore attracted large and often raucous after-hours crowds. From a stint at Jerry Paton's Log Cabin off Seventh Avenue, once home to Billie Holiday, Wilson moved to the Hotcha, on the corner of 134th and Seventh Avenue, and later to the Morocco.

Paris was not on Wilson's mind when he first met Nina Mae McKinney and her husband, Jimmy Monroe, in 1928. She had starred in the film *Hallelujah*, which introduced her as a voluptuous teenage beauty. Four years later, she hired Wilson as her accompanist for a European tour. He joined McKinney and her husband and they sailed for France on 28 November 1932. Their appearance at Chez Florence was, in Wilson's words, a "flop" and only increased his dislike of France (he spoke no French). When McKinney opened at London's Leicester Square Theatre in the musical *Chocolate Cream*, Wilson went too, happy to be invited to do so. After the show closed, they went on to Athens, opening on 7 April 1934 at the Femina, where McKinney was billed as "the black Greta Garbo."

Wilson's return to Britain was brief. Around the turn of 1934–35, difficulties with the Ministry of Labor over a work permit forced a retreat to Paris, where he was booked at Le Bœuf (now in rue Pigalle, in Montmartre). The famous recording Wilson made with Jean Sablon in January 1935 increased his popularity with the Parisian jazz crowds and in turn led to a tour in Britain with the British band leader Jack Payne.[8] After a year on tour Wilson came back to Le Bœuf, on this occasion as accompanist with Una Mae Carlisle, until the end of 1938. He entertained his devotees of artists, literary figures, and men-about-town each night in his own room at the club. Wilson remained based in Paris during 1939 and was playing at Bricktop's when war clouds began to loom over Europe.

For other black musicians, Harlem in Montmartre was the base from which to spread the gospel of jazz to many points on the globe. North Africa, Belgium, and England were temporary ports of call for the musical wanderings of jazz pianist Herman "Ivory" Chittison, the "Sinbad of the Piano."[9] Chittison was born in Fleminsburg, Kentucky, in 1908. After performing in Zack White's *Chocolate Beau Brummels*, Chittison toured as an accompanist with Stepin Fetchit, Ethel Waters, and Adelaide Hall. In 1934 band leader Willie Lewis, with whose band Chittison had played in New York, brought him to Paris.[10] At different times during his stay with Lewis until 1937, Chittison worked and recorded with Louis Armstrong. As a soloist, Chittison played at Chez Florence, joining a long list of talented musicians who contributed to the nightclub's popularity. Between Paris engagements, he lived up to his name "Sinbad" by carrying his distinctive jazz piano style to the Heliopolus Palace in Alexandria and Shepard's Hotel in Cairo. On these journeys Chittison shared the spotlight with close friends and fellow pianists who played the nightclub circuit in Montmartre and elsewhere in Europe, talented entertainers like Teddy Weatherford, Garnet Clark, Garland Wilson, and Tommy Chase. They all belonged to that category of artists "who consistently play[ed] wonderful valid jazz merely for the love of creating music of lasting enjoyment to the listener."[11]

Unlike in la Butte, in Montparnasse's nightclub scene the popular culture of hot black jazz never became firmly implanted. Solo black performers were sometimes engaged for special concerts, as was the blues singer Alberta Hunter, who appeared at the Dingo Bar in November 1936. Wildly popular black orchestras in Paris, including those of Willie Lewis, Arthur Briggs, and Freddy Johnson, had no lengthy bookings in Left Bank nightclubs.

The contrasting styles of jazz-oriented popular culture emanating from opposite sides of the Seine could not have been more striking. Montmartre had the flavor of Harlem—where white patrons went uptown to 135th Street and Seventh Avenue to Connie's Inn or the Cotton Club dressed in their finery for an evening of jazz, dancing, and drinking cheap whiskey at high prices. And going to Montmartre was also a dress affair. Evening clothes and gorgeous cloaks were in order. Doormen in bright uniform ushered patrons through shining glass doors into far-from-cavernous rooms, filled with the sounds of familiar jazz tunes. Montmartre for most people was, as Sisley Huddleston wrote, "a place of colored lights on a midnight sky, of more or less luxurious cabarets. Montmartre is what the French call the Paris du dollar."

By contrast, Montparnasse was more bohemian. It fostered clubs like La Croix du Sud, a lively place popular with artists and fanciers of bohemian atmosphere. "Painters like de Kooning," Bricktop recalled, "would add to the atmosphere by coming in bare feet and short pants. Leaving *de rigueur* at the door, the Prince of Wales often sat in on drums when [Stéphane] Grappelli was on the bandstand playing hot jazz tunes on his hot violin." [12] Montparnasse had no reason to imitate Montmartre's methods of exploitation and profiteering from the tourist trade. It had its genuine artistic elements; its open-air cafés on spacious boulevards catered honestly, and usually well, to a less snobbish though largely sophisticated clientele. The "French state, with its respect for artists and understanding of the attraction they exert, allowed Montparnasse to develop into a 'free zone' with less police surveillance and greater acceptance of unconventional behavior and lifestyles than would have been allowed in other areas of Paris. The police kept Montparnasse free of the unsavory elements that invaded Montmartre: brothels and organized prostitutes were not allowed and criminal elements were kept away." [13]

As Wambly Bald observed, "the sidewalk terrace is a gay witty morgue of a place where drinks are cheap and conversation free. The types suffer far more from conversation than from drink, for sooner or later they all babble the same babble about art and sex and find themselves too tired to do any thing about it. To attract favorable attention, some of them wear fancy rags and let their hair grow long, a device of very lonely people. They do not represent Montparnasse." A blasé attitude and style reigned supreme in the terrace culture. "If Molière were to come strutting along the sidewalk, carrying on his shoulder Eugene O'Neill, he would attract attention only if he slipped and fell." One day Bald observed a young female poet sipping a *crème de menthe* and reading a book on the terrace of La Coupole. "Some one touched her arm and whispered in her ear: 'Charlie Chaplin is sitting in the corner right behind you. He wants to talk to you.' 'Tell him I'm busy,' she snapped, and turned a page." [14]

Montparnasse was content to enjoy and dance to jazz Martinican-style. It had become the home to a new fad introduced to the dancing public at the Colonial Exposition of 1931, the Creole folk dance called *beguine.*

Launched in Paris by black-owned dance halls and cabarets that sprouted like mushrooms in Montparnasse, its vogue was assured by Josephine Baker, who outlined the steps in the revue *Paris qui remue* at the Casino de Paris in 1931.[15] Even in strictly Parisian dance halls, the beguine was the attraction of the evening. Promoted by Antillean musicians and their phonograph records, the beguine's appeal came in part from the sensuousness of the dance steps: performers do not embrace; they mimic the everlasting pursuit of woman by man. The dance differed from the blues, characterized by a swaying of the whole body, and from the Charleston, thought of as a rhythmic exercise. But for Montparnasse's true jazz lovers longing for an evening of Harlem-style jazz, it was Montmartre that beckoned.[16]

The depression was in its second year when Stéphane Grappelli— France's leading jazz violinist—commented on the "luxury" of going to the Colisée once in a while to hear black jazz.[17] Parisians tucked away a few of their hard-earned francs to enjoy the best of black American entertainment at affordable prices. They gave no thought to popular Montmartre cabarets, which still attracted the black-tie French crowd and an ever-dwindling number of British residents and American tourists. More and more, Parisians listened to black American artists who came from Bronzevilles or Britain to perform in the small Parisian concert halls where the price of admission did not empty the family purse of coins needed for daily bread.

In these difficult times J. Turner Layton and Clarence Nathaniel Johnstone, a piano and vocal duo, rode the crest of popularity among French light music-hall patrons. Johnstone, an orthopedic surgeon, and Layton, a pianist and the son of a reputable professor of music, had begun their collaboration in 1924, when they went to England. Early in his career Layton had teamed with Henry Creamer, a professional ballroom dancer and songwriter. Together they wrote "Unhappy," produced in the Ziegfeld Follies of 1917, and a number of well-known songs, including "After You've Gone." In 1922 Creamer and Layton produced the all-black musical *Strut Miss Lizzie.* Toward the end of the decade, performing on the piano and singing in evening dress, Layton and Johnstone displayed a refined musical technique different from that of other black artists appearing in popular clubs in London and Paris. Their mixed repertoire of songs, including "Dinah," "Hallelujah," "Blue Heaven," and "Every Sunday Afternoon," combined a touch of jazz with a nod toward Negro spirituals. They delighted audiences who viewed the popular slam-bang jazz as a profane evolution from plantation songs and spirituals.

Before Layton and Johnstone's first concert at Salle Pleyel on 19 June 1928, their recordings on the Columbia label had enhanced their popularity on both sides of the Channel, creating great interest among the French and a clamor for tickets. Louis Léon Martin's lengthy review in the *Parisien* praised their mixture of singing in the idioms of blues, Charleston, waltzes, and fox-trots.[18] It was jazz in a form unusual for its time, engaging the audience in head-swaying and knee-tapping to lively numbers but without the stomping feet and loud noise characteristic of patrons of hot jazz played in Montmartre nightclubs. Following their sellout performance at Salle Pleyel, the piano-singing duo played at the Palais des Beaux-Arts in Brussels on 20 February 1930, returning to France at Salle Prat in Marseille. Layton and Johnstone continued their popular concert performances throughout Europe. As with many black American entertainers, the singing duo found Berlin, in the early thirties, the most lucrative source for income on the continent and added to their triumphs engagements at the prestigious UFA, the largest film studio in Europe. In February 1931 they starred in a new talking film before returning to Paris and Salle Pleyel.

Layton and Johnstone's popularity among Parisian music-hall audiences also served to remind the black community that Montmartre's growing community of talented stage performers included individuals like those who had produced stellar songs for the Ziegfeld Follies and the musical *Strut Miss Lizzie*. It included people like Ivan Harold Browning, a member of the famous Four Harmony Kings, who had made successful tours of Europe for several years before joining Henry Star, the singer, pianist, and composer who had been featured in the Bal Tabarin revue in Paris and who wrote the musical score for the revue *Jungle Nights in Gay Montmartre*.

The time was ripe for a black musical production in Paris. There had been only two shows, *Blackbirds* and *Revue Nègre*, which displayed the great talents of Florence Mills, Adelaide Hall, and Josephine Baker. This became a topic of conversation during home-away-from-home early-morning meals that Mitchell's served up to musicians and late revelers in Montmartre. The economic depression had not dampened the community's clamor for its own revue, originated by blacks, performed by blacks, and produced by a Race Man. Black Manhattan was producing musicals that had Broadway runs, finally breaking the barrier of racial exclusion from the Great White Way, and black orchestras were playing in fancy white nightclubs in downtown New York as well as in Greenwich Village. Harlem in Montmartre, which was always fed its entertainment talent by the Bronzevilles of America, recognized a challenge to produce a black musical review in the City of Light. Louis Douglas responded to the challenge.

Louis Douglas was no stranger to the song-and-dance world when he launched the Théâtre Nègre. And he was no stranger to Europe, being among the surprisingly large number of the twenties' best jazz tap dancers who visited the continent as part of one or another black shows. Douglas started performing in Europe in 1903, when he was fourteen, first with Belle Davis's Pickaninnies for five years and then with the singer Will Garland in a song-and-dance act. Striking off on his own, Douglas toured Europe as a solo act until 1915. During the war years he made his home in the United Kingdom, starring in revues and forming an association with dancer Sonny Jones. Together they created a large vaudeville act with a chorus of female dancers called the Shurley Girls and took their revue to Paris, where they were booked at the Folies-Bergère in January 1921.

Though not an instrumentalist himself, Louis Douglas had an eye and ear for outstanding musical talent. He knew the most talented of these musicians who found themselves on different sides of the English Channel but at one time had worked together in the Bronzevilles of America, when the best ragtime and early jazz sounds were heard. He came to know Louis Mitchell and his Jazz Kings, who were crisscrossing the United Kingdom, converting a staid British public in clubs and dance halls to the early sounds of jazz. The Jazz Kings included such outstanding musicians as Crickett Smith, Frank Withers, Joseph Meyers, and James Shaw. Abbie Mitchell came over to London to join the orchestra led by Will Marion Cook, whom she later married.[19]

A tap dancer with extraordinary skills—when he danced, only his feet seemed to move—Douglas had appeared on stage at the Alhambra and the Ba-ta-Clan music halls in Paris. "Known locally as the man with the rubber legs, he was admired for his sheer physical dexterity, even though tap dancing was not a much appreciated art in Paris."[20] It was appreciated by Carolyn Dudley, however, who came to enjoy the art from visiting black vaudeville houses on Chicago's south side and chose Douglas as the principal dancer, choreographer, and codirector of her production *Revue Nègre*. His brilliant and artistic tap-dance skills were displayed in the revue's sixth tableau, dedicated to him, "The talking feet" (*les pieds qui parlent*).

Douglas's directing debut, of which he was fully in charge, was his first involving a large spectacle with several tableaux and set the stage for Théâtre Nègre's first revue, *Liza*. A common name in black American folklore, *Liza* was the title of Irvin C. Miller's play presented at Daley's Sixty-third Street Theatre in New York City in 1922. The fact that *Liza* is credited as the first musical comedy owned and produced on Broadway entirely financed by black capital may have inspired Douglas to select that name for the title of his production. It opened at the Théâtre de la Porte-St-Martin for the 1929–30 season. After the first night's performance, French theater critics labeled Douglas's production of *Liza* an *opérette-revue*. The grand spectacle (presented in two acts, eight dramas, forty-five scenes) included an ensemble of sixty artists and the music of black jazz. The role of Liza was played by Valaida Snow. Recognized as a great jazz musician who could play every instrument in the band, she was better known for her artistry on the trumpet. Born into a show-biz family in New York City in 1903, she made her debut at Baron Wilkins's Harlem cabaret in 1922. She toured Europe six times, starting when she was just twelve years old. By the time she was fifteen, she was starring abroad and playing command performances. She had appeared with Josephine Baker in *In Bamville* and *Shuffle Along* (1930), the collaborative efforts of Sissle and Blake.[21]

The story line for *Shuffle Along* depicts Creole Liza being enticed to leave the cotton plantation in Louisiana to board a train at the Plantation Railway Station, heading to Harlem. After joining the Plantation Cabaret in Harlem, she quickly becomes disillusioned and expresses dislike for cabaret life. In short order she returns to Louisiana and the cotton plantation. Bandanas, dandies, dope in Harlem, and bootleg whiskey all make their appearances. Singing and dancing, with spirituals by the Utica Jubilee singers and an introduction to the lindy hop, a dance named after

Colonel Lindbergh, led to a grand finale at the Plantation Cabaret. Providing the musical backdrop for the gala production were the Black Flowers Chorus, Black Flowers Girls, and Black Flowers Jazz directed by B. Winfield. Missing from the revue were "darkey impressions" of the type staged by Josephine Baker in *Revue Nègre* and watermelon scenes staged as clichés of black life. Paul Colin, who had produced the famous *Revue Nègre* posters of Josephine Baker, designed the imaginative scenery of plantation life and big city Harlem, raising the production's visual aesthetics above that commonly seen in music-hall revues. Arousing less harsh reactions from theater critics and the general public than *Revue Nègre* had, *Liza* portrayed a segment of black life, from plantation to big city, replete with undertones of morality and the pitfalls of life in Harlem. *Liza* transcended the wiggling, shaking hips, and acrobatics staged in *Revue Nègre*, though some theater critics bitterly rejected the notion that the production qualified as an *opérette-revue*.[22] Drawing the final curtain after a spectacular run in Paris, Douglas's Théâtre Nègre moved to Marseille and opened *Liza* at the Alcazar Théâtre-Musique, 48 cours Belsunce, in May 1931. Eight months later the revue opened at the Nouveau Casino in Nice.

Hardly had the curtain risen on *Liza* when the second version of *Revue Noire, Hot Stuff,* opened at the Embassy, 136 avenue des Champs-Élysées in May 1930. Billed as "Harlem to the Champs-Élysées," the revue was a promotion composed by S. H. Dudley, Jr., and E. C. Newton. Dudley followed in the footsteps of his father, S. H. Dudley, who had directed *Shufflin' Sam From Alabam'* at the Elmore Theatre in Pittsburgh in 1926. Young Dudley's long aspiration was to produce a show to play in the best white theaters and on the black vaudeville circuit's Theater Owners' Booking Association (TOBA, which black musicians often renamed "Tough On Black Asses"). His aspiration was exceeded when *Hot Stuff,* probably based on his successful *Ebony Follies,* played in Paris. TOBA could boast of the appearance of such artists on the circuit as Ethel Waters, Butter Beans and Susie, Bessie Smith, and Josephine Baker. The Embassy restaurant-dancing-cabaret, though not the big stage of a Parisian music hall, provided a continuum for mounting black mini-stage productions in Paris.[23]

Unlike the popular black musicals, the dramatic face of Harlem's black theatrical talent presented at the Théâtre de l'Avenue on 12 December

1932 created little public interest and was universally panned by theater critics. Private presentations of Eugene O'Neill's *Emperor Jones,* played by James Lowe, and Ridgley Torrence's *Riders of the Dreams,* performed by the American Negro Players, were said by one press reviewer to consist of "terrible, monotonous hallucinations," not helped by two musical numbers sandwiched between the acts.[24] The American Negro Players' unsuccessful attempt to introduce Parisian audiences to serious drama produced by black Americans and performed by black Americans appears to have dampened whatever dreams other black repertory theatrical companies had to mount productions in the City of Light. But concerts by Paul Robeson and Roland Hayes filled the small Parisian halls. These solo performances, presenting classics and spirituals, made no pretense at being one-man Negro dramas. Serious drama was not in the image Parisians had conjured up of black Americans in the entertainment world, an image the black community kept alive in the exuberant idiom of jazz.

The jazz circuit made up of black American musicians and entertainers in the United Kingdom between the wars rivaled the vibrancy of the Parisian *tumulte noir.* But the British circuit lacked what Paris contributed to the making of its jazz scene: a small, tightly knit district that assumed the cultural flavor of a section of Harlem. Montmartre was a community complete with hair dressing shops, a valet shop owned by the actor James Lowe, and William Marshall Winthrop's shop that specialized in the making and selling of fine handmade silk lingerie and shirts at 22 rue Chaptal.[25] A graduate of Howard University, Winthrop, with his French wife, was successful from the start and catered to the growing community of black American musicians earning high salaries on the nightclub circuit. Their lingerie shop was profitable until the Wall Street crash of 1929. Catering then became Winthrop's chief occupation. He opened a restaurant in the American Embassy building and ran it for two and a half years. Until he went back to America in 1936, Winthrop supplied Americans with their favorite "back home" dishes. Another purveyor of soul food specialties was Jack Garner at the Costa Bar, one of several favorite meeting spots in Montmartre like Chez Boudon in rue Pigalle and Café Liseux—all with the "do-drop-in" character of Harlem—where gossip and news from home were freely exchanged. Bloomsbury's cheap bed-and-breakfast hotels that housed many black musicians and entertainers in London had none of the flavor of Harlem in Montmartre.

The rising tide of fascism that would soon engulf western Europe was far from the thoughts of most members of the black community in Paris. Average French citizens too were still clearing away the economic rubble of the Great Depression. They marveled at the spread of comic book culture, grumbled at the creeping influence of American films on French cinema, welcomed the radio programs and the opening of cabarets that featured black American jazz in Montmartre—all despite hard times and the depression blues. In October 1934 kiosks throughout France featured the first issue of *Le Journal de Mickey,* a weekly eight-page comic-strip magazine that immediately captivated a generation of young readers who followed with wide eyes the adventures of Mickey Mouse. Two years earlier, in December 1932, their parents had become devoted adherents of the musical sounds promoted by the Hot Club of France.

Founded by "a few jazz enthusiasts to foster the development of the idiom," the Hot Club of France organized concerts by "the best performers that were available, French or American." [26] And it revolutionized the public presentation of jazz in Paris of the mid-thirties, reaching potential converts who had never visited the small smoky cabarets and jazz clubs in Montmartre. Like high priests in the home mission, Charles Delaunay and cofounder Hugues Panassié gave direction to the Hot Club that enabled the jazz missionaries to spread their gospel and reach an eager flock. Principal among these was Django Reinhardt, who formed the Quintet of the Hot Club of France.

Django Reinhardt, a French-speaking Gypsy, a *manouche,* born 23 January 1910, in Liverchies, near Charleroi, Belgium, was not yet thirteen when he began his career playing banjo with an accordionist at a dance hall in rue Monge. Émile Savitry, a bohemian artist in Montparnasse who frequented Le Dôme and La Rotonde, introduced Django to the music of Duke Ellington and Louis Armstrong on phonograph records, which marked a turning point in his move toward the jazz sounds of black American musicians. And as members of the newly founded quintet, Reinhardt and Grappelli gave the Hot Club of France direction. In large measure, the club's popularity arose from the quintet's jam sessions attended by the black singer Bert Marshall in the early hours after work at the Alsace à Montmartre, the restaurant in rue Fontaine where musicians used to meet for the last time before going home to bed. Recordings of

Reinhardt's style of jazz, a whorl of music like a quiet storm rendered on a string instrument, convinced "the public, which until then had evinced precious little interest in jazz"—according to his biographer—but now "suddenly showed enormous enthusiasm for it. Overnight, almost, jazz records began to sell in their thousands; the public craved 'swing.'"[27]

Hot Club concerts benefited both the gospel message and the collection plate. Pierre Nourry, secretary of the Hot Club of France, arranged an opening concert of the quintet at the École Normale on 2 December 1932. The organizers, Stéphane Grappelli and Django Reinhardt, augmented by Joseph Reinhardt, rhythm guitar, Louis Vola, bass, and guitarist Roger Chaput formed the musical backdrop for popular black musicians who were featured attractions. To a full house, Harry Cooper and his Rhythm Aces, including Booker Pittman and Billy Taylor, performed their concert, "The Harlem Tea Party," a title carrying an obvious double meaning. The price: 10 francs, with discount for Hot Club members.[28] Pianist Herman Chittison's concert at Salle Lafayette demonstrated the spirit of the Hot Club in exposing the jazz-loving public to the best integration of French and black American musicians when it brought to the stage trumpet player Arthur Briggs, Noël Chiboust, Bobby Martin, and Frank "Big Boy" Goudie.

The Hot Club, with the quintet in the vanguard, brought in many converts who appreciated the style of jazz that was slowly shedding the slam-bang, ragtime beat that characterized its origins. "Critics who were usually indifferent or even hostile to jazz," Delaunay remarked, "were struck by the elegance and wit of the [quintet's] music. A great number of [their] records were sold and people were always asking whether new ones had been issued. Agreed, it was not yet a question of international fame, the variety halls and America, but for a jazz group it was an unprecedented departure. . . . Up to then this form of music had been considered 'a cacophony,' 'a series of discords'; it was reserved for Negroes or was said, 'for savages,' and whites only made themselves ridiculous by showing interest in it. . . . With the arrival of the Quintet and the reassuring presence of string instruments, jazz became a more delicate music, one that could be more easily assimilated by outsiders."[29]

Club engagements in provincial France and in Europe thrust the quintet into the role of involuntary missionaries, leading local jazz fans to open chapters of the Hot Club of France. No provincial city could afford *not* to have a Hot Club. Nice, Bordeaux, Marseille, and Nancy, among the earliest to form chapters, were joined by Amsterdam, Utrecht, Milan, and Barcelona. The Hot Club of Königsberg, the first to appear in Germany, promoted jazz through sales of gramophone records, boasting of receiving fifty new titles of discs in the May–June 1935 issue of the club's journal. But in the rapidly changing German political climate, the Königsberg club's proud promotion of jazz records was a short-lived effort.

Paris in 1935 symbolized the awakening of a new era in spreading the gospel of jazz. Of the early jazz scene, Grappelli wrote that "however jazz was defined (and to the confused general public it was almost anything that wasn't a waltz) it was obviously a hit." [30] In the new musical space created by the Hot Club of France and the quintet, French and Race musicians living in Paris used the club and its musical aggregation to arrange concerts in Salle Pleyel near rue des Acacias, Salle Lafayette, Stage B on the boulevard du Montparnasse, and other small venues, featuring black performers brought to Paris from the jazz capitals in America. Stage B was often the home of the lions of French jazz—Léon Vauchant, Philippe Brun, André Ekyan, and Django Reinhardt. Concert appearances did not mean these musicians were absent from the club scene. After a night's engagement, Django might join pianist Freddy Taylor's band at the Villa d'Este, and it was not unusual to find Benny Carter, who was working at Chez Florence, sometimes sitting in on piano with the quintet at the cabaret Grand Écart, in rue Fromentin. And when the Big Apple opened in 1937, the quintet worked regularly as a house band for an extended period, often joined by Eddie South, adding another string instrument to the soft jazz sounds.

Like a musical magnet, Django and his quintet attracted to its bandstand the best of visiting black American musicians, who took great pleasure when invited to improvise for the audience. On such an occasion one night at The Hot Feet, a tiny cabaret in the shape of a triangle in rue Notre-Dame-de-Lorette where the quintet was playing, Duke Ellington was invited to join the group. For a quarter of an hour or more that night his improvisations created a memorable jam session that quickly entered the rich annals of the quintet's folklore.[31]

After closing engagements in the City of Light, visiting bands toured provincial cities giving concerts arranged by local Hot Clubs. Cabarets featuring jazz and thronged with enthusiastic patrons were ideal settings for bouncy tunes, tricky noises, and lots of drums. In the early era, Grappelli noted, ideas of jazz were embodied in such titles as "Ain't We Got Fun," Irving Berlin's "Everybody Step," "C'est Paris," and "Stumbling." To be a jazz lover in Paris in the twenties, "when criticism of the new musical sounds was often nasty and vitriolic," Delaunay said, "was like being an early Christian in Rome."[32] The musical message had changed by the time the first edition of the early "bible," which propagated jazz among the faithful, made its appearance under the title *le Jazz-Hot,* the official organ of the Hot Club of France. That first issue was one page printed on the back of a program for a concert by Coleman Hawkins at Salle Pleyel on 21 February 1935. The copies arrived during intermission.[33]

From their headquarters at 15 rue Chaptal, cofounders Delaunay and Panassié spread the jazz message from the heart of Black Broadway in Black Paris. Delaunay, the new journal's editor-in-chief, explained its origin: *"Jazz-Hot* is the only review that is entirely consecrated to real Jazz Music and appears at the same time in English and in French, actually the countries where this music is most widely known." With release of the journal, the Hot Club's popularity soared. The issues had articles on popular black musicians playing in the great nightclubs of Harlem and Chicago, reviews of the latest American jazz recordings, and members boasted of being the first of their compatriots to hear the new sounds. They stood in line outside Delaunay's office hoping to hear and—if they were among the fortunate few—converse with famous jazz musicians visiting the club. Like a tourist's guidebook to the locations and activities of professional and amateur musicians, as well as the grand and small orchestras and their leaders in Paris and the provinces, the Hot Club's monthly organ advertised the full range of jazz performances by regular and visiting musicians. The jazz critic Helen Oakley was one of the principal correspondents reporting for the journal on the jazz scenes in Harlem and Chicago. Edgar Wiggins, the Street Wolf, covered the jazz scene in Montmartre.

Popular culture inspired by the jazz idiom and the Hot Club of France coincided with the golden age of radio in Paris. New stations began broadcasting to areas of Paris previously served only poorly or not at all. Radio LL became Radio Cité on 29 September 1935. In its new transmission format the station invented the music hall for a young audience, where the popular singer Charles Trenet sang for the first time without his erstwhile partner, Johnny Hess (who would go on to popularize his theme song, "Je suis swing," and present it almost nightly at Jimmy Charter's bar in Montparnasse).[34] Radio Cité and Poste Parisien, a private radio station, opened up opportunities for black American orchestras to spread the message of jazz over the airways. Leon Abbey, who had followed Benny Carter into Le Bœuf sur le Toit, began twice-weekly broadcasts on both stations. So popular was Abbey's radio show that Radio Cité Belgique engaged him to broadcast from the car that the Belgium-Paris intercity train devoted entirely to dancing. And Willie Lewis's Sunday night broadcasts verified to the world of radio listeners his reputation of leading the most popular black American orchestra in France.

Harlem in Montmartre experienced a mini-renaissance of sorts in the two years before war clouds gathered over Paris. And it also experienced a mini-version of *le tumulte noir*. The year 1938 began as Adelaide Hall, the star of Lew Leslie's last *Blackbirds* revue in Paris, was bringing a long-held dream to life: she opened her own nightclub, the Big Apple at 73 rue Pigalle, on 9 December 1937, just in time for the Christmas season. The Big Apple was a comfortable stroll from Josephine Baker's newest club, Le Frontenac, in rue François-Premier. Hall's silent partner, Hetty Flacks, who provided the bulk of the club's financial assistance, was described by the *Chicago Defender's* Street Wolf as "a lovely congenial Jewish lady, whose mother is one of the wealthiest" in Manchester, England. Seven months after a grand opening that attracted the usual crowd of Montmartre celebrity first-nighters, the partnership ended, but not before Adelaide Hall had her chance to sit at the pinnacle of Montmartre cabaret life.

The club's featured attraction was the Big Apple dance step brought over from Harlem and danced nightly by the chorus, with a special review for patrons willing to learn the steps. The theme song, which took the club's name, was especially written for Adelaide Hall by the bandleader Maceo Jefferson. Hall's radio broadcasts on continental hookup every Saturday night from the Big Apple further spread the popularity of Montmartre's newest jazz nightclub. Somewhat less austere than the old Jockey in Montparnasse, the club decorated its walls with four huge designs of a rosy apple and three life-size paintings of a female dancer demonstrating the Big Apple dance step. With a name that had gained currency from her stellar performance in *Blackbirds,* Hall drew the celebrity crowd to the Big Apple. During their nightly outings in Montmartre, Josephine Baker and her third husband, multimillionaire sugar broker Jean Lion, as well as Maurice Chevalier, Leslie Howard, and Mistinguett, made the club their favorite rendezvous.

Adelaide Hall gave her last performance at the Big Apple on 19 June 1938. The Hall-Flacks partnership began on a high note that carried it through January, the dull month for cabarets in Paris. Then trouble began in May when Adelaide and her Trinidadian manager-husband, Bert Hicks (who was also the club's manager and owner of the Florida Club, a private dining club in London's exclusive Mayfair district), decided to go to London. Hall accepted a principal role in the African-based drama adapted from Edgar Wallace's novel *The Sun Never Sets,* at a West End theater. Against the opposition of the Big Apple's financial backers, Hall moved to London, promising to return to Paris each Sunday. At the end of the London show's scheduled run, on 9 September, Hall and Hicks proposed to transfer the Big Apple to London.

Word of the scheme spread throughout Montmartre. Business had declined immediately after Hall's departure, and Flacks hired Bricktop as manager and hostess of the Big Apple. Bricktop's reputation as a popular hostess had made her a celebrity who could bring in a nightclub crowd. On weeknights Myrtle Watkins replaced Hall as the star in the Big Apple's floor show (Watkins had performed in the Paris revues *Hot Stuff* and *Ebony Follies*). The new program also added the tenor Arthur Gaines, former member of the original eight Kentucky Singers, and the dancing Mackey Twins, who were favorites on the Berlin nightclub circuit. An effort to engage the black community's best talent brought Garland Wilson and Una Mae Carlisle as occasional guest artists, though regularly engaged at Le Bœuf sur le Toit. But the Big Apple, which advertised itself as the "only American cabaret in Paris," shut its doors on 10 December 1938, after exactly one year and a day's existence.

Regardless of allegations of Bert Hicks's tyrannical behavior toward the club's financial backers, Bricktop—its manager and hostess—was accused of mismanagement and blamed for the Big Apple's closing after Hall left. There were allegations of Bricktop's involvement in an unscrupulous financial affair, which recalls Alberta Hunter's claim that Bricktop pilfered a telegram meant for her sent from Paris by Bullard offering a job at his Grand Duc. The Big Apple's owners, learning that Bricktop had planned to arrange financial backing to purchase the cabaret, decided to sell it to a Frenchman.

Whatever truth there is in this account reflects the similarities in the two artists' careers: both Adelaide Hall and Josephine Baker had performed on the vaudeville stage, not on cabaret dance floors. In 1927 Hall played in Irvin Miller's *Desire of 1927*, a musical comedy that toured on the TOBA circuit. Her big break in musical theater came with the untimely death of Florence Mills, whom she replaced in *Blackbirds of 1929*. She was still learning to enjoy the bright lights of Paris's musical theaters when she launched the Big Apple venture. Though charming and gracious as hostess to Big Apple patrons, Hall lacked the flair of Florence Jones, Bricktop, or Josephine Baker, who relished playing the role of nightly greeter to the rush of happy, giggling patrons, teasing the rich and famous of Parisian nightlife and welcoming them to the clubs. Hall relished the glare of stage footlights, the curtain calls from an ecstatic audience that signaled a triumphant performance. So throwing caution to the wind, she seized the opportunity to perform in *The Sun Never Sets* at the Drury Lane, in London's theater district. It, too, was a dream long deferred.

By the time of the Big Apple's closing, Freddy Taylor and his partner, Jimmy Monroe (now divorced from the movie star and cabaret singer Nina Mae McKinney), were already working their way past the pitfalls of cabaret ownership in Montmartre. On 11 June 1937 they had opened the cabaret Club Harlem, advertised as the club in France with the only real Harlem atmosphere. To create that atmosphere, the partners brought in well-known characters from the black community. Jimmy Monroe himself acted as master-of-ceremonies for the evening's entertainment. Eugene Bullard brought to his position as general director a long experience of cabaret management; his old boxer friend Bob Scanlon, a regular fixture at Chez Boudon, was the nightly uniformed doorman. To enhance the club's international flavor, Martinicans were hired as waiters and barmen. As required by law, a French orchestra backed the floor show, but the principal stars were from the black community and included Eunice Wilson, Jigsaw Jackson, and Mickey Roller. And for Parisian lovers of black jazz, the club featured hot jazz-swing music by an eight-piece orchestra with Harry Cooper, the trumpeter who had played with Leon Abbey in Europe from early 1928.

On Club Harlem's gala opening night, the stellar attractions of the black community made their conventional appearance among the patrons at the opening show. Bricktop, the entire Cotton Club review with Teddy Hill (only recently arrived from Harlem and now playing at both the Ambassadeurs and the Bal du Moulin Rouge theaters), Adelaide Hall, and Garland Wilson were in the audience. One year later, Club Harlem closed, and immediately Jimmy Monroe opened his Swing Club in the Trinity Palace Hotel.

Amid the flurries of openings and closings, the formidable political challenges facing France and central Europe had begun to mute the clamor and hilarity of Montmartre's nightly street life. By April 1938 the two principal streets of Montmartre for black cabaret life, rue Pigalle and rue Fontaine, were bare and nearly deserted. At the start of 1936 Lila Gray, former wife of Charlie Chaplin, had bought Frisco Bingham's old Montmartre cabaret and renamed it The Don Juan. It had a short life. On 22 May 1937 Henry Dajou opened his Cotton Club in place Pigalle, next to Bricktop's new club; two doors away from Dajou's place, Adelaide Hall and Hetty Flacks opened the short-lived Big Apple. The Cotton Club closed by the end of June 1938. Georgette Huguette and her sister, who were rumored to have "exploited" their financial interest in Freddy Taylor and Jimmy Monroe's Club Harlem, were also forced to close in 1938. Before the end of the year, the famous Chez Florence, acquired by Madame Régine in June 1935, closed its doors.

The loss of several popular Montmartre cabarets brought sadness to the black community and caused a shuffle for employment by displaced black American musicians who turned toward Belgium, the Netherlands, and Denmark. There opportunities were more lucrative, often engagements in nightclubs that had always featured black dancers and singing duos and quartets in their floor shows.

While the economic barometer of cabaret life in Montmartre was falling, there was one cause for celebration. The event was unrelated to nightlife but united the black community's jazz family: Joe Louis's quick defeat of Max Schmeling in defense of his world title in 1938. The fight broadcast was heard at 3 A.M. in Paris. Shortly after the decision was announced, the black community's celebration in Montmartre was joined by a group of German Jewish refugees who had fled from Germany and Austria to France after the rise of Hitler. They came to congratulate the black community for Louis's victory, which they viewed as a symbolic blow against Nazi anti-Semitism. Hetty Flacks, herself Jewish and then owner of Adelaide Hall's Big Apple, gave champagne to the crowd to toast Joe Louis's victory. Harlem in Montmartre had adopted the convention long held in America's Bronzevilles of taking to the streets in wild rejoicing when "the Brown Bomber" defended his titles. In Paris, such street celebrations perhaps began with Battling Siki's victory over Georges Carpentier in 1922, earning him the title of European World Heavyweight champion. In Harlem the victory celebrations ended up at Hotel Theresa, at 125th and Seventh Avenue; in Montmartre's narrow twisting streets, Louis's victory celebrations—and those of other black boxers, like the world's bantamweight champion, Panama Al Brown—were held in the closest open bar a celebrant could enter.

Joe Louis's victory over Max Schmeling had meaning of extraordinary value to the black community. As early as 1935, evidence of creeping anti-Jewish as well as anti–black American bias in the entertainment world had begun to appear in Austria, Germany, and Italy. Creighton Thompson, who had traveled to Paris with Elliott Carpenter's Red Devils as a drummer in 1920, had made a transition from jazz to classical singing, with steady bookings in European capitals. He was one of the several black performers forced out of Germany and back to Paris, his adopted home, when Nazi racial policies excluded non-Aryans from radio and from theaters. Marian Anderson was among the black American artists denied permission to perform in Germany and Austria—including the cancellation of a scheduled recital at the Salzburg festival in Vienna on 18 August 1935—on the grounds of being non-Aryan. In Mussolini's Italy, anti–black American sentiment became so pervasive that the American consul in Rome advised black American entertainers not to accept contracts to appear in Italy, as contracts were likely not to be honored. Lew Lake's musical review *Blackberries,* which was rehearsing at Lake Como for an opening in Rome, received an official notice banning the show. The theater company was forced to return to London.

Vienna had exceeded all other cities in western Europe in the virulence of its reaction against Josephine Baker, who arrived in Vienna at the height of her stardom in 1928 to perform in *Revue Nègre.* Protests by riotous university students marred her arrival, and a police guard was placed around her. The students declared their intention of preventing "colored artists" from playing in the city. Their displaced anger against Baker arose over Ernst Krenek's interracial jazz opera *Jonny spielt auf* (Jonny tunes up [composed in 1926]). In the opera's offending theme Jonny, a black jazz-band violinist, seduces a charming but naive French woman in a subterfuge to steal a precious violin. He intends to play upon it as David played upon the harp and to praise Jehovah, who created men black. Everything good in the world belongs to him, he boasts, and "all white women capitulate to him."[35]

Though squads of armed police contained the rioting students in Vienna, other groups considered Baker's planned revue at the Théâtre Johann Strauss no less immoral and offensive. The Jesuits' *Bulletin ecclésiastique* announced a special service to be held at Saint-Paul's church in the capital to allow those Catholics who attended Baker's revue to expiate the sin. Anticipating the revue's run in Hungary, the Austrian Ministry of Foreign Affairs condemned the theaters in Budapest as immoral to propagate the taste in nudity displayed in Baker's dances.[36] A decade or so later, Josephine Baker would again experience the offensiveness of racial exclusion when the Nazis imposed their new moral order on occupied Paris.

French audiences' reaction to the interracial play *La Joueuse* was in sharp contrast to Viennese responses to *Jonny spielt auf.* The French play presents a voluptuous white woman whose feverish desire for sexual thrills makes her career one of excess and dissipation. A proposed black lover—performed by Habib Bengalia, a celebrated African dramatist and French idol—finally kills her.[37] As Parisian theatergoers were lining up for tickets to *La Joueuse,* Joseph Goebbels, in his recently appointed position as minister of propaganda, was introducing legislation to remove once and for all interracial theater in the Third Reich. Black American jazz too would have to go.

# 6 | LE JAZZ-COLD
## *The Silent Forties*

At 5:30 in the morning on 14 June 1940, German troops entered Paris by the Porte de Villette. At 9:45 they hoisted the first of many black, white, and red swastikas of Nazi Germany to the top of the Tour Eiffel. Under the command of General Dietrich von Cholitz, who had ordered the destruction of Rotterdam and led the siege of the Black Sea port of Sevastopol, the occupying force set its heavy boot on the most beautiful city in the world. At the stroke of noon every day, 250 men of the First Sicherungsregiment began their march down the Champs-Élysées to the place de la Concorde. "Along the graceful arches of the rue de Rivoli, around the Place de la Concorde, in front of the Palais du Luxembourg, the Chamber of Deputies, and the Quai d'Orsay, black, white and red Wehrmacht sentry boxes barred Parisians from the pavements of their own city." [1]

This institutionalized spectacle of conquest and humiliation took place every day for four years. Over a million people fled Paris in the weeks shortly before and after the German occupation. [2] Buses and taxis disappeared, leaving the city's wide boulevards empty. Vélo-taxis became the common mode of public transport in the city; about 250,000 were in use by the close of 1940. A few drivers gained permission to convert their cars to *gazogènes,* burning wood for fuel to power them in wash boilers bolted to their trunks.

By August 1940 Paris was a hungry city. Food shortages were acute and rationing further restricted daily supplies. "Parisians that August would get two eggs, 3.2 ounces of cooking oil, 2 ounces of margarine on their ration tickets. The meat ration was so small that, according to a popular joke it could be wrapped in a subway ticket—provided that the ticket has not been used. If it had, went the joke, the meat might fall through the hole punched in the ticket by the conductor's perforator." The staple of most Parisian diets was the rutabaga, a variety of turnip formerly fed to cattle.[3]

For Parisians with personal savings, or winnings on the National Lottery, or German friends, there was *le marché noir*. On the black market, they could get rationed items like apéritifs, tobacco, household linens, cloth, shoes, electrical batteries, shaving cream—on the rare occasions when the items were available.[4] Newly rich black marketers could enjoy champagne and caviar at Maxim's, the Lido, the Schéhérazade, and a few other cabarets still providing many of the pre-occupation material pleasures symbolic of Parisian life. For them, "life under the boot" was more an irritant than a deprivation. There was no curfew for Corinne, the pretty movie actress and daughter of Jean Luchaire, head of the collaborationist press, as she dined and danced with Nazi bigwigs. Hermann Göring loved Maxim's and gave lavish parties there whenever he was in Paris. Amidst the putative gaiety and libations, a lot of black market business was done at Maxim's as well.[5] But there was no dancing to the black American jazz that Parisians once enjoyed.

A trickle of African Americans began an exodus from Paris when war clouds gathered over western Europe. On 6 October 1939, one month after Germany attacked Poland—and Britain and France declared war against Germany—U.S. Consul General John Woods announced the order from American Ambassador to France William Christopher Bullitt: all Americans who could not prove they had important business in France were to leave. The wrenching bewilderment many in the black community felt in abandoning the city they called home anticipated the despair French citizens felt in their flight nine months later, as German troops were poised on the outskirts of Paris. African American students and teachers enrolled at universities in Paris, Bordeaux, and Toulouse were among the first to leave. Joining the exodus were world travelers like Max Yergen and "Colonel" Hubert Fauntleroy Julian. They were typical of the black Americans who joined the throngs of visitors swinging to the jazz of black musicians each night at Chez Joséphine, Le Grand Duc, and other black-owned nightclubs in Paris's Harlem.

Returning to New York aboard the SS *Manhattan,* Yergen, sometime reporter for *P.M.* and conservative political commentator for the Negro press, held isolationist views about the war. America should not be supporting the imperialistic governments of England and France, he argued, because they had exploited the colored peoples of the West Indies and Africa. The flamboyantly self-styled "Colonel" Julian, a sometime soldier of fortune who boarded the ship at Verdon-sur-Mer, expressed a contrasting view. Julian was going back to America, he said, to raise $1 million from among "colored Americans" so he could send colored nurses, surgeons, pilots—along with hospital planes—off to the French, because of France's democratic attitude toward colored people.[6]

Expatriate African Americans in France shared Julian's perception of France's attitude. Some members of the black community had decided not to seek repatriation even if it were offered. If they could, they would fight for la belle France and strike a blow against racism. In the rush of volunteers at a recruiting station in Paris, Nancy Cunard reported to the *Baltimore Afro-American,* forty of two hundred foreigners in line were French Antilleans. Black Americans were expected to enlist soon.[7]

When the SS *St. John* docked in New York on 3 November 1940, her fifty American passengers included more than a dozen black musicians and entertainers who had lived in Paris for a decade or more. Mustering their talents to form an orchestra, Frank Withers and Leon Abbey gave the passengers a last chance to relive the joy of Harlem-style nightlife in Montmartre. America's racial climate in the 1940s would make it much harder to swing to the talents of black American jazz musicians in the small, smoky cabarets that dotted the streets of Bronzevilles everywhere. Abbey, the bandleader and violinist, was one of the black musicians who had found the doors of concert halls closed to them before leaving America and once in Europe made the transition to jazz from classical music. He began his long and successful career playing light and classical music; he appeared in Paris's popular nightclubs, spreading jazz sounds in European and Asian capitals and in weekly broadcasts over Radio Cité. Abbey was not a jazz soloist but was able to identify and employ in his bands such excellent sidemen as the trumpeter Bill Coleman, when he toured Europe from 1928 to 1939, with Paris his base.[8]

The impromptu shipboard orchestra included Chicagoan Glover Compton, who began his career as a ragtime piano player in some of south-side Chicago's most famous cabarets and had lived in Paris for twelve years. Engaged for the last several years as resident pianist at Harry's New York Bar, he was popular with American tourists. Una Mae Carlisle, who had worked with Fats Waller before coming to Europe and modeled her style of piano playing on his, entertained the SS *St. John*'s passengers with her sultry chanting of "I Can't Give You Anything but Love." Faithful patrons of Le Bœuf sur le Toit on board enjoyed the performances of pianist Garland Wilson, who had held sway at the piano bar in his own room at this popular nightspot. And there was Creighton Thompson. He ended his twenty years' classical musical career in Europe as a concert tenor—"le célèbre chanteur américain," music critics in Paris called him—having been recruited in 1926 as a jazz drummer in pianist Elliot Carpenter's Red Devils (along with Sammy Richardson and Opal Cooper on banjo). Now recrossing the Atlantic, the former choirboy from Chicago's St. Thomas Episcopal church, where his father was pastor, pondered adjustment to the city of his birth in a land still plagued by racial discrimination.[9]

If Harlem had invaded Montmartre before America's engagement in World War I, with Will Marion Cook and the Southern Syncopated Orchestra playing in Paris, now Montmartre came to Harlem with the return of Bricktop (now Ada Smith du Congé). Often billed as Josephine Baker's rival as the toast of Montmartre during her long stay in Paris, Bricktop had joined the exodus of black American entertainers. On 10 November 1939 she landed in New York aboard the SS *Washington,* ending fifteen years of nightclub show business in Montmartre and the Côte d'Azur. Bricktop's own cabaret was now silent, as were other popular nightclubs along rue Fontaine and rue Pigalle, streets made famous by the black community when Harlem in Montmartre was in vogue. These painful memories receded, at least for the moment, when Bricktop arrived at the Mimo Club in downtown Manhattan for a homecoming celebration in her honor. About fifty black entertainers who had left Paris to resettle in New York joined the celebration to welcome Bricktop's return.

The evening's event was orchestrated by Louis Mitchell, who had been the first black American to open a nightclub in Paris.

After the close of the affair, Bricktop and her husband, Peter du Congé, were driven uptown to the Hotel Teresa in Harlem. She had thoughts of opening a nightclub in New York modeled after one she had owned in Montmartre. And perhaps her thoughts wandered to her estate in Bougival, outside Paris, where Eugene Bullard, Arthur Briggs, Mistinguett, Maurice Chevalier, and a number of other popular expatriate and French entertainers owned homes. Pianist Louis Cole lived on the top floor of the mansion on the spacious estate where Bricktop raised chickens—Rhode Island Reds and other prize breeds—to sell to Montmartre nightclubs that adopted the Harlem custom of serving their patrons chicken fricassee, bacon and eggs, or chicken salad sandwiches in the morning after a night of dancing.

Before the move to Bougival, Bricktop had been part of the good times in Montmartre. One such time was the summer of 1935 when she returned to Paris after one of several failed nightclub ventures on the Côte d'Azur. She was often seen "clacking around Pigalle by day in her copper shoes and housecoat, shouting raucously from the street up to the windows of friends, 'Hey, you bitches, watcha doing?' and 'Kiss my ass,' if someone like Alberta Hunter didn't respond." [10] And doubtless Bricktop smiled when she recalled the reactions of nightclub patrons to such episodes as when Kiki volunteered to sing vulgar French songs in her robust Burgundian manner, or when a "French chippy" shot a pianist outside her nightclub. But moments of sadness would punctuate these smiles, as her thoughts turned to her not-too-gentle fall from the pinnacle of nightclub success in Montmartre.

It was Bricktop's hands-on management style to which Robert McAlmon, writer of the Lost Generation crowd, attributed her success. Frequent visits to her nightclub, often in the company of Kaye Boyle, sharpened his views of her colorful managerial skills:

> While she sang and danced now and then, she generally sat at the
> cashier's desk keeping accounts, while at the same time observing
> every action that went on in the cabaret . . . while singing her
> songs, she thinks more of her dancing. It is a great show to watch

her skipping about the floor while rendering "Bon-Bon-Buddie," "The Chocolate Drop," or to listen to her singing a recent blues, torch song, or Cole Porter's latest witty song. . . . She puts across her songs with intelligence and wit.[11]

On one occasion, McAlmon described Bricktop demonstrating her extraordinary talent like a vaudeville performer, juggling several unrelated activities taking place in the club as she responded to patrons' requests for favorite songs.

> In the back room several Negroes were having an argument. Brick sat at the cashier's desk keeping things in order . . . all the while she was adding up accounts, calling out to the orchestra to play this or that requested number, indicating to the waiters that this or that table needed service; and, when asked, she began to sing "Love for Sale," while still adding up accounts. . . . [Interrupting an argument and fight in the back room, she then] continued the song, having missed two phrases, and was back at her desk again adding accounts.[12]

But by late 1939 the accounts were closed, the doors shuttered, and Bricktop had returned to America. And for the next ten years, Harlem was her home.

To some Parisians and African Americans of the musical entertainment community, the prospect of war seemed remote, notwithstanding the 3 September formal declaration and politicians' urgent consultations. Describing Paris about eight months before German forces occupied the city—during the uneasy lull everyone called the *drôle de guerre,* the "phony war"—the journalist Alexander Werth remarked,

> In Paris you would hardly, on the face of it, have thought that there was a war on at all—except, of course, that nearly all the men you knew had been called up. The *Chevaux de Marly* in the Place de la Concorde and the base of the Obelisk were sandbagged (it gave the Obelisk an even more phallic look than usual). . . . And at Lancel's there were terracotta Aberdeen terriers

raising a hind leg over a copy of *Mein Kampf*. . . . But apart from little things like that there was, on the face of it, little in Paris to remind you of the war. . . . Especially since November [1939], life in Paris became quite normal. Theatres and dancings and music halls were open. . . . There were also Maurice Chevalier and Josephine Baker at the Casino de Paris.[13]

Paris nightlife returned to its old form, in a fashion. Freed from the blackout and the ban on dancing imposed three months earlier at the declaration of war, a few nightclubs owned by black Americans and other jazz clubs made popular by black American musicians reopened and turned on their glaring neon signs. Black American musicians who had tossed caution to the wind and decided to "stick it out" were riding the crest of a newfound vogue.[14]

Arthur Briggs and his orchestra were still Parisian favorites, entertaining nightly at Le Club on the Champs-Élysées. In the heart of what was left of Harlem in Montmartre, pianist Maceo Jefferson played at La Silhouette. Harry Miller, the singing guitarist at the American Legion bar, kept spirits alive among American journalists mingling with other patrons to compare notes on the latest news from the phony war. Destitute Americans, of whom there were many, including black American musicians who had thrown away excellent earnings on gambling or philandering and expensive bad champagne, now sought cheap passage on a ship returning home. As for many other former jazz club proprietors in Montmartre, the climate of financial uncertainty forced Jimmy Monroe's once popular Swing Club to remain shuttered.

Eugene Jacques Bullard had his own reasons not to join the exodus of the black community from Montmartre. A decorated World War I hero, he still hated the Germans with a passion. During the phony war he kept open his restaurant-bar Escadrille, at 5 rue Fontaine, which he had bought before he sold Le Grand Duc. It was at Le Grand Duc that he had made his reputation as one of the pioneers of black jazz–cabaret life in Montmartre and where he had hired Bricktop in 1924. He also kept open his gymnasium in rue Mansart, now attracting Parisian men who felt a patriotic need to shed the physical evidence of a life of overindulgence in good food and wine. For some patrons, physical conditioning was considered a preparatory measure, if need be, for defense of the City of Light. Capitalizing on Bullard's own fame as a fighter pilot, Escadrille attracted French and British airmen on leave in Paris. On any night at the crowded bar, one or more of France's World War I aviation heroes appeared, impressing new recruits by weaving tales of daring exploits against German fighter pilots in what they still referred to as the Great War.

Like many Parisians, Bullard dismissed the German invasion of France, firmly believing the French defenses at the Maginot line would repel it. But French critics of the Maginot's defense capabilities asked Bullard to help gather intelligence that might prove useful against German espionage in France. Members of the several Corsican gangs that operated between the wars openly in Montmartre—chiefly "les Corses," "les Parigots," and "les Marseillais"—were thought to be an invaluable aid to suspected plots of sabotage; and Bullard's reopened Grand Duc, with its international clientele, including regular German patrons, was an ideal place to gather information for the underground.

After Consul General John Woods ordered all Americans who could not prove that they had important business in France to leave, Bullard, then forty-five years old, left Paris on foot to join his old regiment, the 170th Infantry, reported to be engaged in fierce fighting at Épinac, southeast of Orléans. On learning that Épinac had been captured, Bullard walked back to Paris.

The 51st Infantry was fighting German advances near Orléans. Bullard headed there, stopping in Chartres, about 50 miles from Paris, where he met his old friend Bob Scanlon, a boxer and comrade from Foreign Legion days. Their last meeting had been in Montmartre, when both worked at Freddy Taylor and Jimmy Monroe's Club Harlem. Finally reaching the 51st at Orléans, Bullard found his old commanding officer, Major Roger Bader—whom he had not seen since the battle of Verdun in 1916—and joined the unit. Bullard was assigned to install machine guns on the left bank of the Loire River to repel German advances that were supported by aerial bombardment and artillery fire. When Bullard was wounded, Bader issued him a safe-conduct pass and directed him to get immediately to unoccupied Bordeaux by way of Angoulême, a twenty-four-hour journey. There he was admitted to hospital, treated, and told to leave France. He went to Biarritz, near the Spanish border, to await passage on a ship bound for the United States and finally sailed from Lisbon for New York aboard the SS *Manhattan* on 9 July 1940.

Having received news three weeks earlier that Nazi troops had occupied Paris, Bullard assumed that Nazi distaste for African American and Jewish jazz music would lead to the closing of his Escadrille and Le Grand Duc. But now he was in New York and "that burst of brightness from Miss Liberty's torch," which he was thrilled to see, quickly dimmed. After almost thirty years in France, he found the attitude of white Americans toward blacks was precisely the one he had experienced in his encounters with them in Montmartre. With limited funds, he rented cheap rooms in Harlem, labored at a number of menial jobs, and worked as a longshoreman. On a visit to Columbus, Georgia, he found the South little changed. Later he toured Europe as a factotum and interpreter for Louis Armstrong, and in 1954 he was among the group of American former legionnaires invited by the French government to return to Paris to relight the eternal flame under the Arc de Triomphe. He eventually found steady employment as an elevator operator in New York's RCA Building. Bullard was living in a ramshackle building at 80 East 116th Street in Harlem when he died on 12 October 1961.[15]

By April 1940 Willie Lewis and his band made up the only black American musical aggregation still in Europe.[16] This was Lewis's second tour of Europe, beginning in March 1934. As he wrote in his dispatch to the *Defender* from The Hague, his mind "was made up to stay right through the entire war (so wish me luck)." Of his band, only Teddy Brock, the first trumpet, returned to America. Lewis's decision to stay doubtless was shaped by his success in obtaining continual bookings at popular jazz nightclubs on his second European tour. In Paris, his band played at Chez Florence and the Restaurant Ambassadeurs for three continuous years. On the Côte d'Azur it was a favorite at Chez Victor in Cannes and the casinos in Monte Carlo.

Each summer since 1936 the band had been booked in Belgium at the casinos in Knokke-Heist and Ostend. They were playing in Ostend when war broke out in September 1939, forcing a loss of half the contract there and the entire contract for the exposition in Liège, Belgium. On the last day of September a contract was signed to play for the Dancing Tabaris, a nightclub in The Hague. Opening on 11 October 1939, the band would remain until May, Lewis wrote, if Hitler's armies did not arrive first (they did). Every evening until then, Willie Lewis and other black American musicians in northern Europe, like the pianist Freddy Johnson at the Negro Palace in Amsterdam, delivered the kind of jazz sounds that kept the thoughts of citizens off the German menace.

The respite was short. The German blitzkrieg swept through the weak defenses of the Netherlands and Belgium in a matter of days. It was a dress rehearsal for the contest on the larger stage of France, with Paris as the prize. As American citizens in the Netherlands, Evelyn and Joe Hayman believed themselves not subject to arrest by the occupying force and were taken by surprise when ordered to report to their district's police station. America was not then at war with Germany. A dancer, Evelyn had come to Paris as a member of Lew Leslie's *Blackbirds*. After leaving the show she traveled through Europe dancing in several musicals, then settled with the children in the Netherlands in 1939. An alto-saxophone man, Joe Hayman came to Europe with other musicians recruited by band leader Claude Hopkins for Carolyn Dudley Reagan's *Revue Nègre*. After the production closed, Hayman joined Louis Armstrong's orchestra but remained in Europe when the group returned to America.

The small black community in the Netherlands dispersed by the Nazi occupation included Ida Johnson and her pianist husband, Freddy, who was once an accompanist for Florence Mills, and their two daughters. In 1927 Freddy Johnson came to Europe with Sam Woodie's band, which played at the Embassy Club on the Champs-Élysées two years later. He was playing at Bricktop's in 1929 when the club began to make its mark in Montmartre, with bandsmen Big Boy Goudie on sax, Peter du Congé on clarinet, Billy Taylor on drums, Herb Flemming on trombone, and Juan Fernandez on bass. Johnson's own group, the Harlemites, formed after he left Bricktop's, was on tour in 1939. The Johnsons were living in Rotterdam with their two daughters enrolled in school when the first Nazi panzer divisions occupied the city in 1940, after the Luftwaffe had nearly leveled it. The family then moved to The Hague, where Johnson played at fashionable cafés largely patronized by high-ranking Nazi army officers. Jazz played by black American musicians had not yet been labeled by the New Order's racist propaganda as "degenerate negro-jewish" music. But when the United States declared war on Germany in December 1941, all Americans in the Netherlands were immediately placed under arrest. After processing by the police, Johnson was interned in Bavaria. Ida Johnson and her two daughters were interned at Amersfoort, a

Dutch camp for women, and were later transferred to another camp at Liebenau, in Germany, near the Swiss border.

In Paris, the detention of all Americans by the Nazis began in earnest after President Roosevelt's speech to Congress and the nation on 8 December 1941, invoking the 7th as a date that would live in infamy and requesting a declaration of war against the Axis powers. Black American entertainers who had defied Ambassador Bullitt's order to all Americans in France to repatriate themselves and had kept the musical sounds of jazz alive in Montmartre during the phony war, appear to have been singled out for arrest and internment immediately after Nazi troops marched into Paris.

The series of proclamations codified by the *Officiel du Spectacle* made good on Hitler's promise after his first visit to Paris on 24 June 1940 that Paris would continue as the world's amusement center. But—in a bizarre twist—no mixed café shows or shows composed of all black American performers or entertainers would ever again entertain in the city. Thus the attacker of Paris assumed the role of its defender, to ensure shows made up of leading performers of the world who would be strictly Nordic.[17] Jim Crow laws canceled work permits for black Americans. All first-class restaurants, cafés, theaters, and hotels were barred to them, some establishments prominently displaying signs in large letters, For Aryans Only. Musicians, actors, and entertainers who once earned high salaries walked the streets, hiding from friends; those with money escaped to Vichy France or Africa.[18]

Six weeks after France fell, the Germans directed a general census of all foreigners. The trumpeter Arthur Briggs was ordered to report to the police to be interned. The order was suddenly canceled but Briggs was arrested and sent to the camp at St-Denis, north of Paris, on 17 October 1940. His devotion to music was such that three days after internment Briggs formed a six-piece orchestra that included Gay Martins, a West African, and Owen Macauly, a black Briton. Soon the orchestra, augmented to twenty-five pieces, became the centerpiece of camp entertainment.

The Nazis' sweep continued. The concert singer Princess Tovalou, formerly Roberta Dodd Crawford from Chicago, a prominent black American figure on the Montmartre scene who had accompanied *Defender* ed-

itor Robert Abbot on his trip to Paris in 1929 and married Prince Tovalou Houénou in 1932, was arrested when the Germans occupied Paris.[19]
The roundup of black Americans also caught the trumpet player Harry
Cooper. Maceo Jefferson, a composer and musician who played at La Silhouette in Montmartre during the nine months of the phony war, escaped the net that snared Briggs and Princess Tovalou. Later Jefferson was
captured and sent to Frontslag 122, a camp about 70 miles from Paris.
Henry Crowder, who had left the Montmartre jazz scene and found lucrative bookings in Brussels and other cities in Belgium, was arrested in
Beverlo in 1942. Valaida Snow, an all-around accomplished musician and
singer who had been performing in Europe and Shanghai since 1929, had
made her last trip to Paris in February 1939 — organizing a ten-piece
female orchestra with French players, spending ten weeks teaching them
swing. After this engagement, she went to Denmark to perform and was
arrested and imprisoned.

Hitler's decree banning mixed café shows by black American performers became effective immediately. Between the second and fourth night
of the occupation of Paris, two nightclubs in Pigalle—Eve and Le Para-
dis—reopened. Soon Chez Elle and L'Aiglon opened their doors, then
other nightclubs followed their example. An April 1941 edition of *Pariser
Zeitung* listed the names of nightclub proprietors granted permission to
publicize the quality of musical performances presented in their establishments. Like tourists agents advertising to visitors, the German press
recommended to occupying soldiers, the Gestapo, and German civilian
bureaucrats posted in Paris that they frequent the "hot points" in Paris:
Chez Elle, Le Bosphore, Ciro's, Le Danube, Don Juan, Eve, Paris-Paris,
Le Jockey, Le Grand Jeu, Liberty's, Chateau-Bagatelle, L'Impératrice, Le
Lido, Schéhérazade, and Le Tabarin.[20]

The scarcity of jazz-swing performances in the press's recommended
nightclubs paralleled the actual scarcity of food that Parisians equally savored. Sacha Guitry composed with humor his New Year's Eve midnight
supper (*le réveillon*) on 31 December 1942, a menu set in terms of the food
shortages: fish eventually; roast presumed; chicken anticipated; vegetables
very likely; salad possible; dessert hypothetical. Wines blue, white, red;
cigarettes individual.

But not even the absence of black jazz-swing or culinary delicacies
could slow the explosion of new nightclubs. Of the four grand poles of

nightclub life, Montmartre was the locale for forty-nine cabarets situated between place Pigalle and adjacent streets of Trinité and St-Lazare. The section of the Champs-Élysées and l'Étoile held thirty-one establishments; there were sixteen on the periphery of the grand boulevards and thirteen in Montparnasse.

Montmartre's traditionally unsavory reputation as the district of pleasure and crime, the fiefdom of Corsican gangsters and high-class mobs, did not change during the occupation. Gangsters and the Gestapo frequented the Chantilly at 10 rue Fontaine, but also the Heure Blue and Le Grand Jeu, neighbors in rue Pigalle. White Russian émigrés became in effect the dispensers of pleasure in the small island of Montmartre dominated by the Corsicans, whose business interests were directed toward other affairs. The newly named Florence, in rue Blanche, was transformed with an Italian flavor. The orchestra at the Royal Soupers, 62 rue Pigalle, where Édith Piaf made her debut before the war, offered sad versions of swing and tap-dancing during the band's intermission. Small nightclubs like Florence, offering second-hand swing, lost popularity to Montmartre cabarets offering more sumptuous evening musical entertainment. Patrons with hard-to-come-by francs could find greater enjoyment at the Liberty, 20 rue de Clichy, or at the Chateau Bagatelle and the Chapiteau, on place Pigalle. Before the occupation, the Chapiteau was the old Abbaye de Thélème, where in 1929 and 1930 the Plantation Orchestra had played and Josephine Baker had performed nightly. For high-ranking German officers and visitors, the grand center of attraction in Montmartre resided at Le Tabarin, in rue Victor-Massé, where nude reviews, claimed to be of great quality, were featured in the nightly spectacles.

The nightclubs of the Champs-Élysées presented a smiling semblance of Paris before the occupation. Tempting slogans gave publicity to Paris-Paris as the city's chic restaurant-cabaret. The Vol de Nuit claimed to be the bar of poets and men of wit. L'Aiglon, boasting of being the conservators of French esprit, was full of German soldiers every night.

The elegant district of the Champs-Élysées had set itself apart from Montmartre as much by the originality of its architecture and decor as by the relatively few nightclubs with jazz played by black American musicians before the occupation. The Bœuf sur le Toit, launched by Jean Cocteau and made famous during the 1920s by French writers, artists, and jazz musicians, could still assure its clientele of impeccable table service, despite a skimpy menu, but could not assure them of the impeccable jazz sounds of Leon Abbey, Bobby Martin, Garland Wilson, or Una Mae Carlisle; they had joined other black entertainers in the exodus from Paris in 1939. (When Montmartre artists gathered to celebrate Le Bœuf's twentieth anniversary in 1941, these musicians back home probably had no news of the event. If they did, missing out on the celebrations would have saddened them.)

Less numerous than the clubs on the Champs-Élysées were the small cabarets in the Opéra district and on the grand boulevards. Typical was Chez Elle in rue Volney, featuring solo guitarists and singing pianists. At La Vie Parisienne, Suzy Solidor sang "Lily Marlene" each night, to the great delight of German patrons.

"Lily Marlene" was out of place in the Latin Quarter. By December 1941, cabaret posters reflected the irreverent spirit of the students, artists, and writers who inhabited the quarter. German-language songs would not have been welcome at Le Caveau de la Bolée, near place St-Michel, which boasted about the realism and joviality of its attractions. Nor at Le Gypsy, in rue Cujas, which claimed to be the temple of traditional French gaiety. Nor at Le Jockey, one of the first nightclubs in Montparnasse to offer jazz. Le Jockey had never enjoyed a steady flow of the talented black American musicians who shaped Montmartre's jazz scene, but before the occupation it was white Americans' favorite nightclub on the Left Bank. Entering the Jockey, patrons now met a poster with a slogan to reflect the wartime mood: Leave All Care Behind.

Jimmy Charter's bar-café in rue Huyghens—where a band featuring Django Reinhardt, Alix Combelle, pianist Charlie Lewis, and Philippe Brun had a long run the winter before the occupation—was rebaptized Chez Jimmy. When Johnny Hess became the attraction at Chez Jimmy singing "Je suis swing," the club heaped late-coming patrons one against another like sardines in a tin. For Johnny Hess represented the new vogue of anti-Nazi jazz-swing music adopted by young Parisians in defiance of the New Order. These young Parisians were called *Zazous*.

Arthur Briggs's arrest and internment at St-Denis in mid-October had stoked the coals of red-hot jazz in Montmartre. Under the watchful eyes of the occupation authorities, Charles Delaunay, cofounder and secretary general of the Hot Club of France, organized a jazz concert to be held at

Salle Gaveau on 19 December 1940. Twenty-four hours after the announcement, all seats were sold. The concert was a protest against the German boot, trampling the Parisian culture of jazz. It was also an evening's musical refuge from the trauma of the present. Delaunay also knew that sooner or later the Nazis would ban jazz, as they did immediately after the United States entered the war.[21] But what the Nazis prohibited was not *jazz* itself; they banned American cultural products. French jazz, filling the vacuum, blazed as never before. In preparation for the concert, Delaunay summoned the most talented French musicians who had played in Montmartre's nightclubs with black American musicians before the occupation. Among the performers were Alix Combelle and his swing group, Hubert Rostaing the clarinetist, and Django Reinhardt and his new quartet. So popular was Delaunay's musical event that spectators demanded a second concert, scheduled for 2 February 1941. It too sold out, and jazz concerts were repeated ten other times.[22]

In these dark days jazz concerts offered alternatives to nightclubs where bands played "approved" swing or to Chez Ledoyen's five o'clock teas. Before each concert Delaunay camouflaged the jazz classics in French titles when he handed in the program to the Propaganda Staffel for the censor's approval. Rebaptism with French names made acceptable popular favorites like "La tristesse de saint Louis" (Saint Louis Blues), "La rose de chèvrefeuille" (Honeysuckle Rose), "Ma chère Suzanne" (Sweet Sue), "L'attaque de train" (Take the A-Train), "La rage du tigre" (Tiger Rag), and "Bébé d'amour" (Some of These Days). The renaming of jazz classics transformed what the Nazis called "American jungle music, jewish, negro and decadent" into French music. It was also Delaunay's form of overt resistance, which matched his covert role at the Hot Club of France headquarters at 14 rue Chaptal. In honor of jazz saxophonist Benny Carter, Delaunay took the code name "Benny" and called the resistance network "Cart."[23] At the same time, Zazous created their own style of resistance to Nazi decrees: Johnny Hess's chorus in his "Je suis swing"—"zazou-zazouzazouzazou hé"—became their defiant chant (the full text is in the appendix).

A dress rehearsal for Nazi interdictions against jazz-swing music in occupied Paris had taken place soon after Germany acquired a new leader. In March 1935 his propaganda minister, Joseph Goebbels, had identified black American hot jazz as a vehicle to promote Nazi ideology. German authorities banished jazz from all radio programs on the grounds that it was a form of musical decadence. The German Broadcasting Company (RRG) informed the press that "the Berlin programme is banning all the dubious dance styles that healthy public opinion calls 'Nigger music,' in which provocative rhythms predominate and melody is violently abused." To further educate the healthy public, RRG's program director outlined the 1935–36 winter program that was to expiate the "disintegrating effects of cultural Bolshevist-Jewry . . . and to eradicate every trace of putrefying elements that remain in our light entertainment and dance music." He proclaimed, "As of today, Nigger jazz is finally switched off on the German radio."[24]

Exactly what jazz *was,* the Ministry of Propaganda failed to state as it broadcast vitriolic propaganda against musical sounds best understood and appreciated by young people. They remained unimpressed by the Reich Chamber of Music's attempt to ridicule hot music in their program—"From Cakewalk to Hot"—replete with criteria for identifying jazz. The program unwittingly won admirers for the new sounds and rhythms, attracting young listeners who had never gone to clandestine swing clubs. As early as 1938–39, jazz-swing music had already become a symbol of resistance for German adolescents who defied the Nazi regime's ban on "jewish-negro" music. In Hamburg the Swing Kids frequented the Café Bismarck and danced to the music of Count Basie, Duke Ellington, Louis Prima, Django Reinhardt, or Eddie Carroll.

Under Goebbels, the Ministry of Propaganda broadened its attack by linking the popular jazz culture to the emergence of new visual art forms. "Expressionism, Suprematism, Constructivism and Dadaism, as well as 'Nigger' music and modernist atonal composition, in short, 'the refuse of a rotting society' were banned. And the perceived source of it all, the jews, could begin to be barred from the life of the Reich."[25] Even more than an affront to the nation's moral standards, American hot jazz was a bitter reminder of the "shame of Versailles" between 1919 and 1925, when French colonial troops were the dominant force in the occupation of the Rhineland. And of course there was an exemplar of "the shame" in Krenek's popular opera *Jonny spielt auf.* Its central character was a sly, black American violinist whose music seduced a white woman.

Anti-Semitism and antiblack racism were intrinsic to German radio propaganda about the "rhythm of belly-dancing Negroes." It was below

German moral standards and aesthetically inferior to German culture. "While black people were supposed to revel naïvely in the perceived erotic ingredient of jazz, Jews were alleged to exploit it as part of the systematic conspiracy to corrupt the 'Aryan' German culture through acts of 'musical race defilement.'"[26] By promoting hot jazz, and mainly that of black American and Jewish musicians, the Swing Kids of Hamburg were deemed to have committed acts of musical race defilement and were subject to arrest and harassment at the hands of the Gestapo. It was a pattern of oppression the Zazous experienced after the occupation of Paris.

By December 1941 these young people began appearing in cafés off the Champs-Élysées and in the Latin Quarter. Zazous' favorite cafés for rendezvous on the Left Bank were the Pam Pam, Dupont-Latin, Soufflot, Grand and Petit Cluny, near the Musée de Cluny on boulevard St-Michel. Off the Champs-Élysées, the small bars in streets adjacent to the grand boulevard, like the Colisée, were favorite places for gathering and planning "surprise parties." Clandestine "surprise parties" created social space in which Zazous could chat, drink, eat, listen to jazz, and above all dance the jitterbug. After-dark gatherings gave Zazous a stage on which to practice their "Je suis swing" impromptu public performances, which staid citizens often preferred to label public nuisances. In the metro one might see a young man or woman board a car, raise a finger in the air and say or cry "Swing" and take a hop, before shouting "Zazou, hé hé hé, za za zou." Then three slaps on the hip, two shrugs of the shoulder, one turn of the head. Finished!

Zazous' public antics were replete with costumes inspired in part by the American "zoot-suit" craze from the barrios of southern California cities.[27] The allure, the costumes, the hairstyles, the makeup, were unmistakably Zazou. Young men wore very large pleated pants, very short, raised to expose colorful socks and the tops of shoes with three soles. Their long sheep-lined jackets with back-belts were fitted with numerous pockets. Each high shirt collar was closed by a narrow tie knotted as tightly as possible. The young Zazou women wore short skirts, large coats (or, in winter, shabby furs), enormous wooden platform shoes, and carried large purselike sacs of fur. Both men and women had multiple accessories like the "Chamberlain" umbrella (Neville Chamberlain's sartorial elegance was in vogue across the Channel) and dark glasses with big lenses. They wore their heavily brilliantined hair high in front and long in the back, curly for male Zazous and straight for female, who also went bareheaded to show off the single lock of a different hue. Young women wore heavy makeup. The Zazous used English expressions, read American literature, and delighted in crooning in the style of Johnny Hess.

The Zazou vogue was a short-lived phenomenon that served the time. Writing in her *Paris Journal* of 21 February 1945, Janet Flanner observed:

> Nothing is left of the proletariat male and female Zazous . . . who had their own special resistance sartorial getup—nothing, that is, except the long, crooked-handled umbrella which all French women now carry, rain or shine. That was only a part of the strange chic of the female Zazous, along with no hat, an artful, absolutely terrific pompadour, a strict tailored suit with a full skirt for bicycling, and hanging from the neck, the inevitable cross. It was not a de Gaulle Lorraine cross; it was a Christian cross. Second-hand shops are now full of them and nobody can explain what they signified. Male Zazous were like the long-coated zoot-suiters except for their pantaloons, which were skintight; no one can explain that either.[28]

"Je suis swing," the jitterbug, and the swing music Zazous adopted as their raison d'être were an affront to the moral values that the New Order attempted to instill in citizens of occupied Paris. (In Vichy, which shrouded its youth in French nationalism sympathetic to Nazi values, Johnny Hess's chant also offended the *révolution nationale*.) At authorized "dance schools," a piano or phonograph was permitted but no orchestra, and the maximum number of couples per session was fifteen. Attempts by the prefect of police to regulate dancing seemed only to encourage flouting the ban on "le bal." Scandals in Paris associated with the Zazous' *bals clandestins* flourished. "In the countryside, the Jeunesse Agricole Chrétienne reported in 1943 that dancing was going on in almost every canton of the Rhone. Not only in isolated barns and remote houses, but even in the small towns. In Paris students danced in bars off the Boul Mich and *la jeunesse dorée* in more sleazy establishments near the Étoile. Dancing, jazz, and outlandish dress became marks of a veritable counter-culture of youth, which differed from that of the Resistance because it was effete, but nevertheless anti-killjoy, anti-prudish, and, in the final analysis, pro-Allied."[29]

In the middle of 1941, the anti-Zazou campaign began to appear in the collaborationist press, and articles against Zazous and swing increased from nine in 1941 to seventy-eight in 1942. By then the association between Zazous and Jews had begun to take on a particularly unflattering profile. Jean Geslin, a frequent contributor to the collaborationist journal *Jeunesse*, peppered his caustic words with images that conveyed the anti-Semitic and racist sentiments of Parisians opposed to the Zazou phenomenon: one attack compared Zazous to the perpetual flowering of unwelcome weeds on the boulevard St-Michel; another charged Zazous and their parents with black market activities—a charge that French citizens believed, in light of the money Zazous spent on costumes and in cafés.[30] Like other collaborationist writers, Geslin argued that jazz was a degenerate, racially impure form of enjoyment. And—even as the collaborationists feared—Zazou refrains about being *swing* "came to symbolize the vitality of resistance in the face of the Vichy moral order . . . denouncing jazz became a sign of toeing the Vichy line, wearing enjoyment on your sleeve—literally the case of the zazous—became a way of publicly opposing Vichy authority."[31] By the end of 1940, the reason for the Vichy powers' objections to Zazous and clandestine jazz-swing parties became clear: French youth were dancing instead of collaborating.

The anti-Zazou attacks in the press overlapped the 29 May 1942 ordinance requiring all Jews in the occupied zone to wear the yellow Star of David. Many non-Jews abhorred the decree and themselves wore a star on which they wrote such slogans as BOUDDHISTE, GOÏ, or VICTOIRE. Many Zazous exhibited their disdain for the ordinance by wearing a star on which they wrote SWING. Nazi action against this affront to the ordinance was swift. Henri Amouroux vividly describes the fate of a young woman, in the company of her Jewish companion passing before the Dupont-Latin café on 6 June 1942, seven days after the ordinance was imposed. The police stopped the couple and demanded their identity card and their food ration card. They asked Alice Courouble, who wore a yellow star, if she was a Jew. When she refused to answer, they took her to the commissariat. There she explained that she wore the star in sympathy for her friend Suzanne.[32]

Alerted to the growing anti-star movement, Obersturmführer Dannecker, the head of Jewish Affairs in the occupied zone, implemented immediate countermeasures against all "friends of Jews." Announcements of their arrests were made in the press and on the radio, and several individuals were sent to the internment camp at Drancy. On 14 June 1942, two weeks after the ordinance was decreed, squads of "bully boys" were ordered to raid the Zazous' favorite places for rendezvous in the Latin Quarter and the Champs-Élysées. Bully boys cropped the hair of any Zazous they could find; the police joined in the hunt. La Jeunesse Populaire Française, a French version of the Hitler Youth, appealed for volunteer barbers to shave the Zazous. So outraged at the association of Zazous and Jews was *Au Pilori,* a leading collaborationist journal, that in its 9 July 1942 edition it editorialized that Zazous who wore the yellow star should be sent to the camps of Jews. In fewer than five days, the article declared, these individuals would get over their compassion for Jews.[33] The editorial was not merely hysterical rhetoric: a certain number of non-Jews who wore the Jewish star, imitated the insignia, or otherwise manifested their sympathy for Judaism were in fact sent to camps.[34]

In the midst of the anti-Zazou campaign, battle lines in a war of swing were drawn in Montmartre, the *quartier chaud.* Cabarets vied with one another by advertising the hottest swing in Montmartre, as in the era when black jazz was in vogue and nightclubs used barkers to cry their wares of good swing. In May 1942 Chez Eve in place Pigalle, a cabaret featuring nude shows and catering to Germans who liked swing, had *Pariser Zeitung's* approval for its latest feature, *Eve . . . zazou, zazou.* Le Grand Jeu, at 58 rue Pigalle, advertised a "tout swing" show for the very particular clientele of French *gestapistes* who were like their German counterparts. Soon to join the swing war, L'Étincelle, 9 rue Mansart, announced its reopening with the revue of the year—*Le swing de l'amour.* And October witnessed the Robinson-Moulin Rouge launch of publicity for the revue *Femmes et rythmes* in two hot acts and swing.[35]

For German soldiers, Gestapo, and French collaborators alike Montmartre offered make-believe fantasies; an escape via swing from the realities of the Axis powers' declining fortunes. The quarter had served a similar function during the phony war for Parisians who flocked to la Butte to hear the final jazz notes from black American musicians before the Germans' arrival.

But the Zazous never understood jazz before the occupation, in part because many were too young to appreciate the hot sounds emanating from Harlem in Montmartre in the 1920s and 1930s. They earned a rebuke from Charles Delaunay at the Hot Club of France, who tried at great personal risk from the Gestapo to promote the connoisseurs of jazz. The club distinguished between the Zazous and lovers of jazz. As one critic said, "the zazous had not been the amateurs of jazz, the connoisseurs, but they had been amateurs of rhythm."[36] Their outlandish dress and wild rhythm expressed through dancing to swing, later provided context for music hall and theater performances with Zazou themes. As late as February 1944 Yves Montand appeared as a Zazou in a musical, and at the Théâtre Édouard-VII the young celebrity Jean Marais played in a production of Racine's *Andromaque* that dramatized the epoch of Zazou. On 10 June 1944 the collaborationist journal *Francisque* praised the "courageous secret police" for intervening to close the production that, in their view, depicted depraved and shameless little Zazous.[37] Perhaps the journal was trying to counter the shock wave that had spread through Nazi occupying forces as word of defeat on other war fronts reached Paris, but praise for the police was badly timed. It came four days after the Allied invasion of Normandy.

When Allied troops advanced to within a few miles of Paris, Zazous began to gather in their favorite cafés along the boulevard St-Michel and the Champs-Élysées. Now ignoring Nazi bully boys, some female Zazous darkened their faces as French women had done over a decade before, to celebrate Siki's victory over Georges Carpentier. In their final gesture of defiance to the Nazi occupation, they looked like actors in extravagant dress rehearsal for a grand finale, like clusters of Bojangles Robinsons ready to usher in the approaching Allied liberators. But their strut was unlike Bojangles's. Zazous entered history jitterbugging all the way.

Louis Armstrong's gravelly voice symbolized as much Paris liberated as General Charles de Gaulle's victory parade down the Champs-Élysées. On 25 August 1944 General Dietrich von Cholitz had just signed the act of capitulation of German forces occupying Paris (though France would not be completely liberated until 8 May 1945). And on that day in August 1944 black American soldiers—having fought German forces a second time in thirty years in order to rekindle the dimmed lights of the city of Paris—stood poised, ready to relish marching in de Gaulle's victory parade. Twenty-six years and seven months earlier, General Pershing had denied permission for the 15th New York Heavy Foot Infantry Regiment, the Harlem Hellfighters, to march in the American Expeditionary Force's victory parade past the Arc de Triomphe and down Paris's most famous boulevard. A second generation of black soldiers had landed at Normandy Beach, seen fierce fighting at St-Malo, and flushed out German troops in villages along the way as they marched toward Paris. Perhaps few of them knew the Hellfighters' history of valor on the battlefields of the Meuse and Argonne, gaining the collective citation of the croix de guerre. And perhaps fewer still of the many thousand Parisians wildly cheering the parade of American soldiers connected the black GIs marching in that parade with jazz in Paris.

The presence of black American soldiers in this historic event would have been unrecorded except for the reports of African American war correspondents on assignments for the Negro press. Observing the parade, Ollie Stewart, correspondent for the *Baltimore Afro-American,* linked the liberation of Paris to the liberation of black American soldiers from the racism of America.[1] Among the grateful Parisians were many mothers who swarmed to thrust their babies in the faces of black soldiers to be kissed, a symbolic act of gratitude for making a safe world for their children. A generation before, mothers in Aix-les-Bains had presented their babies to be kissed by Harlem Hellfighters in James Reese Europe's band as they went off to join combat forces at the front. The euphoria of this recent moment recalled legends in African American folklore about discrimination-free France inspired by the Hellfighters and other black units who fought in the Great War. This generation of black GIs unwittingly became part of the legends when those with musical talent took part in the rebirth of jazz in liberated Paris.

Two days before de Gaulle's victory parade, the Hellfighters jazz trumpeter Arthur Briggs anticipated his own liberation from four years' internment in the Nazi camp at St-Denis. On the night of 24 August, German prison guards opened the camp gates and deserted. The next day the Swiss consul arrived and told the prisoners they were free but to remain in camp until arrangements could be made for transportation, which was to be provided two days later. That same night Nazi troops encircled the camp and bombarded it from a Tiger tank. In the panic that ensued, Briggs and a companion escaped, pushing a cart with their meager belongings five miles to their destination. After reunion with his wife, Briggs joined his old group of musicians and the Hot Club of France in a concert to celebrate the liberation of jazz.[2]

Flight and capture was the war camp tale related by the popular pianist Henry Crowder. His repatriation to the United States on the SS *Gripsholm* in April 1944, two months before the Normandy invasion, finally resolved the mystery of his disappearance from the Montmartre jazz scene before the occupation of Paris. His whereabouts had been unknown even to Nancy Cunard, the British shipping line heiress with whom he had had a turbulent thirteen-year romantic relationship that ended in 1935. Crowder stayed in Europe, keeping afloat with occasional jobs, avoiding the Montmartre jazz scene he had come to detest.[3] During his self-imposed exile, Crowder played in the band that accompanied Louis Douglas's ill-fated all-black revue that disbanded in Liège, Belgium. Some performers returned to Paris with Douglas; Louis Hardcastle and his Eight Black Streaks and the Harlem Truckers, who had introduced the dance called "trucking" in the revue, returned to London. The Four Harmony Kings and Crowder stayed in Brussels through several bookings. He was playing in Brussels when the Nazi invasion of Belgium began. Crowder fled toward Abbeville, where German forces overtook Allied armies before turning north toward Dunkerque and the coast. While waiting at Abbeville to board the "last train" to Paris, he hurried to a nearby café for a drink. In the few minutes of his absence, Nazi planes bombed and strafed the train and station, killing most of the passengers. Fortunate to escape unharmed, he made his way on foot back through German lines to Brussels, a journey of 125 miles, during which he lost thirty-five pounds and was arrested for questioning no less than fifty times. Crowder was taken into custody by military authorities in Brussels, put in an internment camp at Beverlo, Belgium, and later transferred to a camp at Tittmoning, Germany, where he was interned until repatriation.[4]

The SS *Gripsholm*'s crossing with repatriated internees was somber, unlike the voyage of the SS *St. John* in 1940, on which Leon Abbey had organized shipboard entertainment with some of his band members for the uprooted passengers. After the hardships Crowder and his fellow entertainers experienced in Nazi camps, they were too weary to express whatever gaiety they may have felt.

Doubtless Valaida Snow too had been exhausted when she returned to the United States on board the *Gripsholm* in 1943, after about three years in a Nazi internment camp in Denmark. She was a shadow of her former self; ill health had reduced her weight to sixty-eight pounds. Perhaps some other passengers remembered her as the flamboyant five-foot-tall trumpet star—one of the best known jazz women of the pre-swing era—and had seen her riding around Paris in an orchid-colored Mercedes Benz, dressed in an orchid suit, her pet monkey wearing an orchid jacket and cap, with the chauffeur in orchid as well. Like many other black American musicians and entertainers in Paris, Snow ignored warnings to leave and was appearing in the capital with Maurice Chevalier when the Nazis arrived.[5]

Music was not uppermost on the minds of many musicians on the 1944 crossing. The guitarist Johnny Mitchell had played in Baltimore with Joe Rochester and Ike Dixon before he went to France in 1925. He exchanged war camp stories with George Welch, the singer and pianist whose many years' residence in Paris had given him steady bookings in cabarets throughout Europe. Anticipating his return to a country he had not visited in a decade—where, according to the grapevine of gossip in Montmartre, racial relations were almost unchanged—Welch was ill-prepared, he said, to travel again to America's Deep South. The composer Maceo Jefferson, the band leader Freddy Johnson, and Evelyn Anderson, who first came to Paris as a dancer with Florence Mills and the *Blackbirds* review in 1926, all had similar stories to tell. Evelyn Hayman and her two daughters would soon be reunited with her husband, after his release from internment.

When the *Gripsholm* docked in New Jersey, nostalgia for prewar Montmartre's gut-bucket culture gripped these repatriated musicians and entertainers of *le tumulte noir*. The absence of Jim Crow behind the barbed wire had made internment in Nazi camps only slightly less painful: they all agreed, Nazi policy was impartial, serving equally meager and unwholesome daily rations to black and white internees alike and administering equally harsh punishment. Nostalgia for Harlem in Montmartre tugged at them again months later when the Negro press reported on a revival of jazz in Paris by the Hot Club of France. And Arthur Briggs was at the bandstand. The *Chicago Defender* headlined its account on 11 November 1944: "Paris Blossoms Again with Negro Music as the Theme."

Once jazz was liberated, Charles Delaunay's members-only "schools," which educated the younger generation in the prewar art of swing, could boast successful "graduates." Many of the pupils absorbed Benny Carter's style, which had become the predominating influence on alto saxophone players in Paris. It was the style he brought to Europe in 1935 when he began to advance the cause of jazz, and played and recorded with local musicians in France. After liberation, every would-be jazz saxophonist in Paris studied and modeled their playing on Benny Carter's idiom of execution. The saxophone became such an important instrument in postwar France that a professional chair for saxophone was established at the Conservatoire de Musique in Paris.

Just as it had captivated the prewar generation of jazz lovers, jazz-swing music now gripped young Parisians, who no longer felt obliged to carry the sociocultural baggage of the Zazous. Long-held images of prewar jam sessions that young people conjured up during the occupation's jazz-cold years became reality when the Hot Club of France staged a session at the École Normale de Musique in honor of Arthur Briggs, only recently released from prison camp. Jazz fans packed the auditorium to hear Django Reinhardt, André Ekyan, Hubert Rostaing, Robert Mavounzy, Robert Mommarche, and Maurice Mouflard. Allen Morrison, of the American army's military journal *Stars and Stripes,* joined the jam session, symbolizing the American role in shaping the jazz culture in Paris.[6] As if the first postliberation public jam session was a heavenly sign of a new era, French musicians in Montmartre nightclubs rearranged their repertoire of music to include the quarter's celebrated prewar rhythmic jazz beat.

As Paris swayed in rhythmic exuberance, black American GIs with musical talents took part in the rebirth of jazz in American Red Cross clubs set aside for "Negro soldiers."[7] The Potomac Club, near the Bastille, which black GIs nicknamed "the Rue de Poo," was the first club in postwar Paris to offer jazz sounds from black musicians. Spreading the music of liberation to Parisian jazz fans, the formerly all-white Left Bank Club became "Negro-staffed" for exclusive use of "Negro troops." Here nightly jam sessions joined by professional and amateur French musicians rekindled the interracial jazz scene characteristic of prewar nightclubs on both banks of the Seine.

But another Red Cross club, the Rainbow Corner, which occupied the Hôtel de Paris on the boulevard de la Madeleine from September 1944, enforced a "white GIs only" policy, except for the occasional billeting of a "colored officer," and referred black soldiers on leave elsewhere. The Rainbow Corner was on the edge of Montmartre, familiar to the previous generation of black American soldiers who had encountered very different treatment along the Champs-Élysées and the Madeleine.[8] Unwelcomed there, black officers and men confined their dancing and drinking to one or two cabarets in rue Fontaine, but these proved not to be the sanctuary from white racism they hoped for. Squads of military police barged in about midnight each night, raiding the cabarets, ostensibly looking for soldiers absent from base without permission. Mirroring the Nazis' treatment of young Zazous for dancing to swing music—and feeding on old stories of the "black horror on the Rhine"—military police harassed black GIs for fraternizing with French women.[9]

Yet the French people appreciated both the military and musical contribution of African Americans in the liberation of Paris. "Quietly and without fanfare," Roi Ottley wrote, "the American Negro is having a profound influence on war-torn Europe. . . . The Negro soldier has helped to reinforce this . . . in these moments of hardship, he has lifted his voice in song in the clubs and music halls to aid in alleviating the suffering of war-torn people."[10] For Hugues Panassié, director of the reborn Hot Club of France, it was jazz spread by black soldiers moving through towns and cities liberated from defeated German troops that alleviated much of his country's suffering.

In the first postwar issue of *Jazz-Hot,* Panassié described Marseille as the new jazz capital of France. The port city had thousands of black soldiers; hundreds of them were jazz musicians, and at least a dozen orchestras existed. In principle the popular *bals noirs* did not admit whites, and in any case it was not wise to enter without protection.[11] The revues staged by exceptionally talented dancers, singers, and comedians might well have taken place on the Harlem nightclub scene. Sunday morning jam sessions organized by Paul Mansi for the Hot Club of Marseille at the Salon Pélissier, in rue de la Plaine, attracted the best black musicians who joined the sessions more for pleasure than in response to the club's call to perform. Jazz was alive and well in Marseille.

The abundance of young talent that formed Marseille's black military musical groups was not always perfect but often outshone the excellent professional musicians recruited for Red Cross–sponsored entertainment. Some of these amateurs began their musical careers playing with such celebrated performers as Ida Cox, Harlan Lewis, Jay McShann, and Lionel Hampton. Eminent musicians in military orchestras included the trumpet player and singer William Morris and the saxophonist Eddie Williams, formerly with Jelly Roll Morton, whose technique was in the best tradition of Johnny Hodges; also among the best were pianist Roger Williams, and electric guitarist Leon Washington, a student of Charlie Christian. Of the dancers, "Sporty" Johnson modeled his dazzling tap-dance routine after the famous Jimmy Wall.

Marseille and the rest of France celebrated its liberation when Germany capitulated without condition to Allied forces on 8 May 1945. In the ensuing months Americans in military uniform slowly departed from the port city. Twenty-seven years after the last jazz notes sounded in the auditorium at Aix-les-Bains during the Great War, Marseille's Hot Club patrons rinsed their ears to capture the final musical notes of black American amateurs of jazz, after yet another tragic war.

# CODA

The era of Harlem in Montmartre had come to an end. Boarded windows and marred exteriors of buildings that once offered jazz until early morning hours greeted visitors to the nearly deserted streets of la Butte. During four years of neglect, shabbiness acquired its own patina. Nightclub proprietors no longer catered to well-dressed Parisians out for an evening's entertainment that had invariably included swinging to hot jazz played by black musicians, mainly American.

Writing from Paris five months after its liberation, Nancy Cunard observed a city gradually recovering the energy that had fueled the jazz world for two decades. When Harlem in Montmartre was in vogue, Cunard's long romantic affair with jazz pianist Henry Crowder had linked her to that world. For her, Crowder combined the spheres of black jazz and black Americans, opening her vision and understanding of "Negroes," and their precarious status, as exemplified in the Scottsboro trial. Cunard's literary interests focused her concerns on the racial plight of black Americans, not on their music, songs, and dances. Her association with writers and poet friends like Louis Aragon, Sylvia Beach, Richard Aldington, and Walter Lowenfels gave her intellectual comfort. And if Cunard ever visited Montmartre after the liberation, perhaps it was only fleetingly, long enough to confirm, if need be, that everything had changed.

Unlike Harlem in Montmartre, Cunard's literary world of Left Bank cafés survived with remarkably little damage from the occupation. Reflecting on the postliberation café scene, she wrote,

> On the left bank the literary cafés the Deux Magots and the Flore are as full as ever. The latter, one hears, remained a perfect moral fortress against the Boches; the Germans hesitated to enter it. Today, it is a veritable center of intellectual productivity; Sartre sits there writing lengthily when in Paris; there is almost a School of the Café de Flore—that of the most activity of the numerous resistance groups. It is certainly an oasis in the desert of daily difficulties that have to be coped with: Food, transport, lack of time to do things. Despite all these difficulties of transport, of daily living and the hesitation with which one meets friends in the bar or café, where a few drinks can run to several hundred francs, PARIS IS PARIS.[1]

For two decades, cultural ties of music and the literary and expressive arts held together two black communities on opposite sides of the Atlantic. Black Broadway in black Paris drew almost exclusively on the music and entertainment talent of itinerant African Americans from Harlem and other Bronzevilles. Yet the Americans' popularity and success in Parisian nightclubs was also, in part, their failure. Stephen Mougin, the sometimes firebrand music critic and talented pianist, decried the shallow "Negrophilia" that fostered racial posturing over good music in the jazz nightclubs in Montmartre and Montparnasse between the wars.

> One aspect of France's adoption of jazz caused some awkwardness: a postwar wave of Negrophilia swept intellectual and artistic circles with stereotypes about jazz and race. Negritude was in fashion, a foreign echo of the Harlem scene between the wars. Black American veterans and musicians were happy to perform in Paris, enjoying an enhanced social status. Most of them did not expatriate to France nor did they become recognized jazz artists in following years and some French musicians felt that they played poorly. . . . Still, for a group of as yet unproven French jazzmen, the tendency of club owners to present only black American jazzmen spelled trouble.[2]

And "trouble" was the 10 percent law. It, combined with the depression, dampened Harlem in Montmartre's once vibrant jazz-based economy. With the abundance of musical talent coming from America's Bronzevilles, Montmartre was unable to absorb this overflow of entertainers into a shrinking nightclub economy that had reached saturation even before the Great Depression.

Under the banner of the Harlem Renaissance, Charles Johnson and Alain Locke rallied black Manhattan's musicians to the cause of economic, social, and cultural equality with white Americans. They perceived arts in general to be a crack in racism. Artists, writers, musicians, and entertainers came from all parts of the country, having accepted the credo of Alain Locke's *New Negro*. On the role of music in the new movement, one writer observed that "the Harlem Renaissance used and was supported and accompanied by music. The music of the black theater shows, the dance music of the cabarets, the blues and ragtime of the speakeasies and the rent parties, the spirituals and the art songs of the recital and concert halls all created an ambiance for Renaissance activity and contemplation."[3] But renaissance cultural ambience that was so evident when Harlem was in vogue failed to replicate itself in black Paris. The base of artistic creativity in Montmartre was dance music and cabarets, but little else. Thus the banner of the Harlem Renaissance fluttered feebly.

We can only estimate the size of the African American population in Paris at any time between the Great Wars. The black community was small, constantly in flux, and perhaps never exceeded a few hundred individuals in the mid-1920s. Instilled with a sense of adventure mixed with uncertainty about the future, they were mainly itinerant unmarried men in their twenties; if they had families, their wives and children usually remained home. Negro churches, a pillar of Bronzevilles everywhere, were never established in Paris; choirs and spirituals were not features of the musical scene. In the absence of family, the musicians' social life away from the bandstand centered on Chez Boudon, Chez Liseux, or the Flea Pit, and the interminable crap games in Montmartre that Henry Crowder came to despise.

In an apparent effort to maintain ties with other black American children in Paris and their peers in America, Florence Richardson, wife of the banjo player and guitarist Sammy Richardson and mother of two children, set up a Bud Billiken chapter. Named after a mythical godfather of black children, the club sponsored cultural and educational activities that were a unifying social force in Chicago, where the club was founded. Promoted by the *Chicago Defender,* Billiken chapters were established worldwide. Among the twelve children in Paris eligible to join were the daughters of Eugene Bullard, Jacqueline and Lolita.[4] With the folding of Lew Leslie's *Blackbirds* review, many dancers and singers chose to join other productions on the Parisian nightclub circuit, thus increasing the number of black female entertainers in the city; some of the women were married, with children.

To critics of Harlem in Montmartre, the jazz scene exhibited a stereotype that renaissance leaders hoped to eliminate from the image of the new Negro. Robert Abbott and George Schuyler, among other black American civic leaders, held to their view that jazz and the culture that developed round this musical form were but a short distance away from minstrels and cooning. Even popular stage performers joined the chorus, criticizing the scandalous public behavior identified with black representatives of the jazz culture. Newcomers, in hope of making their theatrical mark in Paris, were warned that personality ranked higher than talent in the pursuit of fame in Europe.[5]

Race and color were not enough to create common ground for the various elements of the renaissance movement. Exponents of black literature and expressive arts, on one side, and those of black American jazz, on the other, held their work to be separate and unequal. Black writers of the era resisted the acceptance of jazz. It was not considered the kind of cultural achievement of the race that ought to be mentioned or recommended. Thus "the *Journal of Negro History,* from its inception in 1916 through the issues of 1946, did not publish a single article on jazz or a single review of a book on jazz."[6] And W. E. B. Du Bois ignored jazz in his one-paragraph discussion of American music in *Black Folks Then and Now.*

Langston Hughes's poem "Jazz Band in a Parisian Cabaret" and his body of blues poems, as well as Archibald Motley's painting depicting a jazz scene in a Harlem cabaret, are among the few creative works by Harlem Renaissance writers and artists based on the jazz idiom.[7] Early in their careers both Hughes and Motley had spent time in Paris and rejected the black majority's view of jazz as debasing and harmful to racial advancement ("advancement" toward the white standard in all realms). Harlem in Montmartre—Hughes and Motley argued—enabled black American writers and artists to ignore their own country's race-bound status hierarchy and work on their own, apart from jazz musicians. And in France, jazz music and the dances that accompanied it did not connote immorality and low social status.

The environment of jazz in Montmartre clubs like the Flea Pit did give musicians who had trained in classical music the chance to carry on their studies as they developed a popular musical genre. Toward the end of 1924—at about the same time that Eugene Bullard took over management of Le Grand Duc, and Florence Jones was the nightly attraction— Edmund Thornton Jenkins was living in Paris and working on the libretto for a musical play, which he hoped to get presented at a Paris theater. In Europe he would get his chance to compose classical music, he wrote to his father. Five months later, Jenkins was directing a jazz band of black musicians in Paris called the International Seven. Their nightclub engagements kept resources flowing to support Jenkins's classical music pursuits, which led to the writing of several works, including operettas and dance numbers.[8]

Likewise Creighton Thompson, who came to Paris as a drummer with Elliott Carpenter's Red Devils in 1920 and later deserted jazz music for the concert stage as a classical tenor. The pianist Spencer Williams studied composition and improved his study in Europe. The band leader and violinist Leon Abbey maintained his popularity and demand for bookings in the most famous Parisian nightclubs; he began his career playing light and classical music. Harry Wellman, bandmaster, marvel on the drums, composer, master of syncopation and opera, arrived in Europe in 1909, with bookings in all the large houses in the British Isles. Eventually, his travels took him to Bombay, India, where he conducted the all-white Maurice Bandman Opera company. As a composer he wrote the hit songs "Pearl, My Girl" and "Lindy Lou" and recorded on the Columbia label.

Harlem in Montmartre rightly claimed the title Black Broadway in Black Paris when the Harlem Renaissance was in its most creative phase. And, like most black American musicians in the Parisian community, writers and artists identified with the Harlem Renaissance were single. They made relatively short visits to Paris for study and cultural enlightenment early in their careers. Among the black artists, only Henry Ossawa Tanner had exiled himself to France in 1891. Only there, he was convinced, the color of his skin would not keep him from getting full recognition for his work as an artist. His prediction was accurate. At the peak of his career, with paintings hung at the Musée du Luxembourg, Tanner received the Legion of Honor.

The writer Countee Cullen—whom Michel Fabre calls "the Greatest Francophile"—and other major black American literary figures and artists of the Harlem Renaissance had scholarships to help support them during their short stays in Paris (Cullen was a Guggenheim fellow in 1928). Harold Jackman, a Harlem-based supporter of black writers and artists, often aided struggling black students in Paris with personal loans and gifts. Their sojourns in the City of Light came to a close in 1939, when war clouds gathered over Parisian skies.

Of those individuals whose musical prominence shaped *le tumulte noir* and kept jazz alive during the dark days of the depression, few, it appears, are alive today. Hugues Panassié, whose writings made jazz known and respected in Paris and who was responsible for many of the early jazz recordings in the prewar years in France, died on 8 December 1974. Arthur Briggs died in 1991. Stéphane Grappelli, the jazz violinist who cofounded with Django Reinhardt the Quintet of the Hot Club of France, died on 1 December 1997.

And everything is changed.

## JE SUIS SWING

*Johnny Hess and M. Vandair (1938)*

Negro music and jazz are already old machines
now, to be "in the note," one must have swing.
Swing is not a melody
swing is not a malady
but as soon as you have gotten a taste for it,
It grabs you and doesn't let you go.

I am swing, oh!
I am swing,
zazouzazouzazouzazou hé!
I am swing, oh!
I am swing.
It's crazy! It's crazy how it makes me tipsy!

When I sing a song of love
I spice it with a lot of little thingumajigs around.
I am swing,
I am swing.
Zazou, zazou, it's nice as can be!

I was going to sing an opera, so I went to see the Director.
I wanted to sing Traviata in D Major.
First he asked me some questions:
"Are you a light tenor, singing bass or baritone?"
I answered: "Ah! not at all!"

I am swing, oh,
I am swing,
zazouzazouzazouzazou hé!
I am swing, oh.
I am swing.
It's crazy, it's crazy how it makes me tipsy!

When I sing a little tune
I frighten the *concierge* and the neighbors.
I am swing,
I am swing,
zazou zazou, I'm happy as can be!

I have a mistress named Beatrice, I am the father of her child,
with Simone, I've had two sons in no time,
and last month, with Zouzou,
I had four children at one go!
It's not that I do it on purpose, but what can you do . . .

I am swing, oh!
I am swing,
zazouzazouzazouzazou hé!
I am swing, oh!
I am swing.
It's crazy, it's crazy how it makes me tipsy.

A spirit revealed it to me:
It is the rhythm that makes you go wild.
I am swing, oh!
I am swing,
zazou, zazou, I'm having a wonderful time!

## ILS SONT ZAZOUS

*Johnny Hess and M. Martelier (1943)*

Hair in wild curls
eighteen-foot-high collar.
Ah! They are zazou!
A finger like that in the air
a jacket that drags on the ground.
Ah! They are zazou!

They wear pants of an outrageous cut
that reach a little above their knees
and, in rain or wind they have an umbrella,
large dark glasses, and there, that's all.
They look as if they are sick of it all,
these little crackpots.
Ah! They are zazou!

One day, a good old *notaire* fresh from his *province*
arrived (in Paris) for the big business of executing two testaments.
He looked very dignified but as the fashion of today
is about the same as of 1900,
two young zazous exclaimed when they saw him:

"How distinguished he looks
with his eighteen-foot collar!
Ah! How zazou he is,
this good old *notaire,* jacket dragging on the ground.
Ah! How zazou he is!"

He didn't realize, this very distinguished *notaire,*
that he was, to such an extent, zazou
for all his clothes had come down from his grandfather
the jacket collar and all the rest.
He was very surprised
to be noticed like that
by all the zazous.

Back home, the *notaire* flabbergasted all his friends.
He walked the finger in the air at first but soon it became worse.
This malady was caught by his daughter, his wife,
his clerk, his dog.
In a word the whole family, all of them became zazou.
In the town, when they took a walk, people thought they were crazy.

When they saw them pass by,
the good people exclaimed:
"Ho, Ho! there come the zazous!"
After long reflection
the doctor in consultation
declared: "They are zazous!"

It is a disease a little peculiar,
pretty soon all symptoms will disappear
with a good cure of Polka from our grandmothers.
Then, looking at himself, he said: "Ho, Ho!"

My hair all in wild curls,
my eighteen-foot-high collar.
But . . . But . . . I am zazou
just like the *notaire.*
My jacket drags on the ground
but, then, I am zazou!

And if it is but a question of clothing,
then I am the most zazou among us
for my frock coat drags all the way to the ground.
I must admit:
the doctor had understood
that there resided the spirit of all the zazous.

Zazou.

# NOTES

*1. Making Noise and Stomping Feet*

1. James Weldon Johnson, *Black Manhattan* (New York: Alfred A. Knopf, 1930), 147–48.

2. Ibid., 161.

3. Willie "The Lion" Smith, *Music on My Mind,* with George Hoefer (New York: Doubleday, 1964), 133.

4. Ibid., 75. On the shaping of the black musical tradition in Harlem, see Johnson, *Black Manhattan,* chs. 8–9.

5. Rainier E. Lotz, *Heisse Tanzmusik in Deutschland: Ein Fotoalbum* (Hot dance bands in Germany: A photo album) (Bonn: Jazzfreund-Publikation, 1986), 1:9: "Jarrett and Palmer's American Negro Company was probably the first to stage theatrical interpretations in Germany, in 1879; doubtless the group toured Europe." All translations of foreign languages are my own, unless specified otherwise.

6. Jacques-Charles, *La revue de ma vie* (Paris: Librairie Arthème Fayard, 1958), 118.

7. David Levering Lewis, *When Harlem Was in Vogue* (New York: Alfred A. Knopf, 1982), 32.

8. Robert Kimball and William Bolcom, *Reminiscing with Sissle and Blake* (New York: Viking Press, 1973), 63–64.

9. Len Gutteridge, "The First Man to Bring Jazz to Britain," *Melody Maker* 31 (1956): 6.

10. Robert Goffin, *Nouvelle histoire du jazz: du congo au be-bop* (Brussels: l'Écran du Monde, 1948), 62–63. Note that Goffin identifies Philadelphia as Mitchell's place of birth (60).

11.  Gutteridge, *Jazz to Britain,* 6.

12.  Berry Kernfeld, ed., *The New Grove Dictionary of Jazz* (New York: Macmillan, 1988), 1:114. Mitchell's biographical note states that "the Clef Club Orchestra [was] led by cellist Walter Kildare." But see Johnson, *Black Manhattan,* 123: in 1910, Europe organized the Clef Club and "systematized the whole business of 'entertaining' with black professional instrumental musicians."

13.  John Chilton, *Sidney Bechet: The Wizard of Jazz* (New York: Oxford University Press, 1987), 33.

14.  Eileen Southern, "Will Marion Cook," in *Readings in Black American Music,* ed. Eileen Southern, 2d ed. (New York: W. W. Norton, 1983), 227.

15.  Ibid., 34–35.

16.  Jean-Paul Crespelle, *La vie quotidienne à Montmartre au temps de Picasso, 1900–1910* (Paris: Hachette, 1978), 17.

17.  Ibid., 22.

18.  Ibid., 27–28.

19.  Ibid., 194. Le Chat Noir predated the assemblages of literary figures associated with La Closerie des Lilas, Café Floré, and Deux Magots on the Left Bank later in the century; 201, 206–8, 214. The Hôtel du Poirier was razed and the modern building that replaced it was destroyed by a gas explosion in 1934.

20.  Ibid., 134. Crespelle suggests that naval and colonial officers acquired the opium habit during campaigns in China and Indochina.

21.  Billy Klüver and Julie Martin, *Kiki's Paris: Artists and Lovers 1900–1930* (New York: Harry N. Abrams, 1989), 114.

22.  Jacques-Charles, *Revue,* 26.

23.  Lotz, *Heisse Tanzmusik,* 7, 35. In Great Britain the group was known as the Colored Masters; see Rainier E. Lotz, "The Black Troubadours: Black Entertainers in Europe, 1896–1915," *Black Music Research Journal* 10, no. 2 (fall 1990): 253–67.

24.  Jacques-Charles, *Revue,* 19. It is doubtful that the cakewalk was launched in Paris by "M. et Mme Elkes" at the Nouveau Cirque, as Jacques-Charles claims. The dance step had its origins in Negro minstrelsy in the early 1880s (see Southern, ed., *Readings in Black American Music,* 227–33).

25.  Ibid., 67.

26.  Rainier E. Lotz, "Black Diamonds Are Forever: A Glimpse of the Prehistory of Jazz in Europe," *The Black Perspective in Music* 12, no. 2 (fall 1984): 217–34.

27.  Lotz, *Heisse Tanzmusik,* 83, 87. For a biographical portrait of Arabella Fields, including a chronology of her European performances and a discography, see Rainier E. Lotz, *Black People: Entertainers of African Descent in Europe and Germany* (Bonn: Lotz, 1997), 225–45.

28.  Lotz, *Heisse Tanzmusik,* 71.

29.  Ibid., 51, 75. See Henry T. Sampson, *Blacks in Blackface* (Metuchen, New Jersey:

Scarecrow Press, 1980) for a comprehensive review of early black musical shows and entertainers who, after lengthy tours abroad, settled in Europe; see also the gross caricatures illustrating "Neger Clowns" (14, 31) and the "Cake Walk" (44).

30. Samuel B. Charters, *Jelly Roll Morton's Last Night at the Jungle Inn* (New York: Marion Boyard, 1984), 77. On the offensive character of the "coon song," Margaret Just Butcher described it as "a relic of the worst minstrel days: slapstick farces about 'razors, chickens, watermelons, ham-bones, flannel shirts, and camp-meetings'. . . . The appeal was not what was said but in the rhythm and swing" (*The Negro in American Culture* [New York: Alfred A. Knopf, 1966], 64).

31. Kernfeld, ed., *New Grove Dictionary,* 304. See also Lotz, *Black People,* for a comprehensive biographical review and chronology of Louis Douglas's European performances, including musicals he directed.

32. W. E. B. Du Bois, "The American Negro in Paris," *The American Monthly Review* 22 (1900): 576.

33. The most comprehensive study of black writers of the Harlem Renaissance in Paris is Michel Fabre, *From Harlem to Paris: Black American Writers in France, 1840–1980* (Urbana: University of Illinois Press, 1991).


*2. Jazz from the Trenches*

1. W. E. B. Du Bois, editorial in *The Crisis* 10 (1917): 10 (hereafter cited as *The Crisis*). Reprinted in Julius Lester, ed., *The Seventh Son: The Thoughts and Writings of W. E. B. Du Bois,* 2 vols. (New York: Random House, 1971).

2. Du Bois, *The Crisis* 16 (1918): 60, 164–65.

3. In World War II, black soldiers adopted—and the black press promoted—the "double V" symbol to signify their fight for victory on two fronts.

4. Reid Badger, *A Life in Ragtime: A Biography of James Reese Europe* (Oxford: Oxford University Press, 1995), 141.

5. Arthur W. Little, *From Harlem to the Rhine, The Story of New York's Colored Volunteers* (New York: Covici, Friede, 1936), 12. Little's history of the making of the 15th Infantry Regiment, from the first enlistees to successful campaigns in France, is the standard work on the Hellfighters.

6. Badger, *Ragtime,* 89.

7. "The Negro's Contribution to the Music of America," *The Craftsmen,* February 1913; cited in Alan Schoener, ed., *Harlem on My Mind: Cultural Capital of Black America, 1900–1968* (New York: Random House, 1968), 26–27.

8. Ibid., 132–33.

9. Samuel B. Charters and Leonard Kunstadt, *Jazz: A History of the New York Scene* (New York: Da Capo, 1981), 65.

10. Little, *Harlem to the Rhine,* 120, 122. Reid's nickname may refer to the fortune he made from the manufacture of tin plates supplied to soldiers in their mess kits.

11. Badger, *Ragtime*, 145.

12. Charters and Kunstadt, *Jazz*, 65.

13. Recalling the denial of his petition for permission of the 15th "to make that final farewell parade to little old New York with the 27th Division . . . , Colonel Hayward said 'I felt wounded. I felt bitter. . . . I don't remember whether I actually cried or not, but I know that I wanted to cry'" (Little, *Harlem to the Rhine*, 124).

14. Ibid., 49–50. Mayor Floyd's protest to the War Department over posting black soldiers in Spartanburg was first published in the *New York Times*, 31 August 1917.

15. Emmet J. Scott, *Official History of the American Negro in the World War* (Washington, D.C., 1919), 304.

16. Ibid.

17. Ibid., 305.

18. Charters and Kunstadt, *Jazz*, 68.

19. André Kaspi, "Le temps des américains: premier concours américain à la France en 1917–1918" (Université de Paris I—Panthéon-Sorbonne, Paris, 1976), 185.

20. Charters and Kunstadt, *Jazz*, 68. Little has been written about the several other army bands attached to black American units who served in France; the most noted of them was the 350th Field Artillery Band led by Lieutenant J. Tim Brymm of Philadelphia, Europe's old Clef Club rival. Brymm's band of seventy soloists, nicknamed the Seventy Black Devils, was described as a military symphony engaged in a battle of jazz.

21. Little, *Harlem to the Rhine*, 127.

22. Ibid., 138, 141.

23. Ibid., 143.

24. Scott, *Official History*, 303.

25. "The Black Man in the Revolution of 1914–1918," *The Crisis* (1919): 132.

26. Ibid.

27. Little, *Harlem to the Rhine*, 359.

28. "New York and Environs Turn Out to Give Hayward's 'Hell Fighters' Welcome," *New York Times*, 18 February 1919; "Fifth Avenue Cheers Negro Veterans," *New York Age*, 22 February 1919.

29. Martha Gruening and W. E. B. Du Bois carried out a special investigation of the riot for the NAACP. A condensed version of the report appears in the September 1917 issue of *The Crisis*.

30. Little, *Harlem to the Rhine*, 49.

31. *The Crisis* (1919): 132. Colonel Hayward's transfer of officers hampered Europe's efforts to organize the band (as the colonel had ordered him to).

32. William N. Colson, "An Analysis of Negro Patriotism," *The Messenger* 2, no. 8 (August 1919): 25.

33. Lewis, *Harlem in Vogue*, 15. See also Kenneth R. Janken, *Rayford W. Logan and the*

*Dilemma of the African-American Intellectual* (Amherst: University of Massachusetts Press, 1993).

34. *Baltimore Afro-American,* 25 March 1944.

35. P. J. Carisella and James W. Ryan, *The Black Swallow of Death* (Boston: Marlbourgh House, 1972), 58.

36. See Will Irwin's interview with Bullard, "Voice of Her Fallen Hero Wounded at Battle of Verdun," *The Saturday Evening Post,* 15 July 1916, 12–13.

37. Bullard's other decorations included the Chevalier of the French Legion of Honor, Croix de la France Libre, Médaille Militaire, Cross of the French Flying Corps, Croix de Combatants, Médaille Inter-Alliée, Médaille L'Étoile Rouge and Médaille de la Victoire. See Carisella and Ryan, *Black Swallow;* James Norman Hall and Charles Bernard Nordhoff, eds., *The Lafayette Flying Corps,* 2 vols. (Boston: Houghton Mifflin, 1920), 1:151. See also *San Francisco Chronicle,* 11 October 1992.

Given Bullard's popularity in the black community of Montmartre, he may have met Bessie Coleman, an African American aviatrix from Chicago, if she visited Paris during her training in France. At age twenty-four, Coleman completed a ten-month course of instruction in aviation at the Condrau School of Aviation in Du Crotoy, France (at the time, apparently the only other nonwhite American woman to earn her flying credentials was a Chinese American). She died in a plane crash while performing stunt flying acrobatics, a daring skill for which she was well known in barnstorming and flying circuses (see *Chicago Defender,* 1 October 1921).


*3. Le Jazz-Hot: The Roaring Twenties*

1. Jean-Marie de Busscher, "À l'ombre des monuments aux morts," in *Entre deux guerres: la création française entre 1919 et 1939,* ed. Olivier Barrot and Pascal Ory (Paris: Éditions François Bourin, 1990), 20.

2. Michelle Pierre, "Le journal de Mickey," in ibid., 119.

3. Edward Behr, *The Good Frenchman* (New York: Villard Books, 1993), 110. The "young French chorus girl" was Arletty, who became a celebrated actor during the interwar years; after the occupation, she and many other French actors faced charges of collaboration with the Germans. On the controversy see Patrick Marsh, "The Theatre: Compromise or Collaboration," in *Collaboration in France: Politics and Culture During the Nazi Occupation, 1940–1944,* ed. Gerhard Hirschfeld and Patrick Marsh (Oxford: Berg, 1989).

4. Francis Carco, *De Montmartre au quartier latin* (Paris: Albin Michel, 1927), 157.

5. Southern, "Will Marion Cook," 227.

6. Jeffrey P. Green, "*In Dahomey* in London in 1903," *The Black Perspective in Music* 2, no. 1 (spring 1983): 22–40; see also Johnson, *Black Manhattan,* 106, 121.

7. Johnson, *Black Manhattan,* 120.

8. Badger, *Ragtime,* 30.

9. Phyllis Rose, *Jazz Cleopatra: Josephine Baker in Her Time* (New York: Doubleday, 1989), 68.

10. Kernfeld, ed., *New Grove Dictionary*, 2:307. In some references the spelling for Benton (Benny) E. Peyton is Payton.

11. Sidney Bechet, *Treat It Gentle* (New York: Twayne, 1960), 129.

12. Kernfeld, ed., *New Grove Dictionary*, 1:244.

13. Chilton, *Sidney Bechet*, 36.

14. Robert Pernet, "Some Notes on Arthur Briggs," *Storyville*, no. 84 (1979): 204.

15. Ibid., 205. In Brussels the Bistroville Jazz Kings, founded in 1920, took their name from Louis Mitchell's Jazz Kings.

16. Carisella and Ryan, *Black Swallow*, 202.

17. The club was in rue Pigalle until 1926, in rue Blanche thereafter. "The original premises were closed in autumn 1926 but the club was in operation again by 1928 when the International Five played there" (Kernfeld, ed., *New Grove Dictionary*, 1:182).

18. In a photo of the Royal Box band, circa 1927, Bullard is shown seated at the drums in the orchestra of twenty-nine musicians (ibid., 1:184). See also Carisella and Ryan, *Black Swallow*, 205.

19. Lynn Haney, *Naked at the Feast: A Biography of Josephine Baker* (New York: Dodd, Mead, 1981), 116.

20. Bricktop [Ada Smith], *Bricktop,* with James Haskins (New York: Atheneum, 1983), 86.

21. Carisella and Ryan, *Black Swallow*, 212.

22. Bricktop, *Bricktop*, 86.

23. Rose, *Jazz Cleopatra*, 69.

24. Ibid., 72.

25. Bricktop, *Bricktop*, 86.

26. Ibid., 85.

27. Carisella and Ryan, *Black Swallow*, 213.

28. Bricktop, *Bricktop*, 94.

29. Carisella and Ryan, *Black Swallow*, 208.

30. Bricktop, *Bricktop*, 86, 107, 70. See also Paul Colin, *Le tumulte noir* (Paris: Éditions d'Art, Succès, 1929).

31. Johnson, *Black Manhattan*, 163.

32. Bechet, *Treat It Gentle*, 149.

33. *Pittsburgh Courier*, 27 July 1929.

34. Bricktop, *Bricktop*, 90, 127.

35. Jean-Claude Klein, "La revue nègre," in *Entre deux guerres*, ed. Barrot and Ory, 366.

36. Haney, *Naked at the Feast*, 45–46.

37. Kimball and Bolcom, *Reminiscing*, 128. Baker's salary was $30 per week.

38. Klein, "Revue nègre," 367 n. 3. The musicians—apart from Hopkins, Williams, and Bechet—were Henry Goodwin (trumpet), Daniel Doyle (trombone), Joe Hayman (alto sax), Ernest "Boss" Hill (bass), and Percy Johnson (drums). The dancers were Louis Douglas and Joe Alex.

39. Rose, *Jazz Cleopatra,* 97.

40. Haney, *Naked at the Feast,* 121; see also Tony Allan, *Paris: The Glamour Years 1919–1940* (New York: Bison Books, 1977), 7–11. Perhaps Baker modeled her persona on the Senegalese boxer Siki, who had created a stir strolling through Montmartre with his pet lion cub (mentioned in chapter 4).

41. Haney, *Naked at the Feast,* 125.

42. Chris Goddard, *Jazz Away From Home* (London: Paddington Press, 1979), 83.

43. Klein, "Revue nègre," 374.

44. Marcel Sauvage, *Les mémoires de Joséphine Baker* (Paris: Éditions Corréa, 1949), 193; he quotes Baker as saying that "the first cabaret called Chez Joséphine was in rue Pigalle" and that "Pepito set up the cabaret in rue Fontaine." See also Kernfeld, ed., *New Grove Dictionary,* 1:182.

45. Rose, *Jazz Cleopatra,* 111.

46. Haney, *Naked at the Feast,* 121–22, writes that Baker's financial backer was Pierre Loy, a medical doctor.

47. Josephine Baker and Jo Bouillon, *Joséphine* (Paris: Robert Laffont, 1976), 92.

48. Haney, *Naked at the Feast,* 112, 122.

49. "Siki's Victory Stirs Americans in France to Protest Equality," *Chicago Defender,* 7 October 1922.

50. "Paris Beauties Kink Their Hair in Siki Glory," *Chicago Defender,* 14 October 1922.

51. Janet Flanner, *Paris Was Yesterday, 1925–1939,* ed. Irving Drutman (New York: Viking, 1972), 182–83.

52. Jean-Paul Crespelle, *La vie quotidienne à Montparnasse à la grande époque, 1905–1930* (Paris: Hachette, 1976), 126–27; Jean-Paul Crespelle, *Montparnasse vivant* (Paris: Hachette, 1962). Le Dôme, opened as a café-tabac, was already in existence when La Rotonde opened, circa 1911. In this year President Poincaré inaugurated boulevard Raspail.

53. Wambly Bald, "Montparnasse Today," *Vanity Fair,* July 1932, 31, 58.

54. Klüver and Martin, *Kiki's Paris,* 11.

55. Robert McAlmon, *Being Geniuses Together: 1920–1930,* with Kay Boyle, rev. ed. (San Francisco: North Point Press, 1980), 92.

56. Sisley Huddleston, *Back to Montparnasse: Glimpses of Broadway in Bohemia* (Philadelphia: J. P. Lippincott, 1931), 139; Klüver and Martin, *Kiki's Paris,* 126–27, 154–55; Crespelle, *Montparnasse,* 241–42. See also descriptions of Le Jockey in André Warnod, *Fils de Montmartre* (Paris: Librairie Arthème Fayard, 1955).

57. Crespelle, *Vie quotidienne à Montparnasse,* 130. Irene West, a white American booking agent for several African American musical entertainers who performed in Paris and

Berlin during the 1930s, was also an occasional contributor to the *Baltimore Afro-American*. Her experience in Montmartre's "Lesbian Colony" was reported under the title "Paris Underworld the Worst," *Baltimore Afro-American*, 16 December 1944.

58. Frank C. Taylor, *Alberta Hunter: A Celebration in Blues*, with Gerald Cook (New York: Mc Graw-Hill, 1987), 89.

59. Ibid., 70. A similar anecdote in 1935 reportedly had Bricktop "swiping a message from a woman who had seen Alberta perform at Fred Payne's Bar in Paris and invited her to an engagement in Budapest. . . . Bricktop got off the train in Budapest . . . the woman understood what had happened . . . took one fierce look at the light-skinned, freckle-faced Bricktop and shouted, "you get on the next train and go back because you are not the nigger I sent for."

60. Ibid., 149.

61. Henry Crowder, *As Wonderful As All That? Henry Crowder's Memoir of His Affair with Nancy Cunard, 1928–1935* (Navarro, Calif.: Wild Tree Press, 1987), 55.

62. Kernfeld, ed., *New Grove Dictionary*, 2:481.

63. Crowder, *As Wonderful?*, 58.

64. Anne Chisholm, *Nancy Cunard* (New York: Alfred A. Knopf, 1979), 118.

65. Ibid., 127; Crowder, *As Wonderful?*, 74.

66. Bechet, *Treat It Gentle*, 153–54. Crowder writes that Bechet and McKendrick received sentences of fifteen months (Crowder, *As Wonderful?*, 80).

67. Louis Chevalier, *Montmartre, du plaisir et du crime* (Paris: Robert Laffont, 1980).

68. Chisholm, *Nancy Cunard*, 140.

69. Ibid., 149, 154. On Nancy Cunard's personal history of Hours Press, its publications, and the destruction wrought to La Chapelle-Réanville, which was requisitioned by Nazi troops during the occupation of Normandy, see *These Were the Hours: Memories of My Hours Press Réanville and Paris, 1928–1931*, ed. with a foreword by Hugh Ford (Carbondale: Southern Illinois University Press, 1969). Crowder's *Henry Music* is deposited in the Howard University Library.

70. Ibid., 154.

71. Crowder, *As Wonderful?*, 99.

72. I am unable to verify this statement in Edgar Wiggins's report in the *Chicago Defender*, 25 April 1936. Doubtless Mrs. Crowder was aware of rumors alleging that Crowder had taken on another "wife" (see Crowder, *As Wonderful?*, 193).

73. Claude Arnaud, "Autour du Bœuf sur le toit," in *Entre deux guerres*, ed. Barrot and Ory, 300; Maurice Sachs, *The Decade of Illusion: Paris 1918–1928*, trans. Gladys Matthews Sachs (New York: Alfred A. Knopf, 1935), 14.

74. Arnaud, "Autour du Bœuf," 289.

75. James Harding, *The Ox on the Roof* (New York: St. Martin's Press, 1972). Noting American music culture's influence on France in the decade of the 1920s, Paul Gagnon wrote that "the spectacle of the Jazz Age was not encouraging. Rather than building upon

and adding to her legacy of brave deeds and generous ideals, America seemed to be rejecting them in complacent enjoyment of a new jealously-guarded island of prosperity" (Paul A. Gagnon, "French Views of the Second American Revolution," *French Historical Studies* 2, no. 4 [fall 1962]: 430–49).

76. Harding, *The Ox,* 72.

77. Goddard, *Jazz Away,* 116.

78. Sachs, *Illusion,* 15.

79. Described in a Paris guidebook in 1925, quoted by McAlmon, *Being Geniuses,* 113.

80. Klüver and Martin, *Kiki's Paris,* 104.

81. Harding, *The Ox,* 84.

82. In 1928 Le Bœuf moved to rue de Panthièvre. One of its managers, Jacobi, moved to the United States and opened a nightclub (see Bricktop, *Bricktop,* 157.) During the peak of *le tumulte noir* in Montmartre, a larger Bœuf was opened at 66 rue Pigalle in November 1931. Six years later it moved to 43bis Avenue Pierre-1er-de-Serbie in July 1937. Since 1951 it has been at 34 rue du Colisée.

83. Allan, *Glamour Years,* 45.

84. Ralph Nevill, *Days and Nights in Montmartre and the Latin Quarter* (New York: George H. Doran, 1927), 14. The Clover Club was renamed Maurice's.

85. Basil Woon, *The Paris That's Not in the Guide Books* (New York: Brentano's, 1926), 174, 25.

86. Nevill, *Days and Nights,* 16.

87. Woon, *Paris That's Not,* 230. It is puzzling that Woon, a close observer of Paris nightlife, would report that the White Lyres played the first jazz ever heard in Paris. Even if the statement is qualified to read "heard publicly," it overlooks the tour by James Reese Europe's band in 1918.

88. Ibid., 231.

89. Jeffrey P. Green, *Edmund Thorton Jenkins: The Life and Times of an American Black Composer, 1894–1926* (Westport, Conn.: Greenwood Press, 1982). See also chapter 6.

90. Woon, *Paris That's Not,* 173–74.

91. Langston Hughes, *The Big Sea,* introduction by Arnold Rampersad (New York: Hill and Wang, 1933), 161–62.

92. This report on Bingham's giving expensive Charleston lessons to wealthy white Americans in Paris was excerpted from *Paris Soir,* between 1–7 October 1926, and reprinted in the *Pittsburgh Courier,* 9 October 1926.

93. Nevill, *Days and Nights,* 43.

94. Hughes, *Big Sea,* 161.

95. Julian Street, *Where Paris Dines* (New York: Doubleday, Doran, 1928), 142.

96. Nevill, *Days and Nights,* 42, 48. There is no record of Le Perroquet ever being located in the rue Blanche as Nevill states. Of the "two strident bands" Nevill mentions, "one of

them composed of negroes [who] play in turn," suggests a reference to Crickett Smith's Real Jazz Kings. See also Kernfeld, ed., *New Grove Dictionary,* 1:183.

97. Nevill, *Days and Nights,* 27.

98. Goddard, *Jazz Away,* 20.

99. Ibid., 123.

100. P. Darius, "Le chef du jazz," *Comedia,* 6 August 1926.

101. See the collection of articles on the jazz debate in the Bibliothèque de l'Arsenal, Paris (hereafter Arsenal) Ro 585.

102. *New York Herald–Paris,* 21 February 1924.

103. MacKinley Helm, *Angel Mo, and Her Son Roland Hayes* (Boston: Little Brown, 1942).

104. See "L'arrivée des Black-Birds," *Press Review,* 1 June 1929 (Arsenal RO 585).

105. The brief biography written by her husband, U. S. Thompson ("Florence Mills," in *Negro Anthology,* ed. Cunard), gives this age, but Sampson (*Blacks in Blackface,* 402) cites the age of eight for the Bijou Theatre engagement.

106. Aida Walker, who married George Walker, of the famous Williams and Walker comedy team, formed Black Patti Troubadours.

107. Sampson, *Blacks in Blackface,* 403.

108. Hugh Ford, ed., *The Left Bank Revisited: Selections from the* Paris Tribune *1917–1934* (University Park: Pennsylvania State University Press, 1972), 236–37.

109. For the theatrical and press reviews of *Blackbirds* in which several critics draw comparisons with *La Revue Nègre,* see Arsenal Microfiche no. 89/3256.

*4. Jim Crow:* Sans Domicile Fixe

1. Claude McKay, *A Long Way From Home* (1937; reprint, London: Pluto Press, 1985), 110, 227.

2. William N. Colson, "Propaganda and the American Negro Soldier," *The Messenger,* July 1919, 24–25. The author, who had been an officer in the all-black 367th Infantry, contributed to the journal several articles on black soldiers and their service in World War I.

3. Mercer Cook, "Booker T. Washington and the French," *Journal of Negro History* 40 (October 1955): 318; Booker T. Washington, "On the Paris Boulevards," *New York Age,* 13 July 1899.

4. Du Bois, *The Crisis* 18, no. 1 (April 1919): 7–9. The U.S. State Department refused Du Bois permission to hold the congress and intended to deny passports to his delegation; Britain too planned to deny passports to a delegation from British colonies. Prime Minister Clemenceau of France gave permission to hold the congress in Paris.

5. Allan, *Glamour Years,* 13.

6. See for example "Countee Cullen on French Courtesy," *The Crisis* 36, no. 6 (June 1929): 193. With respect to black and white relations, Cullen wrote, "a politeness of the French variety cannot conceivably exist in a section of the country where one group despises the other and merely grudgingly tolerates its continued existence."

7.  M. Cornnick, "France, America—Which Is Symbolic of Democracy?" *Chicago Defender,* 25 February 1922, pt. 2.

8.  "Britain Will Investigate Color Line," *Chicago Defender,* 7 September 1929.

9.  Robert S. Abbott, "My Trip Abroad: Paris," *Chicago Defender,* 9 November 1929. See also the comments of George S. Schuyler on this subject. After writing that "the only time I knew I was Colored in Europe was when I came into contact with certain types of white Americans," Schuyler went on to say that many black Americans "have abused their privileges, so that some public places, largely frequented by white Americans, have grown bold enough on occasion to say frankly that their patronage was not wanted. It is true that some of our boys have drunk like pigs, run wild and whipped French women, but . . . such are in the minority" ("Europe Gives Race Actors Better Chance Than U.S.," *Chicago Defender,* 30 December 1930).

10.  "Colored Frenchmen and American *Métèques*," *The Literary Digest,* 1 September 1923. *Métèque* is a contemptuous term applied to a foreigner. Several variations of the Kojo incident have been reported without specific date or place, making the prince's ejection a generic instance of racist phenomena. Though often referred to as a "prince," Tovalou Houénou was not an heir to the kingship.

11.  Abbott, "My Trip Abroad," 1 February 1930.

12.  Albert Guérard, "The Black Army of France," *Scribner's Magazine,* March 1925, 238.

13.  Claude McKay, "What Is and What Isn't," *The Crisis* 27, no. 6 (April 1924): 259.

14.  "U.S. Daily in Paris Stirs Race Strife," *Chicago Defender,* 14 August 1926. See also "Americans Take Hate to Paris," *Chicago Defender,* 11 August 1923.

15.  *Chicago Tribune,* 2 January 1923.

16.  Albert Curtis, "Court Ends 'Dirty Way' of Tribune," *Chicago Defender,* 16 June 1923. Bullard's version was printed in the *Paris Tribune* edition of 24 May 1923.

17.  "Mystery of Brutal Murder Is Solved by Confession of 18-Year-Old Suspect," *Chicago Defender,* 13 March 1926. See also Smith, *Music on My Mind,* 147.

18.  "France Chokes Klan Attempt at Lawlessness," *Chicago Defender,* 6 January 1923. In America nine months later, Valparaiso (Indiana) University was acquired by the Ku Klux Klan to teach "100% Americanism." For a description of the university's proposed curriculum and philosophy, see *The Literary Digest,* 15 September 1923, 42–46.

19.  Graham Smith, *When Jim Crow Met John Bull* (London: I. B. Tauris, 1987), 17.

20.  Lotz, "Black Diamonds Are Forever," 233. Norris Smith died on 25 December 1967 in Burnley, England, at age 85. On retirement his occupation was that of a railway guard.

21.  "Find U.S. Guests Incited Jim Crow," *Chicago Defender,* 12 May 1934.

22.  Letter from Cyclone Billy Warren, Dublin, Ireland, to Tony Lunnon, entertainment editor, *Chicago Defender,* 7 August 1920.

23.  Showbill reputed to have been circulated in what is apparently a fictitious London suburb, Springburn, for a night of entertainment at the New Kinema (*Chicago Defender,* 5 April 1930).

24.  McKay, *Long Way,* 304.

25. Robert Forrest Wilson, *Paris on Parade* (New York: Robert M. McBride, 1932), 287. Wilson writes that "shortly after Armistice the proprietor of a Montparnasse cabaret harkened to the American protest and threw out a party of colored men who entered the place. One . . . proved to be a prince of Dahomey . . . at any rate an official visitor to France." The French government closed the resort for one year. This account is distinct from the well-known incident in Montmartre involving Prince Kojo and described by McKay, "What Is," 259–63; and "Colored Frenchmen."

26. Ralph Matthews, "William Monroe Trotter," *Baltimore Afro-American,* 2 September 1944.

27. "French Citizens Appeal for Scottsboro Boys," *Chicago Defender,* 17 February 1934. Among the 35 signers of the appeal were Louis Aragon, Marcel Cohen, Georges David, Francis Jourdain, Henry Lefebre, and André Malraux.

28. Paul Morand, *Magie noire* (Paris: Ferenczi et Fils, 1936), 91.


*5. The Golden Age: The Thirties*

1. *New York Age,* 8 February 1919. The article went on to claim that "having fallen willing victims to the melody dispensed by race military bands the music-loving public in Paris is eager to hear a colored orchestra from the States."

2. *Chicago Defender,* 10 June 1922, page 7.

3. The 10 percent law was to be become effective in October. See "Jazz Players to Lose Paris Jobs," *Chicago Defender,* 22 July 1922, page 6.

4. Edgar Wiggins, stationed in Paris, reported regularly on African Americans in the entertainment world in France and especially in Paris, through his column "Montmartre," for the *Chicago Defender* from about 1933 to the German occupation of Paris. See his report "Where 'Smart Boys' Go to Learn How Dumb They Are," *Chicago Defender,* 14 October 1933.

5. Carter G. Woodson, " 'Chocolate Dandies' Give Paris an Eyeful," *Chicago Defender,* 21 October 1933. Woodson, the founder of the Society for the Study of Negro Life and History, was editor of the *Journal of Negro History.* Robert Abbott, editor, *Chicago Defender,* in his report of travel to Europe (9 November 1929), including several days in Paris, severely criticizes the behavior of black Americans.

6. This list suggests an approximate size for the African American entertainment community in Paris at the start of 1934 but omits all those entertainers who happened to be engaged elsewhere when Edgar Wiggins compiled it ("Paris Well Stocked with Ace Talent," *Chicago Defender,* 1 January 1934):

| | |
|---|---|
| Leon Abbey | Jimmy Bell |
| Freddy Allen | "Frisco" Bingham |
| Marino Barreto | Bricktop and mother, Mrs. Hattie Smith |
| Ruth Batcon | Arthur Briggs |

Theodore Brock

Panama Al Brown

Eugene Jacque[s] Bullard

Henri William Burns

Roy C. Butler

"Cherokee"

Louis Cole

Kid Cole[s]

Glover Compton

Sterling Conaway

Opal Cooper

Joe Cork

Charles Diggs

"Dinah"

Marion Douglas

"Eddie and Danny"

"Snow" Fisher

The Five Hot Shots

Herbert Flemming

William Frisby

Sidney Garner

"The Great Greek"

Alberta Hunter

Zadie Jackson

"The Jackson Brothers"

Ralph James

Maceo Jefferson

Freddy and Mrs. Johnson

Robert Lee Jones

Sadie Kincaid

Kent and Manya

Kentucky Singers

Art La Nier

George Latamore

Louis Legondt

Charles (Dizzy) Lewis

Joseph Lewis

Doris Colbert Marino

Nina Mae McKinney

Mike Meighly

Mergerson

George Mitchell

Jimmy Monroe

Frank Morgan

Joseph Nelson

Benny Payton

B. T. W. and Mrs. Pittman

Alfred and Mrs. Pratt

Herbert Robinson

Maude Rumford

Cle Saddles

Bob Scanlon

Neeka Shaw and Family

Norris Smith

Fred Taylor

Creighton and Mrs. Thompson

Kid Tunero

"Vensey and Payton"

Seth Weeks

Elizabeth Welch

Henry and Mrs. Wessels

Harry White

A. [Edgar] Wiggins

Grant Williams

Garland Wilson

William Marshall Winthrop

7. Starring in the floor show were Snow Fisher, Elizabeth Welch, Louise Cole, Lavina Mack, Glennie Chessman, Jackie Young, Lillian Brown, Clarice Knopp, Murray Watkins, Fanny Cotton, Norma Davis, Hazel Shepard, Lucile Tlyvor, and Evelyn Dickerson.

8. Howard Rye, "Visiting Fireman 11: Garland Wilson," *Storyville*, no. 119 (1985): 183.

9. G. W. Kay, "Herman Chittison: Sinbad of the Piano," *Jazz Journal and Jazz Blues*, no. 18 (1965): 14–15, 38.

10. M. Jones, "Chittison: Jazz Pianist in Alexandria," *Melody Maker* 25 (1967): 12. Here June 1933 is cited as the date Chittison first went to Europe. However, Kernfeld (*New Grove Dictionary*, 1:207) gives the date of 1934 and also cites Chittison's birth date as 1908. See also G. W. Kay, "Herman Chittison, 1913–1967," *Storyville*, no. 10 (1967): 24.

11. Kay, "Sinbad of the Piano," 14.

12. Bricktop, *Bricktop*, 43.

13. Klüver and Martin, *Kiki's Paris*, 11.

14. Bald, "Montparnasse Today," 31.

15. Andrée Nardal, "Étude sur la béguine créole," *Revue du monde noir*, no. 2 (1932): 51–53.

16. Huddleston, *Back to Montparnasse*, 69.

17. Raymond Horricks, *Stéphane Grappelli* (New York: Da Capo Press, 1983), 13.

18. See Henry S. Robinson, "In Retrospect: J. Turner Layton, Musical Ambassador to London," *The Black Perspective in Music* 12, no. 2 (fall 1984): 235–41. See also the press reviews in *Volonté, Candide,* and that by Robert Brisacq in the *Galerie du carnet,* 23 September 1928 (Arsenal RO 586). Layton and Johnstone celebrated their tenth anniversary of concerts in England at the Holborn Empire in June 1934.

19. On the pioneering efforts of Louis Mitchell on the London jazz scene, see Gutteridge, "The First Man to Bring Jazz," 6. James Shaw was one of several musicians based in London who occasionally sent dispatches describing the entertainment scene and engagements of black performers in the United Kingdom and Paris in 1920 to the *Chicago Defender*. And in May 1920 monthly dispatches from Norris Smith, an entertainer-singer who performed under the team name Marino and Norris and lived at 56 Broad Street, Bloomsbury, London, began to appear under the title "Special European Theatrical Representative."

20. Rose, *Jazz Cleopatra*, 20.

21. Publicity credits for the *Revue Nègre* list Douglas as assistant director. However, he had produced smaller revues such as *Black People* in Berlin, *Chocolate Kiddies* in Munich, and *Black Follies* in Brussels. These revues toured several major cities in Europe. *Liza* seems to have first appeared in Berlin under the title *Louisiana* and was revised before opening

in Paris for the 1929–30 season (see the biography of Louis Douglas in Lotz, *Black People*, 297–389). The cast of *Liza* featured Arabella Fields playing Liza's mother; father, Ralph Thomas; Pastor Jones, Francis Mores; New York dandy, Ferdinand Jones; Rastus, Louis Douglas.

22. In a caustic review of *Liza*, with racist undertones, the writer demanded an explanation for use of the term "opérette." The reviewer argued that the term should not be applied to gay animalistic dancing but does praise Douglas as a true artist, exquisite actor and dancer. See Netty de Larnage, "Le théâtre nègre: opérette," *La Revue europénne*, August–September 1930, 787–89. For a more tempered review of *Liza* and critique of the use of *opérette-revue* in reference to the production see Gabriel Timmory, "Paris au théâtre," *Paris Revue*, 19 June 1930 (both in Arsenal [RO 585?]).

23. The song and dance numbers in *Ebony Follies* featured Elizabeth Welch, El Brown, Myrtle Watkins, Jackie Young, Livina Mack, Glennie Chessman, Lois Fuller, and Snow Fisher (see theatrical reviews in *Volonté, Paris Midi, Revue noire, Paris Revue,* and *Galerie du carnet* in Arsenal RO 585). Louis Cole, with his melancholy chants, the sole male member of the revue, had been popular with the Parisian music-hall public when he appeared in song with Adelaide Hall in *Blackbirds* at the now-defunct Moulin Rouge.

S. H. Dudley, Jr., coproducer of *Hot Stuff* and other black musical reviews that appeared through the TOBA, was unrelated to Carolyn Dudley, who produced *La Revue Nègre*. Her husband was Donald Reagan, the commercial attaché at the American Embassy in Paris.

24. Henri Philippon, "Théâtre dramatique nègre," 14 December 1932; René Lalou, untitled review, 21 December 1932 (both in Arsenal RO 585).

25. Rayford W. Logan, "Howard University Grad Now Shopkeeper in Paris," *Chicago Defender*, 21 February 1925; Edgar Wiggins, "Across the Pond," *Chicago Defender*, 2 May 1936.

26. Charles Delaunay, *Django Reinhardt*, trans. Michael James (New York: Da Capo Press, 1981), 62.

27. Ibid., 67, 101.

28. See the review of Cooper's concert in *Jazz-Hot*, no. 2 (April 1935); also Arsenal RO 585.

29. Delaunay, *Django*, 70–71.

30. Geoffrey Smith, *Stéphane Grappelli* (London: Pavilion Books, 1987), 24.

31. Delaunay, *Django*, 97.

32. Ibid., 30.

33. Mike Zwerin, *La Tristesse de Saint Louis* (New York: William Morrow, 1985), 137.

34. René Duval, "Radio Paris," in *Entre deux guerres*, ed. Barrot and Ory, 144.

35. "Guard Josephine Baker: Vienna Police Protect Negro Dancer from Hostile Mobs," *New York Times*, 2 February 1928 (Arsenal RO 15816). For an extensive review of the controversial opera and the extraordinary subterfuges and excuses made in Europe and America to render the opera acceptable for color prejudices, see Harry S. Keelan, "Jonny Tunes Up," *The Crisis* 36, no. 6 (June 1929): 191–209.

36. "Les Jésuites organisent un service d'expiation à l'église Saint-Paul," *Information,* 12 March 1928; "Un comité hongrois va examiner dans quelle mesure Joséphine Baker est nue," *Rumeur,* 30 May 1928 (both in Arsenal RO 15816).

37. Edgar Wiggins, "Europe Raves Over Play Sharing Mixed Players," *Chicago Defender,* 16 June 1934.

## 6. Le Jazz-Cold: *The Silent Forties*

1. Larry Collins and Dominique Lapierre, *Is Paris Burning?* (New York: Simon and Schuster, 1965), 15.

2. Hervé Le Boterf, *La vie parisienne sous l'occupation* (Paris: Éditions France-Empire, 1974), 7 n. 1.

3. Collins and Lapierre, *Paris Burning?,* 16.

4. See, for example, Jacques Delarue, *Trafic et crimes sous l'occupation* (Paris: Librairie Arthème Fayard, 1968).

5. Willis Thornton, *The Liberation of Paris* (New York: Harcourt, Brace and World, 1962), 39; Le Boterf, *Vie parisienne,* 131–41.

6. Harry B. Webber, "Seven Escape the War Zone," *Baltimore Afro-American.*

7. Nancy Cunard, "French Rush to Volunteer," *Baltimore Afro-American,* 7 October 1939.

8. Bill Coleman, *Trumpet Story* (Boston: Northeastern University Press, 1989).

9. For Creighton Thompson's reflections on returning to America after a long residence in Paris, see Floyd G. Nelson's report in the *Chicago Defender,* 11 November 1939. The *St. John's* passengers included other popular black American members of the Paris jazz scene: Benny Payton, Joe Turner, Norma Davis, Percy Green, and Harvey White.

10. Taylor, *Alberta Hunter,* 130.

11. McAlmon, *Being Geniuses Together,* 281.

12. Ibid. Bricktop returned to Paris in 1950 and opened a new club at 26 rue Fontaine. J. Hugh Shannon was booked as a piano player–singer (*Bricktop,* 243–44).

13. Alexander Werth, *The Last Days of Paris. A Journalist's Diary* (London: Hamish Hamilton, 1940), 14–17.

14. In his report for the *Chicago Defender* on 27 January 1940, Wiggins comments on the brief return of Paris nightlife and black American musicians in it. Wiggins joined the American volunteer Iroquois Ambulance Corps stationed at Ville-d'Avray, in the château de la Ronce. After the occupation of France, he was arrested and interned for four years.

15. See "First Black American Combat Pilot to be Honored," *San Francisco Examiner,* 11 October 1992. Bullard was reunited with his two daughters, Lolita and Jacqueline, who arrived in New York City aboard the SS *Exeter* on 3 February 1941. They reported that his gymnasium and club l'Escadrille had been taken over by a young German living in Paris before the war who was discovered to be a fifth columnist (*Pittsburgh Courier,* 15 February 1941).

16. The band's personnel included Henry Mason and Louis Bacon (trumpets); Maurice Poons (piano); Tommy Buford (guitar); John Mitchell (bass); June Cole (alto sax); Johnny Russell (second tenor sax); Billy Burns and Roscoe Burnett (trombone); Willis Lewis (leader and tenor sax). A photograph of the band at The Hague appeared in the *Chicago Defender,* 6 April 1940.

17. *Chicago Defender,* 20 July 1940.

18. Edward B. Toles, "Nazi Enforced Strict Jim Crow Rules in France During Long Occupation," *Chicago Defender,* 25 November 1944.

19. Prince Tovalou died of typhoid fever in Porto Novo, Benin, in 1933 (*Baltimore Afro-American,* 1 September 1945).

20. In the following discussion I have drawn freely on Le Boterf (*Vie parisienne,* 2:129–50) for description of cabarets in Paris during the occupation.

21. Zwerin, *La Tristesse,* 145.

22. Jean-Claude Loiseau, *Les zazous* (Paris: Sagittaire, 1977), 30; Le Boterf, *Vie parisienne,* 1:326.

23. Emmanuelle Rioux, "Les zazous: un phénomène socio-culturel pendant l'occupation" (master's thesis, Université de Paris—X, Nanterre, 1987), 52; Loiseau, *Zazous,* 41 n. 1.

24. Horst J. P. Bergmeier and Rainer E. Lotz, *Hitler's Airwaves* (New Haven: Yale University Press, 1997), 138–39. The program was first broadcast on 9 December 1935.

25. Ibid., 137.

26. Bergmeier and Lotz, *Hitler's Airwaves,* 137. The German adolescents who resisted Nazi oppression are the subject of the film by Thomas Carter, *Swing Kids.* Carter, himself a swing kid, frequented the Café Bismarck and was arrested by the Gestapo. See the film review in *Le Nouvel Observateur,* 30 September–6 October 1993, 50–51.

27. Rioux's claim that the term *zazou* and its fashion craze were invented by Cab Calloway, his zoot suit, and the jitterbug dance is disputed by Hugues Panassié in *Monsieur Jazz* and by Loiseau, *Zazous,* 48. They give credit to Freddy Taylor, the famous dancer and trumpet player, for launching the chant and style of clothes before the war. Valerie Steele, *Paris Fashion: A Cultural History* (New York: Oxford University Press, 1988), 271, writes that Zazou fashion was primarily a working-class and masculine fashion and shows similarities with the English "Teddy Boys" and Californian zoot suits. However, unlike in these examples, the Zazou fashion also reflected textile rationing and other shortages of manufactured cloth after the fall of France.

28. Janet Flanner, *Paris Journal, 1944–1965,* ed. William Shawn (New York: Atheneum, 1965), 16.

29. W. D. Hall, *The Youth of Vichy France* (Oxford: Clarendon Press, 1981), 176–78.

30. Rioux, "Les zazous," 74, 123.

31. Matthew F. Jordan, "Jazz Changes: A History of French Discourse on Jazz from Ragtime to Be-Bop" (Ph.D. diss., Claremont Graduate School, Claremont, Calif., 1998), 324.

32. The ordinance on the yellow star was issued on 29 May 1942. After 11 November 1942, the yellow star was not imposed on Jews living in the Free Zone. Henri Amouroux, *La vie*

*des français sous l'occupation* (Paris: Librairie Arthème Fayard, 1961), ch. 14. See also Alice Courouble, *Amie des juifs* (Paris: Bloud et Gay).

33. Quoted in Amouroux, *Vie des français,* 162.

34. Loiseau, *Zazous,* 163.

35. Ibid., 177.

36. Rioux, "Les zazous," 164, quoting from an interview with George Guetary, 20 December 1986.

37. Loiseau, *Zazous,* 196.


*7. Final Notes: The Liberation of Jazz*

1.   Ollie Stewart provided weekly reports regularly of black soldiers in the North African and European theaters of operation, beginning with the invasion of Tunisia, then Sicily, in southern Italy, and finally Normandy. He was the first African American war correspondent to reach the North African fighting front in August 1942 and covered the campaign in which General Rommel was defeated in North Africa. In France, he covered the breakthrough at St. Malo and entered Paris with the first Americans. In his report to the *Afro-American* on 2 September, Stewart wrote that four "colored [American] truck drivers drove General de Gaulle's party into the French capital." See also Carl Murphy, *This Is Our War* (Baltimore: The Afro-American, 1945).

2.   Rudolph Dunbar, "Briggs Trumpet Player, Free After 4 Years in Nazi Camp," *Chicago Defender,* 23 September 1944.

3.   Chisholm, *Nancy Cunard,* 227.

4.   *Baltimore Afro-American,* 1 April 1944.

5.   Linda Dahl, *Stormy Weather: The Music and Lives of a Century of Jazz Women* (New York: Pantheon Books, 1984), 82. See also Sally Placksin, *Jazz Women, 1900 to the Present: Their Words, Lives and Music* (London: Pluto Press, 1982), 93–95.

6.   Ollie Stewart, "Nazi-Free Paris Swaying to Swing," *Baltimore Afro-American,* 9 September 1944.

7.   Channing Tobias, national secretary of the NAACP, took violent exception to an American Red Cross Report that "made reference to the apparent satisfaction on the part of Negro troops with segregated facilities for recreation . . . [based] upon comments made to [the report's author] by officers and men with whom he came into contact." Channing "drew a sharp distinction between accepting the conditions imposed and being satisfied with them" (National Archives, Washington, D.C., Record Group 3, Records of the American Red Cross, 900.02, 2 August 1944).

8.   By September 1944 two other Red Cross clubs were opened in the heart of Paris: the Columbus Club at the Regina Hotel and the Lafayette Club in the Hotel de Louvre. Several smaller hotels adjacent to these centers were taken over as dormitories for soldiers on leave (ibid., Recreation 1944–46, 8 September 1944).

A persistent problem the Red Cross faced was to supply enough African American personnel for clubs. It wrote in a narrative report that "a great many negroes are coming overseas, and several of the clubs managed by white girls are patronized by a large majority of colored soldiers. Where previously the colored troops were scattered among the white, of late the army tends to concentrate them so that many of our clubs which have a sprinkling of colored troops are now entirely taken over by colored. They need Red Cross clubs badly but they should be staffed with colored personnel if they are to do an adequate job" (ibid., Narrative Report, 900.08, May 1945).

9. Ollie Stewart, "Nazi Tactics Against Tan GI's in Paris," *Baltimore Afro-American*, 16 June 1945. On the white racist hysteria that had erupted after the armistice in America and Germany, see Kaspi, "Le temps des américains," ch. 5.

10. Roi Ottley, *Pittsburgh Courier*, 7 April 1945. A war correspondent for the *Courier*, Ottley published his memoir of the peculiar character of Nazi racial policy and practice in occupied France and the general racial climate in postwar Europe under the title *No Green Pastures* (New York: Charles Scribner's Sons, 1951).

11. Hugues Panassié, "Marseille nouvelle capitale du jazz," *Jazz-Hot*, n.s., no. 1 (October 1945). Panassié may have been referring to the American Red Cross club set aside for Negro troops, the Canebière Club. On the racial climate affecting American forces, Max Johnson described Marseille as "now one part below the Mason-Dixon line—American and one part hungry France." Black American soldiers were prohibited from patronizing two clubs operated daily by the army's special service division as entertainment features for American GIs: the Delta Rhythm and Savoy, formerly French cabarets. "White GI's resented the presence of colored soldiers accompanied by French girls at dances and affairs and the measure was intended to prevent any racial clashes" (*Baltimore Afro-American*, 9 December 1944).

*Coda*

1. Nancy Cunard, "Letter From Paris," *Horizon* 11, no. 61 (January 1945): 396–407.

2. William H. Kenny III, "The Assimilation of American Jazz in France, 1917-1940," *American Studies* 25, no. 1 (spring 1984): 12. See also Jody Blake, "Le Tumulte Noir: Modernist and Popular Entertainment in Jazz Age Paris, 1900–1930" (Ph.D. diss., University of Delaware, 1992).

3. Samuel A. Floyd, Jr., "Music in the Harlem Renaissance: An Overview," in *Black Music in the Harlem Renaissance*, ed. Samuel A. Floyd, Jr. (New York: Greenwood Press, 1990), 3.

4. Bud Billiken, the mythical godfather of black children everywhere, was the creation of David Kellum, social editor of the *Chicago Defender*. On the report to establish the Paris chapter of the Billikens, see the *Defender*, 12 October 1929.

5. Ivan Browning, "Artists Must Have More Than Talent when Seeking Fame," *Pittsburgh Courier*, 9 September 1936.

6.   Morroe Berger, "Jazz: Resistance to the Diffusion of a Culture Pattern," *The Journal of Negro History* 32, no. 4 (October 1947): 466.

7.   See the essays on writers and music, and on art and music during the Harlem Renaissance in Floyd, *Black Music in the Harlem Renaissance.*

8.   See Green, *Edmund Thornton Jenkins.*

# BIBLIOGRAPHY

ARCHIVES

Bancroft Library, University of California, Berkeley
Bibliothèque de l'Arsenal, Paris
Bibliothèque de la musée de Montmartre
Bibliothèque du centre Pompidou
Bibliothèque historique de la ville de Paris
Bibliothèque nationale, Paris and annexe de Versailles
Hoover Institution Library and Archives, Stanford, California
National Archives, Washington, D.C.
Schomburg Center for Black Culture, New York Public Library, New York
Woodruff Library, Clark-Atlanta University


NEWSPAPERS: THE NEGRO PRESS

*Baltimore Afro-American,* 1939 – 45
*Chicago Defender,* 1920 – 44
*New York Age,* 1899, 1919
*Pittsburgh Courier,* 1926 – 36

Abbott, Robert S. "My Trip Abroad: Paris." *Chicago Defender,* 9 November 1929.

Abrams, M. "Django Reinhardt: The Jazz Gypsy." *Storyville,* no. 77 (1978): 163–70.

Allan, Tony. *Paris: The Glamour Years 1919–1940.* New York: Bison Books, 1977.

Allen, Frederick Lewis. "When America Learned to Dance." *Scribner's Magazine,* 1937, 11–17.

"Americans Take Hate to Paris." *Chicago Defender,* 11 August 1923.

Amouroux, Henri. *La vie des français sous l'occupation.* Paris: Librairie Arthème Fayard, 1961.

———. *La grande histoire des français sous l'occupation: quarante millions de Pétainistes, juin 1940–juin 1941.* Paris: Robert Laffont, 1977.

Arnaud, Claude. "Autour du Bœuf sur le toit." In *Entre deux guerres: la création française entre 1919 et 1939,* ed. Olivier Barrot and Pascal Ory. Paris: Éditions François Bourin, 1990.

Attali, Jacques. *Bruits: essais sur l'économie politique de la musique.* Paris: Presses universitaires de France. 1977.

Badger, Reid. *A Life in Ragtime: A Biography of James Reese Europe.* Oxford: Oxford University Press, 1995.

Baker, Josephine, and Jo Bouillon. *Joséphine.* Paris: Robert Laffont, 1976.

Bald, Wambly. *On the Left Bank, 1929–1933.* Athens: Ohio University Press, 1987.

———. "Montparnasse Today." *Vanity Fair,* July 1932.

Barker, J. Ellis. "The Colored French Troops in Germany." *Current History* 9 (1921): 594–99.

Baschet, Roger. "Nouveaux dandys." *L'Illustration* 211 (1942): 217.

Bechet, Sidney. *Treat It Gentle.* New York: Twayne, 1960.

Behr, Edward. *The Good Frenchman.* New York: Villard Books, 1993.

Bercy, Anne de, and Armand Ziwès. *À Montmartre . . . le soir: cabarets et chansonniers d'hier.* Paris: Bernard Grasset, 1951.

Berger, Morroe. "Jazz: Resistance to the Diffusion of a Culture Pattern." *The Journal of Negro History* 32, no. 4 (October 1947): 466.

Bergmeier, Horst J. P., and Rainer E. Lotz. *Hitler's Airwaves.* New Haven: Yale University Press, 1997.

"Black Musicians Freed by Army." *Baltimore Afro-American,* 8 July 1944.

Blake, Jody. "Le Tumulte Noir: Modernist and Popular Entertainment in Jazz Age Paris, 1900–1930." Ph.D. dissertation, University of Delaware, 1992.

Bourget, Pierre, and Charles Lacretelle. *Sur les murs de Paris et de France, 1939–1945*. Paris: Hachette, 1980.

Bricktop [Ada Smith]. *Bricktop*. With James Haskins. New York: Atheneum, 1983.

"Bricktop Returns." *Chicago Defender*, 29 November 1939.

"Britain Will Investigate Color Line." *Chicago Defender*, 7 September 1929.

Brown, Rae Linda. "William Grant Still, Florence Price, and William Dawson: Echoes of the Harlem Renaissance." In *Black Music in the Harlem Renaissance*, ed. Samuel A. Floyd, Jr. New York: Greenwood Press, 1990.

Browning, Ivan. "Artists Must Have More Than Talent when Seeking Fame." *Pittsburgh Courier*, 9 September 1936.

Butcher, Margaret Just. *The Negro in American Culture*. New York: Alfred A. Knopf, 1966.

Carco, Francis. *De Montmartre au quartier latin*. Paris: Albin Michel, 1927.

Carisella, P. J., and James W. Ryan. *The Black Swallow of Death*. Boston: Marlbourgh House, 1972.

Castle, Irene. *Castles in the Air*. New York: Doubleday, 1958.

Cazalis, Anne-Marie. *Mémoires d'une Anne*. Paris: Éditions Stock, 1976.

Charters, Samuel B. *Jelly Roll Morton's Last Night at the Jungle Inn*. New York: Marion Boyard, 1984.

Charters, Samuel B., and Leonard Kunstadt. *Jazz: A History of the New York Scene*. New York: Da Capo, 1981.

Chevalier, Louis. *Montmartre, du plaisir et du crime*. Paris: Robert Laffont, 1980.

Chilton, John. *Sidney Bechet: The Wizard of Jazz*. New York: Oxford University Press, 1987.

Chisholm, Anne. *Nancy Cunard*. New York: Alfred A. Knopf, 1979.

Coleman, Bill. *Trumpet Story*. Boston: Northeastern University Press, 1989.

Colin, Paul. *Le tumulte noir*. Paris: Éditions d'Art, Succès, 1929.

Collins, Larry, and Dominique Lapierre. *Is Paris Burning?* New York: Simon and Schuster, 1965.

"Colored Soldiers and American *Métèques*." *The Literary Digest*, 1 September 1923.

Colson, William N. "Propaganda and the American Negro Soldier." *The Messenger*, July 1919, 24–25.

———. "An Analysis of Negro Patriotism." *The Messenger* 2, no. 8 (August 1919): 25.

Cook, Mercer. "Nazi Racial Ban on French Theatres." *Baltimore Afro-American*, 1 August 1940.

———. "Booker T. Washington and the French." *Journal of Negro History* 40 (October 1955): 318.

Cornnick, M. "France, America—Which Is Symbolic of Democracy?" *Chicago Defender*, 25 February 1922.

Courouble, Alice. *Amie des juifs.* Paris: Bloud et Gay.

Crespelle, Jean-Paul. *Montparnasse vivant.* Paris: Hachette, 1962.

———. *La vie quotidienne à Montparnasse à la grande époque, 1905–1930.* Paris: Hachette, 1976.

———. *La vie quotidienne à Montmartre au temps de Picasso, 1900–1910.* Paris: Hachette, 1978.

Crowder, Henry. *As Wonderful As All That? Henry Crowder's Memoir of His Affair with Nancy Cunard, 1928–1935.* With Hugo Speck; introduction and epilogue by Robert L. Allen. Navarro, Calif.: Wild Tree Press, 1987.

Crowther, B. "The Forgotten Ones: Eddie South." *Jazz Journal International* 36, no. 8 (1983): 12.

Cullen, Countee. "Countee Cullen on French Courtesy." *The Crisis* 36, no. 6 (June 1929): 193.

Cunard, Nancy. "French Rush to Volunteer." *Baltimore Afro-American*, 7 October 1939.

———. "Black American Army War Volunteers." *Baltimore Afro-American*, 31 March 1940.

———. "Letter From Paris." *Horizon* 11, no. 61 (January 1945): 396–407.

———. *These Were the Hours: Memories of my Hours Press—Réanville and Paris, 1928–1931.* Ed., with a foreword by Hugh Ford. Carbondale: Southern Illinois University Press, 1969.

Curtis, Albert. "Court Ends 'Dirty Way' of Tribune." *Chicago Defender*, 16 June 1923.

Dahl, Linda. *Stormy Weather: The Music and Lives of a Century of Jazz Women.* New York: Pantheon Books, 1984.

Darius, P. "Le chef du jazz." *Comedia* 8 (1926).

de Busscher, Jean-Marie. "À l'ombre des monuments aux morts." In *Entre deux guerres: la création française entre 1919 et 1939*, ed. Olivier Barrot and Pascal Ory. Paris: Éditions François Bourin, 1990.

de Larnage, Netty. "Le théâtre nègre: opérette." *La Revue européenne,* August–September 1930, 787–89.

Delarue, Jacques. *Trafic et crimes sous l'occupation.* Paris: Librairie Arthème Fayard, 1968.

Delaunay, Charles. *Django Reinhardt.* Trans. Michael James. New York: Da Capo Press, 1981.

Deliss, Clementine Marie. "Exoticism and Eroticism: Representation of the Other in Early Twentieth-Century French Anthropology." Ph.D. dissertation, School of Oriental and African Studies, University of London, 1988.

Du Bois, W. E. B. "The American Negro in Paris." *The American Monthly Review* 22 (1900): 576.

Dunbar, Rudolph. "Briggs Trumpet Player, Free After 4 Years in Nazi Camp." *Chicago Defender,* 23 September 1944.

Dutourd, Jean. *Au bon beurre.* Paris: Librairie Gallimard, 1952.

Duval, René. "Radio Paris." In *Entre deux guerres: la création française entre 1919 et 1939,* ed. Olivier Barrot and Pascal Ory. Paris: Éditions François Bourin, 1990.

Émile-Bayard, Jean. *Montmartre Past and Present.* Trans. Ralph Annington and Tudor Davies. New York: Brentano, 1926.

Europe, James Reese. "A Negro Explains 'Jazz.'" *The Literary Digest,* 26 April 1919, 28–29.

Fabre, Michel. "Autour de Maran." *Présence africaine* 86, no. 2 (1973): 165–72.

———. *From Harlem to Paris: Black American Writers in France, 1840–1980.* Urbana: University of Illinois Press, 1991.

Faulkner, Anne Shaw. "Does Jazz Put the Sin in Syncopation?" The *Ladies' Home Journal,* August 1921, 16.

"Find U.S. Guests Incited Jim Crow." *Chicago Defender,* 12 May 1934.

"First Black American Combat Pilot to be Honored." *San Francisco Examiner,* 11 October 1992.

Flanner, Janet. *Paris Journal, 1944–1965.* Ed. William Shawn. New York: Atheneum, 1965.

———. *Paris Was Yesterday, 1925–1939.* Ed. Irving Drutman. New York: Viking, 1972.

Floyd, Samuel A., Jr. "Music in the Harlem Renaissance: An Overview." In *Black Music in the Harlem Renaissance,* ed. Samuel A. Floyd, Jr. New York: Greenwood Press, 1990.

Ford, Hugh. *Nancy Cunard: Brave Poet, Indomitable Rebel, 1896–1965.* Philadelphia: Chilton Book Co., 1968.

———, ed. *The Left Bank Revisited: Selections from the* Paris Tribune *1917–1934.* University Park: Pennsylvania State University Press, 1972.

"France Chokes Klan Attempt at Lawlessness." *Chicago Defender,* 6 January 1923.

"French Citizens Appeal for Scottsboro Boys." *Chicago Defender,* 17 February 1934.

"French Government Sends Actors Home." *Chicago Defender,* 29 November 1940.

Gagnon, Paul A. "French Views of the Second American Revolution." *French Historical Studies* 2, no. 4 (fall 1962): 430–49.

Gaillard, Lucien. *Marseille sous l'occupation.* Marseilles: Ouest-France, 1982.

Goddard, Chris. *Jazz Away From Home.* London: Paddington Press, 1979.

Goffin, Robert. *Nouvelle histoire du jazz: du congo au be-bop.* Brussels: l'Écran du Monde, 1948.

Gordon, Allan M. "Interaction between Art and Music during the Harlem Renaissance." In *Black Music in the Harlem Renaissance,* ed. Samuel A. Floyd, Jr. New York: Greenwood Press, 1990.

Green, Jeffrey P. *Edmund Thorton Jenkins: The Life and Times of an American Black Composer, 1894–1926.* Westport, Conn.: Greenwood Press, 1982.

———. "*In Dahomey* in London in 1903." *The Black Perspective in Music* 2, no. 1 (spring 1983): 22–40.

———. "The Negro Renaissance in England." In *Black Music in the Harlem Renaissance,* ed. Samuel A. Floyd, Jr. New York: Greenwood Press, 1990.

Guérard, Albert. "The Black Army of France." *Scribner's Magazine,* March 1925, 236–42.

Gutteridge, Len. "The First Man to Bring Jazz to Britain." *Melody Maker* 31 (1956): 6.

Hall, James Norman, and Charles Bernard Nordhoff, eds. *The Lafayette Flying Corps.* 2 vols. Boston: Houghton Mifflin, 1920.

Hall, W. D. *The Youth of Vichy France.* Oxford: Clarendon Press, 1981.

Haney, Lynn. *Naked at the Feast: A Biography of Josephine Baker.* New York: Dodd, Mead, 1981.

Harding, James. *The Ox on the Roof.* New York: St. Martin's Press, 1972.

Harrington, Oliver W. *Why I Left America and Other Essays.* Ed., with an introduction by M. Thomas Inge. Jackson: University Press of Mississippi, 1993.

Helm, MacKinley. *Angel Mo, and Her Son Roland Hayes*. Boston: Little Brown, 1942.

"Henry Crowder: Flight, Capture, and Internment." *Baltimore Afro-American,* 1 April 1944.

Hoefer, George. "The Magnificent Gypsy." *Down Beat* 9 (1966): 14.

Horricks, Raymond. *Stéphane Grappelli*. New York: Da Capo Press, 1983.

Huddleston, Sisley. *Paris Salons, Cafés, Studios*. Philadelphia: J. Lippincott, 1928.

———. *Back to Montparnasse: Glimpses of Broadway in Bohemia*. Philadelphia: J. P. Lippincott, 1931.

Hughes, Langston. "Jazz Band in a Parisian Cabaret." In *Fine Clothes to the Jew*. New York: Alfred A. Knopf, 1927.

———. *The Big Sea*, introduction by Arnold Rampersad. New York: Hill and Wang, 1933.

Huygens, G. "Valaida Snow." *Le Point du jazz* 20 (1986): 14.

"Ida Johnson Family Freed." *Pittsburgh Courier,* 2 September 1944.

Irwin, Will. "Voice of Her Fallen Hero Wounded at Battle of Verdun." *The Saturday Evening Post*, 15 July 1916.

Jacques-Charles. *La revue de ma vie*. Paris: Librairie Arthème Fayard, 1958.

Janken, Kenneth R. *Rayford W. Logan and the Dilemma of the African-American Intellectual*. Amherst: University of Massachusetts Press, 1993.

"Jazz Players to Lose Paris Jobs." *Chicago Defender,* 22 July 1922.

Johnson, James Weldon. *Black Manhattan*. New York: Alfred A. Knopf, 1930.

Jones, M. "Garland Wilson: Self-Portrait of a Jazz Pianist." *Melody Maker* 5 (1954): 13.

———. "Chittison: Jazz Pianist in Alexandria." *Melody Maker* 25 (1967): 12.

Jordan, Matthew F. "Jazz Changes: A History of French Discourse on Jazz from Ragtime to Be-Bop." Ph.D. dissertation, Claremont Graduate School, Claremont, Calif., 1998.

Kaspi, André. "Le temps des américains: premier concours américain à la France en 1917–1918." Paris: Université de Paris I—Panthéon-Sorbonne, 1976.

Kay, G. W. "Herman Chittison: Sinbad of the Piano." *Jazz Journal and Jazz Blues*, no. 18 (1965): 14–15.

———. "Herman Chittison, 1913–1967." *Storyville*, no. 10 (1967): 24.

Keelan, Harry S. "Jonny Tunes Up." *The Crisis* 36, no. 6 (June 1929): 191–209.

Kenney, William Howland. *Chicago Jazz: A Cultural History, 1904–1930*. New York: Oxford University Press, 1993.

Kenny, William H., III. "The Assimilation of American Jazz in France, 1917–1940." *American Studies* 25, no. 1 (spring 1984): 12.

Kernfeld, Berry, ed. *The New Grove Dictionary of Jazz*. 2 vols. New York: Macmillan, 1988.

Kimball, Robert, and William Bolcom. *Reminiscing with Sissle and Blake*. New York: Viking, 1973.

Klein, Jean-Claude. "La revue nègre." In *Entre deux guerres: la création française entre 1919 et 1939*, ed. Olivier Barrot and Pascal Ory. Paris: Éditions François Bourin, 1990.

Klüver, Billy, and Julie Martin. *Kiki's Paris: Artists and Lovers 1900–1930*. New York: Harry N. Abrams, 1989.

Le Boterf, Hervé. *La vie parisienne sous l'occupation*. Paris: Éditions France-Empire, 1974.

Lester, Julius, ed. *The Seventh Son: The Thoughts and Writings of W. E. B. Du Bois*. 2 vols. New York: Random House, 1971.

Lewis, David Levering. *When Harlem Was in Vogue*. New York: Alfred A. Knopf, 1982.

Lewis, Harold O. *Negro Year Book, 1941–1946*. Tuskegee: Tuskegee Institute, 1947.

Little, Arthur W. *From Harlem to the Rhine, The Story of New York's Colored Volunteers*. New York: Covici, Friede, 1936.

Logan, Rayford W. "Howard University Grad Now Shopkeeper in Paris." *Chicago Defender*, 21 February 1925.

———. "The Confessions of an Unwilling Nordic." In *The Negro Caravan*, ed. Sterling A. Brown, Arthur P. Davis, and Ulysses Lee. New York: Dryden Press, 1941.

Loiseau, Jean-Claude. *Les zazous*. Paris: Sagittaire, 1977.

Lomax, Alan. *Mister Jelly Roll: The Fortunes of Jelly Roll Morton, New Orleans Creole and "Inventor of Jazz."* New York: Duell, Sloan and Pearce, 1950.

Long, Richard A. "Interactions between Writers and Music during the Harlem Renaissance." In *Black Music in the Harlem Renaissance*, ed. Samuel A. Floyd, Jr. New York: Greenwood Press, 1990.

Lotz, Rainier E. "Black Diamonds Are Forever: A Glimpse of the Prehistory of Jazz in Europe." *The Black Perspective in Music* 12, no. 2 (fall 1984): 217–34.

———. *Heisse Tanzmusik in Deutschland: Ein Fotoalbum,* vol. 1. Bonn: Jazzfreund-Publikation, 1986.

———. "The Black Troubadours: Black Entertainers in Europe, 1896–1915." *Black Music Research Journal* 10, no. 2 (fall 1990): 253–67.

———. *Black People: Entertainers of African Descent in Europe and Germany.* Bonn: Lotz, 1997.

McAlmon, Robert. *Being Geniuses Together: 1920–1930.* With Kay Boyle. Rev. ed. San Francisco: North Point Press, 1980.

McKay, Claude. "What Is and What Isn't." *The Crisis* 27, no. 6 (April 1924): 259–63.

———. "Once More the Germans Face Black Troops." *Opportunity* 17 (1939): 324–28.

———. *A Long Way From Home.* 1937. Reprint, London: Pluto Press, 1985.

Maillard, Nadja. "Le jazz dans la littérature française (1920–1940)." *Revue littéraire mensuelle* 820–21 (1997): 46–57.

Malartic, Yves. *Au pays du Bon Dieu.* Paris: La Table Ronde, 1947.

Marès, Antoine. *Le pays des étrangers: depuis un siècle.* Paris: Imprimerie nationale, 1989.

Marsh, Patrick. "The Theatre: Compromise or Collaboration." In *Collaboration in France: Politics and Culture During the Nazi Occupation, 1940–1944,* ed. Gerhard Hirschfeld and Patrick Marsh. Oxford: Berg, 1989.

Martin, Florence. "Tony Morrison fait du jazz." *Revue littéraire mensuelle* 820–21 (1997): 95–103.

Matthews, Ralph. "William Monroe Trotter." *Baltimore Afro-American,* 2 September 1944.

*Montparnasse—Quartier latin,* 4 October 1930, 183.

Moore, George. "Marseilles Red Cross Clubs." *Pittsburgh Courier,* 22 September 1945.

Morand, Paul. *Magie noire.* Paris: Ferenczi et Fils, 1936.

Murphy, Carl. *This Is Our War.* Baltimore: The Afro-American, 1945.

"Mystery of Brutal Murder Is Solved by Confession of 18-Year-Old Suspect." *Chicago Defender,* 13 March 1926.

Nardal, Andrée. "Étude sur la béguine créole." *Revue du monde noir,* no. 2 (1932): 51–53.

"Nazis' Strict Jim Crow Rules." *Chicago Defender,* 30 November 1940.

Nevill, Ralph. *Days and Nights in Montmartre and the Latin Quarter.* New York: George H. Doran, 1927.

"New GI Club Opens on World-Famous Paris Street." *Chicago Defender,* 5 April 1945.

"No More Mixed Shows in Paris." *Chicago Defender,* 20 July 1940.

Ottley, Roi. *No Green Pastures.* New York: Charles Scribner's Sons, 1951.

Panassié, Hugues. "Marseille nouvelle capitale du jazz." *Jazz-Hot,* n.s., no. 1 (October 1945).

"Paris Beauties Kink Their Hair in Siki Glory." *Chicago Defender,* 14 October 1922.

"Paris interdit." *La France Libre,* 15 January 1942, 147–54.

Paxton, Robert O. *Vichy France: Old Guard and New Order, 1940–1944.* New York: Alfred A. Knopf, 1972.

Pernet, Robert. "Some Notes on Arthur Briggs." *Storyville,* no. 84 (1979): 204–9.

Pierre, Michelle. "Le journal de Mickey." In *Entre deux guerres: la création française entre 1919 et 1939,* ed. Olivier Barrot and Pascal Ory. Paris: Éditions François Bourin, 1990.

Placksin, Sally. *Jazz Women, 1900 to the Present: Their Words, Lives and Music.* London: Pluto Press, 1982.

Pryce-Jones, David. *Paris in the Third Reich: A History of the German Occupation, 1940–1944.* New York: Collins, 1981.

Rioux, Emmanuelle. "Les zazous: un phénomène socio-culturel pendant l'occupation." Master's thesis, Université de Paris—X, Nanterre, 1987.

Rioux, Jean-Pierre. "Ambivalences en rouge et bleu: les pratiques culturelles des français pendant les années noires." In *Politiques et pratiques culturelles dans la France de Vichy.* Paris: Institut d'histoire du temps présent, 1988.

———, ed. *La vie culturelle sous Vichy.* Cahier de l'Institut no. 8. Paris: Institut d'histoire du temps présent, 1988.

Robinson, Henry S. "In Retrospect: J. Turner Layton, Musical Ambassador to London." *The Black Perspective in Music* 12, no. 2 (fall 1984): 235–41.

Rose, Phyllis. *Jazz Cleopatra: Josephine Baker in Her Time.* New York: Doubleday, 1989.

Roy-Loustanou, Claude. *Suite française.* Paris: René Julliard-Sequana, 1943.

———. *Les yeux ouverts dans Paris insurgé.* Paris: René Julliard-Sequana, 1944.

———. *Eight Days that Freed Paris.* London: Pilot Pres, 1945.

Rye, Howard. "Visiting Fireman 8: Eddie South." *Storyville,* no. 108 (1983): 21.

———. "Visiting Fireman 11: Garland Wilson." *Storyville,* no. 119 (1985): 183.

Sachs, Maurice. *The Decade of Illusion: Paris 1918–1928.* Trans. Gladys Matthews Sachs. New York: Alfred A. Knopf, 1935.

———. *Au temps du Bœuf sur le toit.* Paris: Nouvelle Revue critique, 1939.

———. *La chasse à courre.* Paris: Librairie Gallimard, 1948.

Sampson, Henry T. *Blacks in Blackface.* Metuchen, N.J.: Scarecrow Press, 1980.

Sargent, Winthrop. *Jazz: Hot and Hybrid.* New York: E. P. Dutton, 1946.

Sauvage, Marcel. *Les mémoires de Joséphine Baker.* Paris: Éditions Corréa, 1949.

Schoener, Alan, ed. *Harlem on My Mind: Cultural Capital of Black America, 1900–1968.* New York: Random House, 1968.

Schuyler, George S. "Europe Gives Race Actors Better Chance Than U.S." *Chicago Defender,* 30 December 1930.

Schwerké, Irving. "Le jazz est mort! Vive le jazz!" In *Kings Jazz and David.* Paris: Les Presses Modernes, 1927.

Scott, Emmet J. *Official History of the American Negro in the World War.* Washington, D.C., 1919.

Seigel, Jerrold. *Bohemian Paris: Culture, Politics, and the Boundaries of Bourgeois Life, 1830–1930.* New York: Viking, 1986.

"Siki's Victory Stirs Americans in France to Protest Equality." *Chicago Defender,* 7 October 1922.

Smith, Geoffrey. *Stéphane Grappelli.* London: Pavilion Books, 1987.

Smith, Graham. *When Jim Crow Met John Bull.* London: I. B. Tauris, 1987.

Smith, Willie "The Lion." *Music on My Mind.* With George Hoefer. New York: Doubleday, 1964.

Southern, Eileen. "Will Marion Cook." In *Readings in Black American Music,* ed. Eileen Southern. 2d ed. New York: W. W. Norton, 1983.

Speck, Ernest B. "Henry Crowder: Nancy Cunard's 'Tree.'" *Lost Generation Journal* 6 (1976): 6–8.

Steele, Valerie. *Paris Fashion: A Cultural History.* New York: Oxford University Press, 1988.

Stewart, Ollie. "Nazi-Free Paris Swaying to Swing." *Baltimore Afro-American,* 9 September 1944.

———. "Nazi Tactics Against Tan GI's in Paris." *Baltimore Afro-American,* 16 June 1945.

———. "Why Negroes Leave America." *Negro Digest,* March 1949, 8–11.

———. *Paris, Here I Come.* Baltimore: The Afro-American, 1953.

Stoner, H. "Can't We Talk It Over [Valaida Snow]?" *Storyville,* no. 66 (1976): 213.

Street, Julian. *Where Paris Dines.* New York: Doubleday, Doran, 1928.

Sweets, John F. *Choices in Vichy France: The French Under Nazi Occupation.* Oxford: Oxford University Press.

Taylor, Frank C. *Alberta Hunter: A Celebration in Blues.* With Gerald Cook. New York: Mc Graw-Hill, 1987.

Thomson, Virgil. "Jazz." *American Mercury* 2 (1924): 465–67.

Thornton, Willis. *The Liberation of Paris.* New York: Harcourt, Brace and World, 1962.

Timmory, Gabriel. "Paris au théâtre." *Paris Revue* 6 (1930).

Toles, Edward B. "Nazi Enforced Strict Jim Crow Rules in France During Long Occupation." *Chicago Defender,* 25 November 1944.

"U.S. Daily in Paris Stirs Race Strife." *Chicago Defender,* 14 August 1926.

Walter, Gérard. *La vie à Paris sous l'occupation, 1940–1944.* Paris: Armand Colin, 1960.

"War Refugee Musicians." *Baltimore Afro-American,* 16 December 1940.

Warnod, André. *Visages de Paris.* Paris: Firmin-Didot, 1930.

———. *Fils de Montmartre.* Paris: Librairie Arthème Fayard, 1955.

Washington, Booker T. "On the Paris Boulevards." *New York Age,* 13 July 1899.

Webber, Harry B. "Seven Escape the War Zone." *Baltimore Afro-American.*

Werth, Alexander. *The Last Days of Paris. A Journalist's Diary.* London: Hamish Hamilton, 1940.

———. *The Twilight of France, 1933–1940.* New York: Harper and Brothers, 1942.

Wiggins, Edgar. "Where 'Smart Boys' Go to Learn How Dumb They Are." *Chicago Defender,* 14 October 1933.

———. "Europe Raves Over Play Sharing Mixed Players." *Chicago Defender,* 16 June 1934.

———. "Across the Pond." *Chicago Defender,* 2 May 1936.

Wilson, Robert Forrest. *Paris on Parade.* New York: Robert M. McBride, 1932.

Wintz, Cary D. *Black Culture and the Harlem Renaissance.* Houston: Rice University Press, 1988.

Woodson, Carter G. "'Chocolate Dandies' Give Paris an Eyeful." *Chicago Defender,* 21 October 1933.

Woon, Basil. *The Paris That's Not in the Guide Books.* New York: Brentano's, 1926.

Yaki, Paul. *Le Montmartre de nos vingt ans.* 1941. Paris: Éditions Le Vieux Montmartre, 1981.

Zwerin, Mike. *La Tristesse de Saint Louis.* New York: William Morrow, 1985.

Crawford, Roberta Dodd (Princess To-valou), 113–14

Creamer, Henry: "After You've Gone," 87; *Strut Miss Lizzie,* 87, 88; "Un-happy," 87

Creole Five, 29

Crespelle, Jean-Paul, 142 n.20

Le Cri-Cri (Paris), 41

*Crisis, The,* 11

La Croix du Sud (Paris), 86

Crowder, Henry, 44–48, 114, 125–26, 131, 133, 148 n.66; *Henry Music,* 46–47

Crowder, Mrs. Henry, 48, 148 n.72

Cuban musicians, 80–81, 83

Cullaz, Maurice, xv

Cullaz, Vonette, xv

Cullen, Countee, 10, 48, 136, 150 n.6

Cunard, Nancy, 45–48, 105, 125, 131–32; "Henry Crowder," 46

dadaists, 40–41

Dago Frank's (Chicago), 42

Dajou, Henri, 82, 100

Dancer, Jenny, 84

dancing, 51–56; beguine, 80–81, 86–87; Big Apple dance step, 97–98; blues, 41–42, 87, 88; cancan, 55–56; by the Castles, 3; Charleston, 54, 88; dance schools, 120; vs. dining, 55; fox-trot, 3, 88; jitterbug, 120, 157 n.27; Lindy Hop, 90–91; objections to, 3; rumba, 80–81; swing, 118, 122 (*see also* Zazous); tap dancing, 89–90; "truck-ing," 126; waltz, 9, 88

Dancing Tabaris (The Hague), 111

Daniel, Jimmy, 37

Dannecker, Obersturmführer, 121–22

Le Danube (Paris), 114

"darkey impressions," 91

Darrow, Clarence, 69

David, Georges, 152 n.27

Davis, Dixie, 9

Davis, Norma, 154 n.7, 156 n.9

Deauville (France), 36

De Braithe, Jaçon Frank (De Broit), 17

De Bronte, Frank, 17

*Déclaration des droits de l'homme,* 70, 75

de Forest, Maude, 35

de Gaulle, Charles, 124

Delaunay, Charles, 93, 94, 96, 116–17, 123, 127

Delta Rhythm (Marseille), 159 n.11

Deluxe Club (Chicago), 42

*Demoiselles d'Avignon* (Picasso), 8

Dempsey, Jack, 38

Denmark, 100

Depression, xvii–xviii, 76–77, 87, 93, 133. *See also* stock market crash

Derain, André, 50

Derval, Paul, 36

Deschanel, Paul, 50

*Desire of 1927* (I. C. Miller), 99

Detroit Red, 84

Les Deux Magots (Paris), 39–40, 142 n.19

Diaghilev, Sergey, 51

Diamond Tony's (New York City), 2

Dickerson, Evelyn, 154 n.7

Diggs, Charles, 152 n.6

*Dinah,* 35

"Dinah" (Johnstone and Layton), 87–88

"Dinah" (performer), 152 n.6

Dixie Kid, 23

Dixon, Ike, 127

Dodds, Warren ("Baby"), 42

Dodge, Horace, 32

Dolly sisters, 32

Le Dôme (Paris), 39–40, 147 n.52

Don Juan, The (Paris), 100, 114

Dorsey, Jimmy, 58

"double V" symbol, 143 n.3

Douglas, Louis: arrives in Europe, 9–10; *Black Follies,* 154 n.21; *Black People,* 37, 154 n.21; *Chocolate Kiddies,* 154 n.21; and Crowder, 48; dancing of, 88–89, 155 n.22; and Sonny Jones, 72; *Liza,* 90–91, 154 n.21, 155 n.22; returns to Paris after WWII, 125–26; in *Revue Nègre,* 35, 90, 147 n.38, 154 n.21; Thé-âtre Nègre, 88, 89–91

Douglas, Marion, 152 n.6

Douglas Club (New York City), 2–3

Doyle, Daniel, 147 n.38

Dreamland Café (Chicago), 42, 61

Drinkard, Bob and Teddy, 81

*drôle de guerre,* 108–9
drug trafficking/use, 7, 39–40, 142 n.20
Du Bois, W. E. B., 65; *Black Folks Then and Now,* 134; Pan-African Congress convened by, 64, 75, 150 n.4; on Paris Exposition exhibit of black history, 10; St. Louis riot of 1917 investigated by, 144 n.29; on World War I, 11–12
Duchamp, Marcel, 50
Dudley, Carolyn, 8, 35, 90; *Revue Nègre,* 112
Dudley, S. H., Jr.: *Ebony Follies,* 91, 155 n.23; *Revue Noire, Hot Stuff,* 83, 91
Dudley, S. H., Sr.: *Shufflin' Sam From Alabam',* 91
Dufy, Raoul, 6
Dunbar, Rudolph, 132, 136
Duncan, Isadora, 60–61
Dunn, Johnny, 59–60
Du Pont-Latin (Paris), 119
Durante, Jimmy, 2
Durey, Louis, 49
Dvořák, Antonin, 5

*Ebony Follies* (S. H. Dudley, Jr.), 91, 155 n.23
École Normale de Musique (Paris), 128
Eddie and Danny, 152 n.6
Edward VIII, king of Great Britain and Ireland, 28
Eight Black Streaks, 126
8th Illinois National Guard Regiment band, 14
Ekyan, André, 95, 128
Elite Café (Chicago), 61
Elite no. 2 (Chicago), 42
Ellington, Duke, 73, 93, 95, 118
Élysée Montmartre (Paris), 56
Embassy cabaret (Paris), 91
*Emperor Jones* (O'Neill), 92
Épinac (France), 110
l'Escadrille (Paris), 109–10, 156 n.15
L'Étincelle (Paris), 122
Europe, James Reese: Carnegie Hall concerts of, 13; Clef Club Orchestra founded/led by, 1–2, 4, 12–13, 142 n.12; death of, 24; and 15th New York Infantry Regiment band, 3, 15, 17, 144 n.31, 149 n.87; influence of, 4; military enlistment of, 12, 13–14; "One-Step" created by, 3; reputation/influence of, 13–14, 18; Tempo Club Orchestra founded by, 13; and Victor Records, 13
*Eve . . . zazou, zazou,* 122
"Every Sunday Afternoon" (Johnstone and Layton), 87–88
Exposition Four, 72

Fabre, Michel, 136
Fargue, Léon-Paul, 50
Fauset, Jessie, 10
*Femmes et rythmes,* 122
Fernandez, Juan, 112
Fetchit, Stephen, 85
Fields, Arabella, 9, 154 n.21
15th Heavy Foot Infantry Regiment (Harlem Hellfighters), xvi, xviii, 3, 124, 125; fame of, 12; in France, 18–20, 149 n.87; and the French Army, 20, 22; members of, 17–18; origins of, 12–16; parades in New York, 20–21; popularity of, 19–20; racism toward, 16, 21–22, 144 n.13; in Spartanburg, S.C., 16–17, 21–22. *See also* 369e régiment d'Infanterie U.S.
51st Infantry, 110
Fisher, Snow, 152 n.6, 154 n.7, 155 n.23
Fisk Jubilee Singers, 8, 59
Fitzgerald, F. Scott, 32; *Tender Is the Night,* 65
Five Hot Shots, The, 152 n.6
Five Musical Dragons, 29
Flacks, Hetty, 97, 98, 100, 101
Flanner, Janet, 39, 120
Flea Pit (Paris), 42, 46, 133, 135
Flemming, Herbert, 112, 152 n.6
Le Florence (Paris), 43, 115
Florida (Paris), 55, 56
Florida Club (London), 98
Floyd, J. T., 16
*La Folie du Jour,* 36
Folies-Bergère (Paris), 8, 36, 50
Ford, Dolores, 82

Pilsen, Barry, 32
Pinkard, Maceo: "Sweet Georgia
  Brown," 42
Pittman, Booker, 94
Pittman, B. T. W. and Mrs., 152 n.6
Plantation Club (New York City), 35,
  59–60, 62
Plantation Orchestra, 115
*Pocahontas,* 18
Poincaré, Raymond, 39, 78, 147 n.52
Poland, 104
Poons, Maurice, 157 n.16
Porter, Cole, 30
Porter, Horace, 64
Poste Parisien, 97
Potomac Club (Paris), 128
Poulenc, Francis, 49
Pratt, Alfred and Mrs., 152 n.6
Prieur, Gaston, 37–38
Prima, Louis, 118
Prince Kojo incident. *See* Houénou,
  Prince Kojo Tovalou
prince of Wales (Edward VIII), 32, 49,
  60, 86
Prohibition, 84

*quadrille excentrique* (cancan), 55–56
Quintet of the Hot Club of France,
  xviii, 93–95, 136

race relations, in U.S. vs. Europe, xiii–
  xiv, 9. *See also under* France
race riots, 5, 16, 21–22, 71, 144 n.29
Racine, Jean: *Andromaque,* 123
racism, 63–75; and African American
  migration to the North, 63; and African American tourists in Paris,
  66–67; in America, 105, 106; of the
  American press in Paris, 68–70; black
  men accused of raping white women,
  64, 75, 152 n.27; and black men's relations with white women, 64, 70,
  71, 128–29; and criticism of black
  community in Paris, 66–67, 79–80,
  151 n.9, 152 n.5; in entertainment, 101;
  French rejection of, 64, 66–69, 71,
  74–75, 105, 150 n.6, 152 n.25; in Germany, 101, 118–19; in Great Britain,
71; Jim Crow laws, 22–23, 113; Ku
  Klux Klan violence against Southern
  African Americans, 63; in London,
  66–67, 73–74, 151 n.23; and Montmartre's racial incidents, 67–68; race
  riots, 5, 16, 21–22, 71, 144 n.29; and
  Scottsboro boys' trial, 75, 131, 152 n.27;
  segregation, 128–29, 158 n.7, 159 n.11;
  and Siki, 70–71, 73; in Spartanburg,
  S.C., 16–17; of white American tourists in London, 73; of white American
  tourists in Paris, 64–65, 67–68, 70,
  74–75; in World War II, 118–19, 121.
  *See also* Ku Klux Klan
Radiguet, Raymond, 49
radio, xvi, 96–97, 101, 118, 157 n.24
Radio Cité ( *formerly* Radio LL), xvi,
  96–97
Radio LL (*later named* Radio Cité), xvi,
  96–97
ragtime, 2, 57
Rainbow Corner (Paris), 128
Rainbow Division, 16
Rainey, Ma, 61
boulevard Raspail (Paris), 147 n.52
Le Rat Mort (Paris), 7
Ravel, Maurice, 50
Ray, Nora Holt, 81
Reagan, Carolyn Dudley. *See* Dudley,
  Carolyn
Real Jazz Kings. *See* Mitchell's Jazz Kings
Rector, Eddie, 62
Rector's Country Club (Shanghai), 81
Red Cross. *See* American Red Cross clubs
Red Devils, 56, 101, 106, 135
Reed, Ogden, 69
Régine, Madame, 80, 83, 100
Reich Chamber of Music, 118
Reid, Daniel G. ("the Tin Plate King"),
  14, 143 n.10
Reinhardt, Django, xviii, 93–94, 95, 116,
  117, 118, 128
Reinhardt, Joseph, 94
Renoir, Jean, 7
Restaurant Ambassadeurs (Paris), 111
Reuter, Ronald, 69
*Revue Nègre* (Paris), 34–37; Baker in,
  xvii, 8, 27, 35–36, 37, 61, 88, 91; clos-

| | |
|---|---|
| Designer: | Steve Renick |
| Text: | 11/14 Adobe Garamond |
| Display: | Adobe Garamond, Gill Sans |
| Compositor: | G & S Typesetters, Inc. |
| Printer and binder: | Haddon Craftsmen, Inc. |